CHILDREN IN RECOVERY

Rosalie Cruise Jesse, Ph.D.
CLINICAL PSYCHOLOGIST
PRIVATE PRACTICE
SAN DIEGO COUNTY,
CALIFORNIA

W.W. NORTON & COMPANY • *NEW YORK* • *LONDON*

A NORTON PROFESSIONAL BOOK

Published simultaneously in Canada by Penguin Books Canada Ltd.,
2801 John Street, Markham, Ontario L3R 1B4

Printed in the United States of America.

First Edition

Library of Congress Cataloging-in-Publication Data

Jesse, Rosalie Cruise.
   Children in recovery / by Rosalie Cruise Jesse. — 1st ed.
     p. cm.
   "A Norton professional book."
   1. Problem children. 2. Children of alcoholics. I. Title.
  [DNLM: 1. Alcoholism. 2. Family Therapy. 3. Parent-Child
Relations. 4. Personality Disorders — in infancy & childhood. WM
274 J58c]
RJ506.P63J47 1989
618.92'86 — dc19
DNLM/DLC   88-37155
for Library of Congress   CIP

ISBN 0-393-70074-7

W. W. Norton & Company, Inc., 500 Fifth Avenue, New York, N. Y. 10110
W. W. Norton & Company Ltd., 37 Great Russell Street, London, WC1B 3NU

1 2 3 4 5 6 7 8 9 0

This book is dedicated to my son, Rick . . . .
and
to all the children in recovery over the years
who have been my teachers — and to their parents, who cared enough to demonstrate that
recovery is really a process for making the
world a better place.

Acknowledgments

During the writing of this book there were many people who made important contributions—often in ways that they didn't even realize at the time— and they deserve to be mentioned. However, that long list would obscure the special importance of two individuals and their significant contributions. Each has my deepest gratitude.

First, to my editor, Susan Barrows, for her belief in me as a writer and for her vision which made *Children in Recovery* possible. The honor of having been chosen to write a Norton Professional Book stands alongside the privilege of having worked with Susan. Her standard of excellence blends with great sensitivity.

Next, to my husband, Roger Purnelle, for his gentle way of providing a caring milieu where my creative spirit could flourish. From the first, Roger was an unwavering source of enthusiasm and encouragement, always positive and affirming. He certainly deserves my special recognition for his love and loyalty during the many long hours that work on this book required of me: *a ma tendre moitié, je t'aime.*

Contents

Preface

My personal experience with alcoholic and addictive processes began in my family of origin and undoubtedly formed the foundation for my later interest in children of alcoholics and the processes of recovery. However, my earliest professional exposure to work with alcoholics began in the late 1950s in a large, urban medical center where patients were being treated for the secondary and tertiary physical manifestations of final stage alcoholism. (To admit patients to an acute general hospital for a primary diagnosis of alcoholism had not even been considered until after a 1956 American Medical Association decision.) So compelling was the advanced diseased condition of the men on my ward that it did not occur to me at the time to wonder about the status of their children.

A decade later the AMA had identified alcoholism as a complex disease which required attention from all members of the health professions. This decision was followed by an economic backlash. Working within the California hospital system, I observed the debate about whether or not a primary diagnosis of "alcoholism" was reimbursable by health insurance. An important step forward was taken within alcoholism treatment circles when major insurance carriers agreed to underwrite the cost of inpatient care.

By the early 1970s, my clinical work in the field of psychology was showing me alcoholics who presented to outpatient settings with marital problems or parent-child problems while their alcoholism remained undiagnosed and untreated. Centers for the specific treatment of alcoholism were then a rarity, although, with insurance carriers picking up the tab, a growing number of hospitals were designating beds for acute alcoholism care. The inclusion of the spouse in treatment was a relatively new idea, whereas the suggestion that the child also needed care was so innovative as to be considered heretical.

From my commonsense observations during earlier conjoint therapy work with alcoholic families, I could see that the children were being affected in profound ways. However, it was not until I came across a book, *The Forgotten Children*, by Canadian social worker Margaret Cork that my consciousness was raised to the point where I began to take action. I prepared to advocate for these children by attempting to establish the first children's program in the Navy inpatient alcoholism facility where I worked. This effort was tolerated as a harmless, though superfluous, experiment by the agency staff, who continued to view the Navy alcoholic as the identified patient. When the spouse was included in treatment, it was because research showed that the presence of the spouse had some statistical association with the successful treatment outcome for the Navy alcoholic.

"But what about the children?" I continued to ask, sounding very much like a character from an Ibsen play.

Even within my own discipline of psychology, the support for my project with children was secondary to experimental research with alcoholics. For example, a room which had been designated for "The Children's Program" was soon reassigned in favor of biofeedback *machines* where research with alcoholics was conducted. This attitude prevailed in subsequent years when I worked in alcoholism treatment both within neighborhood recovery centers in the civilian community and in the criminal justice system.

While the economics of publicly funded alcoholism treatment programs accounted for some of the disparagement of children's services, another phenomenon appeared to be contributory. Without an agency requirement that the child accompany the alcoholic parent into treatment, agency staff simply did not educate the parent about the child's need for recovery. Without education, the recovering parent and spouse did not voluntarily refer their children for assistance.

Although parents did not focus on the problems of their children during the early recovery phase (first 90 days of sobriety), several months later these recovering alcoholic parents *would* begin to request that a youngster be seen for evaluation. I did not then fully understand what I now realize to be the alcoholic parent's increased ability after several months of recovery to *see* the child. With decreasing self-absorption and increasing physical and emotional recovery, the treated alcoholic parent was beginning to function as a trained observer not only of his own character disturbance but also of problems within the family system.

Another situation appeared to account for the child referrals from recovering parents. After the parent had been sober several months, a formerly quiescent child would begin to demonstrate increased behavioral and psychological problems. This phenomenon, which I was able to demonstrate empirically in research with children of recovering alcoholic parents (Jesse, 1977) was stated, "The mere fact of parental abstinence does not seem to improve the life of the child."

In some cases, the life of the child actually appeared to have worsened with the parent's sobriety. These youngsters showed sudden, abrupt changes which were accompanied by bold, dramatic acting-out behavior that frankly baffled their parents. What was the child trying to communicate through such troubled conduct?

My goal was not to group these youngsters into discrete categories based on symptoms or role behaviors. Rather, I sought to better understand alcoholic family life from the unique perspective of each child, for I firmly believe that any intervention, to have a lasting effect with a child, must facilitate the full expression of that child's inner self. To move beyond superficial roles and symptom façades, I accepted the challenge of devising assessment procedures which could unobtrusively access a child's inner world. Within a developmental framework, this assessment flowed from a determination of the major issues for the years of middle childhood.

The findings of this study, which are discussed in Chapter 5, were not fully understood until a year later, when I became acquainted with the theory of self psychology articulated by Chicago psychoanalyst Heinz Kohut. Suddenly the behavior of the child of the alcoholic in relationship to this parents and significant others was explainable from a theoretical perspective which integrated the development and organization of the self with the potential for addictive disorders.

Although my observations had not been informed by self psychology at the time they were made, the self as a central psychological construct had been the guiding feature of my research.

In the 12 years since I have been applying the principles of self psychology to my clinical work with children of alcoholics — often treating a child in recovery off and on over a long period of time — I have found that there is a congruence between the theoretical assumptions and the psychotherapeutic realities. Whether we view the child of the alcoholic from the perspective of symptoms, defenses, or roles, these are believed to be but expressions of an underlying disorder in the child's ability to self-regulate. This is a shift in orientation from psychopathology and social adaptation to the selfhood of the child. The model, while emphasizing the child's subjective experience, does not exclude the other members of the alcoholic family system. Indeed, the parents or caretakers and even the siblings are discussed as integral to a child's sense of self. However, these significant others are viewed from a self psychological perspective which emphasizes the child's need to draw from others a variety of important self-regulating functions. The overall family system provides the context within which these interactions take place.

As demonstrated in my earlier study, the presence or absence of caretaking functions becomes a part of a child's intrapsychic reality. While these functions are necessary for psychological well-being and self cohesion in *all* children, they appear to be virtually lacking in the child of the alcoholic. How these functions become distorted and constitute the basis of problems in self-regulation even into adulthood will be the primary focus of the discussion to follow. It is believed that self cohesion disorders not only affect younger children of alcoholics but also explain the dilemma of adult children of alcoholics and the potential for addictive disorders.

During the past 30 years, we have made gargantuan strides within the alcoholism treatment field. Treatment centers abound where services to the alcoholic include some form of care for the spouse and children. However, we are still neonates in our search for a better understanding of the problems before us.

We have come full circle, it seems, from the recognition of alcoholism as a complex disease to the most recent dispute which claims that this is all a big *myth*: "Alcoholics simply drink *too much booze* and should be ashamed of themselves for such impropriety!" This type of moral indictment of alcoholics was common during the prohibition era and recently revived when the Veterans Administration labeled alcoholism as "willful misconduct." The V.A. position was upheld by the Supreme Court in a decision on April 20, 1988, which ruled:

"Medical opinion is strongly divided on whether alcoholism is a disease." The High Court is believed to have been strongly influenced by a professor of *philosophy*, Herbert Fingarette of the University of California, who has written that *his* evaluation of the "bulk of scientific evidence" does not support the disease concept of alcoholism. As we bear in mind that philosophers specialize in defining *moral* issues, we also must recognize that they are not medical or scientific experts in the identification and classification of pathological processes.

Once again, economics seem to be dictating whether or not this most serious of public health problems will be viewed as respectable enough to warrant rehabilitation. (It is worthwhile to pause long enough to see just *how far* back in time this moral view of alcoholism will take us. Two centuries ago, the father of the American public health movement, Dr. Benjamin Rush, established that habitual drunkenness is an *addiction* and, specifically, a *disease*.)

While the researchers continue to debate why some folks are so intemperate, we must direct our concern to the consequences of excessive alcohol and drug use for the affected members of their families and their children. We must recognize the critical nature of the work before us with the youth of our nation. I believe that this work must be cognizant of the phases of recovery in the parent and must actively involve the education and participation of the parent in the child's treatment. Our children remind us that we cannot *afford* to be so pompous as to consider alcoholism simply a matter of weak will when our society provides the breeding ground for addiction.

Over the years, I have been most interested in providing assistance to children of alcoholics during their middle childhood years. Children between the ages of seven and eleven usually are not able to speak with the language of adults when they are troubled. Normally quiescent children during these years live within a psychologically separate world of childhood, interacting with peers and siblings and offering little more than a passing nod—sometimes—to the adults around them. It is not surprising that these latency years tend to be the most overlooked and least understood of all developmental periods. However, problems which occur during this period—if not remediated—erupt into more serious disturbances during the teen years.

I am hopeful that the following discussion of the problems of school-aged children from alcoholic/addictive families will be useful in facilitating work with these children in a more in-depth manner. It is my belief that a model of children in recovery is also a model for the prevention of adult addictive disorders.

The usage of the pronouns "he" or "she" throughout this book was chosen first for ease of readability. There was never a deliberate intent to sexually stereotype children or parents. In most instances, the masculine or feminine use of a pronoun is really interchangeable.

PART I

The Traumatization
of Children

The children had been marching all night. They were headed unchaperoned towards the nation's capital, an estimated fifty thousand of America's youth below the age of twelve. They carried banners and placards which were crudely lettered in childish print:
"HELP. HELP. HELP. WE NEED YOUR HELP."
"LOOK AT US AND SEE. KIDS HAVE TO BE."
"START THE WAR. START THE WAR. WHO WILL START THE WAR?"
Militant children? Marching towards the nation's capital? Unchaperoned? Farfetched . . . perhaps.

After working with the children of alcoholism and addiction for the past 15 years, I am convinced that, if children could, they would wage a war. If there were resources which empowered children to organize and protest, that is exactly what one out of three American children would be doing right now. The war they would be starting, of course, would begin within their own families. This would be the war against an alcohol ravaged family culture — a substance-abusing, chemically dependent society which leaves in its wake the lives of its devastated young.

But, of course, children cannot organize, and their protest is barely audible. It is left up to the adult caretakers and interveners to take up the banners and the placards, to begin to make some sense of what children are trying to tell us through their troubled behavior and their desperate acts of self-destruction.

This is an effort to bring to light the problems of younger children from alcoholic and addictive families. We are still lagging in our preventive mental health efforts with these youngsters, who remain at high risk for serious emotional disorders and substance abuse problems. Before the child's cries for help become a cacophony of mental health problems, we must recognize the child has a need for recovery parallel to the parent's need for ongoing recovery from alcoholism and addiction. The practicing alcoholic/addictive parent (PAAP) syndrome, which I will discuss in Chapter 8, can be seen in children during their middle years of childhood. These disturbances to the normal course of development require acute intervention when the parent begins treatment. The acute phase of any type of chemical dependency treatment is *only* a beginning, however, not a panacea.

Children in recovery need to be understood from a model of psychophysiological *trauma*. This model recognizes the process of childhood development as proceeding from a complex interplay of psychophysiological factors. Interferences in development can occur when a child encounters either general or specific traumas. The model emphasizes the *general trauma* which these children experience from ongoing, chronic parental addictive practices and interactions. Then, the model delineates the *specific traumas* from among those hazards commonly experienced by these children. Physical abuse, sexual abuse, emotional and psychological abuse, parental violence and promiscuity, abandonment, neglect, and actual child substance abuse are typical distortions of alcoholic/addictive family life.

A parent's chemical dependency is in and of itself psychologically disruptive to the developing child. Parental alcoholism as a single factor has had a measureable, deleterious effect in the lives of school-aged children (Nylander, 1960). Nevertheless, in the past 25 years, researchers have continued to debate these typical questions.

- Are the problems which are *seen* in children of alcoholics more likely due to some aberration of their genes or to their environment?
- If there *really* are environmental effects upon a child because of the parent's drinking, is it because the parent drinks (a little, moderately, a lot)?
- What, if any, are the positive effects of growing up in an alcoholic family?

The last question, perhaps the most scientifically detached of them all, accentuates the gap between research interests and the realities of pressing clinical problems. However, as these nature versus nurture questions continue to be argued in the years to come, they may be expected to gather all the intensity of the Scopes versus Darwin monkey trials.

With a certain type of professional denial we do not want to see what is before our very eyes. Meanwhile, the children of alcoholism and addiction continue to be bruised, battered, and scarred mentally and physically as their general and specific traumas go untreated. *Professional denial* means that we refuse, as helpers, to ask the difficult questions.

Claudia Black, one of the leading advocates for children of alcoholics, has made an observation about the denial of parental alcoholism among mental health professionals who work with child abuse:

> A social worker who was a caseworker in a county juvenile detention center told of how she repeatedly worked with several children from the same family because of their delinquent behavior. Physical abuse by the father was identified. Alcohol abuse was mentioned several times by the children. The children were dealt with individually, not as a family unit, and the *father's treatment for alcoholism was not considered as a remedy for the physical abuse or the children's behavior. The drinking was never* discussed in a manner which could have identified it as alcoholic drinking. Thus, the dynamics of alcoholism and how it contributed to the delinquent behavior of the children was left unexplored and untreated. Had this social worker been knowledgeable about alcoholism, the correct resources could have been utilized and the children helped to a healthier lifestyle. (1981, p. 167; italics mine)

Although I would argue that the father's treatment for alcoholism is not *the remedy* for physical abuse or the children's behavior, it is the point where treatment must begin. More accurately, the intervention for any type of abuse of a child must begin with an *assessment* of parental alcoholism and addiction. But the treatment of the chemically dependent parent is *only* a beginning; it does not constitute the basis of recovery for the child. The emotional pain of a damaged child-self cannot be healed in a few short weeks.

In this section, I will be emphasizing a type of professional denial which I believe is the reverse of that portrayed in the preceding vignette by Claudia Black, though equally pernicious. This is the professional denial that encompasses the parent's treatment for alcoholism and addiction. There is a tendency to deny all but the most obvious forms of abuse which already have begun to cripple a child's existence, as well as to see the parent's treatment as the panacea that will also repair the child's trauma. But the rent in a child's fractured psyche cannot be repaired without ongoing, individual attention for the child, as well as ongoing work which seeks to heal the damaged parent-child relationship.

In the chapters which follow we consider the various forms of traumatization of children from alcoholic and addictive families. Chapter 1 discusses the effects of substance abuse, while Chapter 2 discusses physical abuse, sexual abuse, psychological maltreatment, and neglect.

The Poly-Addicted Family

Boys and girls can legitimately blame parents when, after bringing about their existence, they do not furnish them with that start in life which is their due.

—*D. W. Winnicott, 1986, p. 124*

The traumatic effects of alcoholic and addictive family life begin with a child's *exposure* to a variety of mood-altering, toxic substances. Before this child is able to exercise free will—even before this child is born—parental substance abuse commences to exert an influence upon the life of the child. I am not talking about problems which only occur in utero, such as fetal alcohol syndrome. I am talking about the genetic influences which will be brought to bear upon a child's life as a result of a parent's chemical dependency. We have the dramatic evidence of the abuse to an unborn child which occurs when a pregnant mother continues to drink alcohol or use heroin. However, the abuse which an alcoholic father may contribute when he has been drinking and using heavily at the time of conception still needs to be demonstrated scientifically. Denial of the father's role in transmitting childhood disorders will persist until science provides more exacting information *or* until there is a shift in our cultural value system. Meanwhile, we must concentrate on those environmental traumas which can be *seen* as a result of the parent's ongoing addictive practices in the home.

During the past 15 years as I have worked with alcoholic families and their children, I have been led to an expanded awareness of the dynamics of *addiction*. Rarely, if ever, have I seen a "pure alcoholic" type parent or family. (I am doubtful if such a phenomenon even exists in our culture today.) After working with these families through the process of recovery, often over long periods of time, I have seen the ongoing struggles of the sober alcoholic parent as well as the other family members with various addictions, often in combination. These addictive practices encompass both street and prescribed drugs, nicotine, caffeine, food, sex, exercise, hobbies, shopping, spending, working, entertaining, relationships, and just about every aspect of human living.

Although there are a number of current definitions of addiction, which vary only slightly, the one I most favor has been abstracted from a recent edition of Webster's (1988): *"Addiction: To give oneself up or over to a constant practice, to apply habitually as one's mind to a constant practice."* Addiction is the surrendering of one's very *selfhood* to the substance, activity, or person. The practice is compulsive in nature and, despite life threatening consequences, is sustained by a life of its own.

A family who practices an alcoholic/addictive way of life rarely does so with respect to only one substance or activity. The term "poly-addicted family" is used to describe the numerous addictions which occur, either at the same time or serially among the members.

Alcohol continues to be our nation's most commonly abused drug; however, one-third of those who use alcohol also abuse other drugs. These statistics do not include other "respectable drugs" such as prescribed medications, nicotine, and caffeine. Of those individuals who abuse illicit drugs, about two-thirds also have an abuse/dependence problem with alcohol. Another way of viewing these statistics is that, while alcohol continues to be our most commonly abused drug, problems with other drugs involve the concomitant use of alcohol (Norton & Noble, 1987).

ALCOHOLISM

The abuse of a child as a result of familial alcoholism can take the form of either psychological or physiological maltreatment. Direct physiological maltreatment occurs when a child engages in self-destructive alcohol consumption at an early age, either through self-administration or through being served alcoholic beverages by a parent figure. The alcoholic family system also contributes deviant parental interactions and behaviors which appear to produce psychological trauma for a child.

Early research which attempted to show the connection between chronic alcoholism in a parent and children's psychological reactions was conducted by Nylander (1960), who compared a matched, non-alcoholic control sample to a group of 229 children, ages four to twelve, whose fathers were undergoing treatment for alcoholism in Stockholm. Children of alcoholics evidenced three symptoms per child for both boys and girls, although for girls the number of symptoms increased with age. Among girls there was a higher frequency of physical symptoms (tiredness, headache, nausea, vomiting, etc.), while boys showed a greater number of speech and conduct disorders.

More recently, the heightened psychological risk for all children with alcoholic parents was investigated by Steinhausen, Godel, and Nestler (1984). Children between the ages of one and eighteen years were studied in order to determine the specific connections between parental alcoholism and psychological disorders. Children whose fathers were alcoholic tended to show a greater frequency of conduct disorders, whereas children with an alcoholic mother tended to show more emotional problems. When both parents were alcoholic, children were affected equally by conduct disorders and emotional problems. When the children were compared according to their sex, the boys had significantly higher scores overall as well as higher scores for conduct disorders and hyperactivity. There was a clear trend for the boys with conduct disorders to be from families with an alcoholic father.

When we turn from the empirical research findings to ongoing clinical observations, we are led to the same conclusion. Over the years I have found that even the most dutiful child from an alcoholic family will signal distress by subtle and not so subtle attention-gaining mechanisms. A good little girl from an alcoholic home may complain of a vague stomachache, for example, when she is feeling overwhelmed by the stresses of alcoholic family life. It is left up to the discerning adult to translate these symptoms into a statement of family dysfunction.

During ongoing aftercare and recovery programs for alcoholics, many of which last as long as one to two years, there is little provision for intensive work with children who have suffered the traumas of parental addiction. These high-risk children constitute the *majority* of the children from alcoholic/addictive families. Here I am emphasizing an apparent disagreement with Black's (1981) observations that the majority of school-aged children from alcoholic families do not draw enough attention to themselves to be identified as "in need of special attention." Although the data base for Black's observations is unclear, she appears to be making inferences from statements made to her by adult children of alcoholics who have remembered that they were well behaved during childhood and did not draw attention to themselves. Numerous consultations with trained school personnel over the years have convinced me that they *can* reliably detect the child from a substance abusing family. Behavior problems in boys of the seven to nine age group or emotional intensity among high achieving girls is usually a reliable clue.

The portrayal of children of alcoholics as a silent majority of overcompensated, well-behaved high achievers is not borne out by the research and long-term clinical findings. It is more likely that children are not *identified* as being from alcoholic/addictive families and in need of special assistance because their pleas for help (conduct problems, somatic distress, intense need to please) are not met with empathic attunement by the potential helper. It should be remembered that children of the years of middle childhood will *rarely* use *words* to ask for assistance. This psychological separation of children from the world of adults is even more pronounced in youngsters from chemically dependent families.

While a child may be genetically predisposed to develop alcoholism in later life, it seems that in many instances *exposure* to alcohol is the catalyst activating that predisposition. As the basic biosocial unit, the family is responsible for the child's early socialization. This obligates the family to see that a child has the freedom of choice about whether or not to engage in an alcohol-related lifestyle; however, children of alcoholics do *not* have this choice. Their lives involve family gatherings and rituals, as well as problem-solving situations, where the drinking plays a prominent role (Steinglass, Bennett, and Wolin, 1987).

> The children of alcoholics are vulnerable. They are vulnerable to the effects of poor or inadequate models who are alcoholics and who happen to be their parents. They are exposed to complex patterns of behavior that show adults coping with stress by the use of alcohol, and they are exposed to mass media that encourage alcohol use as a necessary accompaniment of human pleasure and socialization. When the

child is younger, excessive alcohol use may appear as an effective social stimulant and an anxiety-reduction substance, and thus set the stage for the later elicitation of similar behaviors by the grown child. By the time the social or physical decay of chronic alcoholism is apparent, the child may be so reinforced and patterned toward excessive alcohol use that the outcome is certain. If thought of in this way, it is surprising that *all* the children of alcoholics do not become alcoholics themselves. (Burk, 1972, p. 195)

Adults with a strong alcohol-orientation towards life will not have the slightest idea about the destructive effects of the drug upon the delicate physiological system of a child.

Case Illustration — Andy

Andy, a three-year-old boy, was brought to his first therapy session by his distraught mother, who was the adult child of an alcoholic (ACA). This mother was gravely concerned about some recent behavior problems in Andy, which she believed were in some way related to Andy's having consumed alcohol to the point of intoxication a few months earlier. She claims that Andy had been given the alcohol by his maternal grandmother, a practicing alcoholic. While left in the care of this grandmother during his mother's vacation, Andy had come down with a chest cold. The alcoholic grandmother, in characteristic style, had looked for treatment remedies in her liquor cabinet, medicating the child with a mixture of sugar, lemon, and bourbon. Andy's reaction to the "hot toddy" was to become giddy with drunkenness, performing for his grandparents in a cute and silly manner. Unwittingly, the grandmother had shared this "cute" information with Andy's mother upon her return, only to be stunned by her daughter's irate reaction.

We can only surmise what will be stored in Andy's memory from this deeply impressionable age about the relief available in the drug, ethanol, and about the warm, physiological soothing which transforms pain into fun and celebration.

Exposure to alcohol, where children begin ingesting various forms of ethanol at a very young age, is commonly reported to me by the children of alcoholics in recovery. Fond, warm memories of sharing a sip from a father's beer are often among the only recollections of closeness with an alcoholic parent that a child may have. The conditioned learning which is likely to take place will undoubtedly involve "beer" in the child's later associations to intimacy. Statistics indicate that 30% of fourth graders experience pressure to try alcohol, while 33.4% of the nation's sixth graders have tried beer or wine. Alcohol use among sixth graders more than doubled from 1983 to 1987 (Harrity and Christensen, 1987). We often assume that these children drink under the influence of peer pressure; however, it is often the very parents who should be protecting them from substance abuse who initiate them and continue to supply their alcohol and drugs.

Parents who are consuming large amounts of alcohol or drugs become lost in their own self-absorption. Rarely do they know about many of their children's difficulties. Often, if they do know, they shrug or look the other way. Many children linger around to sip at leftover drinks after the parents pass out from intoxication. Bottles stolen from a liquor closet are rarely missed.

A school-aged child who misbehaves and then sees her mother reach for a glass of wine develops a set of perceptions about the nature of reality. She sees that her misbehavior leads to parental substance use. When, under the influence of the alcohol, the parent continues to belittle and chastise the child, there will be no doubt in that child's mind about *why* that parent is drinking. "My Mom doesn't like me. She thinks I'm a creep. She has to drink wine because I make her so unhappy." Such perceptions are extremely resistant to change.

When a family enters treatment and we tell a child that none of the previously disturbing parent-child interactions was caused by *her* or that *she* was "not to blame," we must be aware of the implications of our message. That child has been told repeatedly by the primary caretaker that she *is* the problem. Even though we may educate a child about the parent's problem and explain that the disease is the problem, that child's internal belief system is not likely to change until new, improved parent-child interactions have been sustained over many months.

Children need to know early on that their difficult internal feelings states *are* valid. We must share their outrage at being used and abused by their parent's alcoholism. While we can attribute the cause to the disease of addiction, we must be cautious about discounting the child's perceptions. By sharing the child's hurt and outrage, we acknowledge the value of the *experiencing self*. By contributing to a child's denial, we perpetuate the cycle of addiction.

> Eventually, all the child's bottled-up rage at being humiliated, deprived of respect, misunderstood, and left alone is turned against herself in the form of addiction. (Alice Miller, 1983, p. 113)

When do children begin to perpetuate the cycle of addiction? Children of ten and eleven reported getting drunk at least once a week, according to the National Council on Alcoholism (Lipsitt, 1988c). Alcohol, the drug most typically abused by children, can be linked to parental drinking. Whether one or both parents drank was the best predictor of a child's use of alcohol. Of the 28.6 million children of alcoholics in the U.S. today, about one-third are under the age of 18. These children have a risk four times greater than do children from the general population of becoming alcoholic.

Another survey which was conducted by the Center for Science in the Public Interest (CSPI) examined children's awareness of alcoholic beverages. General information questions were presented to children between the ages of two and twelve years. Questions included the names of presidents, measurements and other information which a child commonly would retain from environmental learning. Although this study did not screen for parental alcoholism, we are led to an important conclusion about the addictive nature of our society as mirrored in our youth. Children could provide as many names (and sometimes more) to different types of alcoholic beverages as to the names of presidents. Other general information questions, such as how many inches in a foot, were sometimes unknown even by the older children who, nevertheless, could list various brands of beer and wine. According to one of the sponsors of the survey, "There's something drastically wrong when kids can name as many alcoholic products as presidents" (Lipsitt, 1988d, p. 7). One of four eighth graders were reported to drink five or more alcoholic drinks on a single occasion in the two weeks prior to a similar survey.

These studies demand our recognition that alcohol is a regular part of the lives of many children during the years of middle childhood, and then typically leads to the use of other drugs.

ILLICIT DRUGS IN THE FAMILY

Parents who use drugs both within and outside the home usually choose from an array of available street drugs, prescription drugs, and over-the-counter medications. During my work with the families of alcoholism and addiction, I have seen parents who have been dependent on any one or a combination of drugs, including traditional street drugs such as heroin, "designer" drugs, physician-prescribed medications, and other products which can be purchased off the drugstore shelf. Although a parent may select one of these as the primary drug of choice, alcohol may be used abusively as well. Often these parents appear to be attempting to self-regulate emotions, for example using cocaine when an energy boost is needed or the weakened self seeks to feel powerful and then, to stop soaring, using alcohol, or marijuana, or both. This is life in the fast lane—where the media still heralds the message to look outside oneself for quick relief—in a shockingly addicted American family culture.

Designer Drugs

Designer drugs are chemical substances with molecular structures which can be altered in home laboratories to produce powerful synthetic substances. One such drug which is produced widely in San Diego, California, and is affecting adults and young alike is methamphetamine. Known commonly as *crystal* (or *crank*, or *meth*) this drug has become the second most abused drug in the southwestern United States. Carried in small glass or plastic vials or folded slips of paper, the drug is snorted into the nostrils. The effects of crystal are those of other amphetamine derivatives—anorexia, alertness, a sense of well-being, and pleasant memories. Addiction rapidly develops from experimentation through dependency, with severe mood disturbance, paranoia, weight loss, chronic tension, and insomnia. Crystal is commonly used by young adults in the twenties and thirties, an age group often comprising parents of children in the middle years of childhood.

Other designer drugs include "china white," a synthetic heroin-type drug; "ecstasy," a cocaine-like substance; and "crack," which is a cocaine distillate. Crack has been described as "the nation's newest— and most frightening—job program" for youthful inner-city pushers (Lamar, 1987). However, privileged children are also being affected, as they form the clientele of the inner-city dealers. According to Lamar, "There is a terrible symbiosis between the wealthy addicts and the inner-city dealers." Children in the years of middle childhood are already being recruited into the cadre of inner-city drug dealers. "Some of the latest abusers are barely out of babyhood. . . . a Detroit drug program is preparing to treat children as young as six" (Lamar, 1987, p. 24).

The Culture of Addiction

Although the impact of street drugs on the lives of children appears to follow some type of socioeconomic pattern, *all* of today's youth are being affected in some way or another. Music, films, television, and dress style all mimic the drug heroes and heroines of the street. Drug-related juvenile arrests have more than tripled in certain major cities (Detroit, New York) during the 1980s, while in Los Angeles they have climbed from 41 arrests in 1980 to a staggering 1,719 in 1987. The number of crack users is said to be increasing at a rate of 2,000 per day. Among the years of middle childhood, 25% of children in the fourth grade say they feel pressured to use drugs, while 11% of sixth graders begin to use drugs while they are in that grade. Many junior high school age children already know the drug dealers in their community, but most begin their drug use through being given drugs by members of their family, friends, or baby-sitters (Harrity and Christensen, 1987).

Illicit drugs commonly used by parents in the middle-class American household include marijuana, cocaine, heroin, and any one or a combination of the designer drugs. Often parents make the drugs in the household available for a child's use. Or the child is exposed to the parents' use and secretively gains access to these drugs during the parents' absence. Ziegler-Driscoll (1979) examined the family characteristics of two groups of substance abusers—alcoholics and drug dependent individuals—both in their late twenties or early thirties. A major similarity of the two groups was the high rate of substance abuse, particularly alcohol, among their families of origin. These researchers found that the behavior of the children of the substance abusers was an effective barometer of the parent's recovery process. Antisocial behavior and poor academic performance in a child accompanied the parents' return to substance abuse.

In most metropolitan areas, one out of every three children is from a substance-abusing family. This means that parents, who are preoccupied with their own alcoholic/addictive practices, often are completely unaware of the extent of a child's drug involvement. Other times parents are the ones who are responsible for turning a child on to drugs. In many cases, a parent simply looks the other way.

The following is a rather macabre warning from one metropolitan police department to those responsible for the custodial care of younger children.

FROM YOUR LOCAL POLICE DEPARTMENT

*** D A N G E R   A L E R T ***

Attention: PARENT, GRANDPARENTS, OR OTHER CONCERNED PERSONS

There is a community danger for the children in the form of a tattoo called "BLUE STAR", and is sold all over the United States. It is a small sheet of white paper containing blue stars the size of a pencil eraser. Each star is soaked with LSD.

Each star can be removed and placed in the mouth. The LSD can be absorbed through the skin simply by handling the paper. There are also brightly colored paper tabs resembling postage stamps that have pictures of Superman, butterflies, clowns, Mickey Mouse, and other Disney characters on them.

These stamps are packaged in a red cardboard box wrapped in foil. This is a new way of selling ACID by appealing to *young children*. A young child could happen upon these and have a fatal TRIP. It is also learned that little children could be given a free tattoo by older children who want to have some fun or cultivate new customers.

PLEASE, PLEASE ADVISE YOUR CHILDREN
ABOUT THESE DRUGS.

If you or your children see any of the above, DO NOT HANDLE.

CALL THE POLICE

Symptoms include: hallucinations, severe vomiting, mood change, change of body temperature. If you are aware of these symptoms in your child, get the child to the hospital at once.

When a parent is in a drug-induced state, that parent is not able to be responsive to the child's needs. Whether or not the child has direct observation of the drug abuse, there is an awareness of the aberrant nature of the parent's interactions that strongly influences the child.

Case Illustration — Buff

What I most remember about this cute, pudgy boy of seven was the difficulty he had attempting to self-regulate during our first several sessions. Buff interrupted his activities in the play therapy room at least six times in the course of a half-hour to go to the water cooler for a drink. He also chewed nervously on the taffy candy which bulged inside his pockets. His play was chaotic and disorganized, indicating an inner state that was filled with turmoil.

Buff, a second grader, had full knowledge of his mother's drug-related activities. He had seen her snorting and shooting up cocaine and crystal methamphetamine. He had seen her coming down with alcohol. He complained about the smoke when she used "weed" to calm herself. He had filled a towel with ice cubes and taken it to ease her headaches when she was hungover. He had defended her in the presence of her various boyfriends when violence was threatened. During the last days of his mother's using, when she had become increasingly paranoid, Buff had fled with her in the middle of the night to another state, where he had stood watch, reassuring her that her imaginary pursuers were nowhere in sight.

Buff himself, as it turns out, was not that sure about these fantasized pursuers. When he and his mother began child recovery work during her third month of abstinence, Buff needed to ask her to explain. With embarrassment, his mother explained that there had been no one in reality; her paranoia was a result of her heavily drugged condition. Buff sucked on an all-day lollipop, fidgeting back and forth in his chair as his mother continued to try to explain about the influence of the drugs. During the discussion, Buff recalled how his mother had often given him as much as ten dollars at a time to go off to the store and buy treats when she had not wanted to be bothered. Most often he would buy a Big-Stick Slush Bar, a box of Jelly-Bellies, a bag of corn chips, M and M's, and some baseball cards. That would last him a few hours. . . .

By the end of his mother's sixth month of abstinence, she had become willing to discuss her physical and psychological abuse of

Buff. Work with her own damaged, abused childhood freed this mother to become deeply empathic with her son. However, she continued to have difficulty depriving him of the junk food he constantly craved. She felt "mean" and withholding until she had been educated about the drug-like effect of sugar consumption on Buff. Buff's diet was changed and he, too, was educated, both in therapy and by his mother. Healthier treats now included nuts, popcorn, fresh fruit, yogurt, cheese and crackers. By the time the mother had completed one year of abstinence, Buff had calmed considerably. Not only was he able to remain in a play therapy session without leaving the room, but he was able to sit through a full talking session and converse attentively.

During recovery work, a parent is often shocked to find that her drug use, which she believed she had kept secret from the child, was known all along.

Case Illustration — Claudine

Claudine, an eleven-year-old, was an incest victim of her alcoholic stepfather. Her mother was addicted to crystal methamphetamine. When this family entered treatment after the molestation had come to light, Claudine's mother insisted that she had protected her daughter from knowledge of her drug use — just as she had protected her three youngest daughters from incest. This mother was extremely angry with Claudine for becoming involved in a rivalrous relationship with her husband. She had a great deal of difficulty seeing that the stepfather was in any way responsible. Why, she demanded, was she being accused of a failure to protect her child?

During the fifth month of therapy, Claudine authored a picture story which indicated that she was aware of the nature and implications of her mother's drug involvement. One of the pictures showed a couple huddled over a table with a child's face peering from behind a door. The caption read:

"One night when my sisters wouldn't go to sleep, I went out to tell Mom. It was very quiet out there, so I stood and watched. My Mom and Step-Dad had straws up their noses. Then, my Mom looked around and screamed at me, 'You little bitch, get back in your bedroom.'"

Claudine's second drawing showed a bedroom scene with her stepfather reaching for her. The caption read:

" . . . and so, after that, my Mom would go out to her friends' to use her drugs. When she was out to their house, my Step-Dad would drink lots of beer, and then tell me to get the other kids to sleep, and then he would motion for me to come to bed with him. . . . "

Children *are* aware of the horrors of alcoholic/addictive family life. Although a child may disavow the full emotional significance of her mother's abandonment of her, she does perceive accurately. These perceptions become registered and, as a result of the little child's impressionable state, later act as determinants of behavior.

The problems which Claudine later demonstrated with self-regulation were very similar to Buff's initial problems with candy and junk food. Indeed, as Claudine's incest work proceeded and she became flooded with feelings, her junk food consumption escalated and became problematic. In her group work at another agency, where she was in therapy with other incest victims her age, Claudine became disruptive and hostile, running in and out of the group to the vending machines to buy candy and soft drinks.

Not unlike that of her mother (who had been the victim of a long, incestuous relationship with her natural father), Claudine's substance abuse was reflective of her inner state. The mother chose a synthetic amphetamine to overstimulate herself abusively as had been done to her by the father of her childhood. In the same way, Claudine binged addictively on junk food at a particular time in her recovery work when she felt out of control and could not regulate her feelings.

The Trap of Professional Denial

To have been misled initially by Claudine's very organized, ultra responsible behavior (she was the family caretaker) would have been to fail to do the necessary work of recovery. Indeed, Claudine's façade of self-reliance had been part of the problem. She had carried her lonely incest secret for many months before turning to an adult. To adults lacking the sensitivity to see beyond the rigid defensive style of her role behavior, Claudine's inner world was inaccessible. Also, focusing on this family as simply "an alcoholic family" or "an incest family" would have oversimplified the complex nature of intergenerational processes in poly-addicted families.

When this case was examined by another evaluator for juvenile court proceedings, he was highly critical of the fact that the child had been in therapy for one year. "A year is too long for any kid!" he reasoned. This evaluator claimed that *brief intervention* should be the therapy of choice with "any kid" and stated that he simply did not believe in such "nonsense" as dissociative processes, which commonly affect young incest or physical abuse victims and which may leave the child with problems in self cohesion that last a lifetime or even ultimately with a severe adult problem, such as multiple personality disorder. "Nonsense!" the evaluator said, "There's never more than the *one* personality you see right before your eyes. If you can't see it and count it, then it doesn't exist."

Claudine's self cohesion was strengthened by therapy, despite the evaluator's disclaimer, "*Playing* with a kid is not therapy!" As Claudine became increasingly empowered, she sought verbal channels to express her outrage. She told the therapist that she was still angry and mistrustful of her stepfather, who was drinking wine with dinner even though he claimed to be abstinent. She stated that she preferred to remain in foster care. "Then the therapy is not working," the evaluator said. "If a kid is still *mad* at one of her parents after all this therapy, then the therapy is not working!"

Why did the male evaluator have difficulty seeing that the therapy really *was* working? For Claudine to be able to verbalize her misgivings about her stepfather and to refuse return to the home while he was still drinking alcohol was a triumph over the potential for victimization. Why did the evaluator not *see* this?

Professional denial leads to difficulty in seeing a child victim as a real person, with an independent center of initiative. The retraumatization of a child by a professional "helper" happens not only every day but every few hours of every day, when decisions are made irrevocably. The question of "what is in the best interest of the child" often becomes an accommodation to "due process" for the parent and "parental rights."

Case Illustration — Dirk

When eleven-year-old Dirk literally swaggered into therapy, it was at the urging of his mother. Dirk had lived in a split custody arrangement since the age of ten, alternating weeks between the homes of his mother and his father. Dirk's mother was a fastidious woman who was very successful as a real estate agent, and she placed rigid demands on Dirk's behavior. However, she did not suspect that his verbal abuse of her, his lying, and his stealing were related to his drug use. More accurately, she was in denial.

While in the custody of his father, Dirk was often left to care for himself. The father, who refused to come in for therapy with Dirk, was said to be an alcoholic who also used cocaine. He was an occasional drug dealer who lavished Dirk with material benefits. He worked sporadically at a used car lot owned by his father, but the family business allowed him to be lax about his work schedule.

Dirk's mother was interested in changing the split custody arrangement so that she could have full-time physical custody of her son. She hoped that a psychological evaluation would support this process by showing that the father's laxity was responsible for the boy's problems.

During our work together, Dirk bragged to me that he was free to use the drugs in his father's home: "Hey, he has parties almost every night. It's no big deal if I get high. Who's gonna notice?"

Dirk's flippant attitude indicated that the effects of the cocaine were furthering a grandiose sense of self-importance. Dirk was powerful — except when his father cut him down to size. The only problems in his life, Dirk said, as he stifled a yawn, *were* his parents. His Mom nagged, and his Dad would "go off" on him, yelling and belittling him. But then, said Dirk, his Dad could "really mellow out," and things got "pretty cool." His Mom, however, was *always* "uptight."

When this case went before Family Court, Dirk told the conciliation counselor that he preferred to live with his Dad. Against his mother's protestations about the drug using and dealing environment in his father's home, Dirk told the counselor that his Mom was "a nag." Dirk's mother was told that the decision of the court — to place Dirk full-time with his father — was based on "what is in the best interest of the child." Her son preferred to be with his father. The boy was clearly expressing a need, the court stated, to have "a consistent male role model" on a full-time basis.

Further, the court ruled against the mother about the boy's need for counseling. That decision — counseling for Dirk — would have to be made by the custodial parent, in this case, Dirk's father.

In the process of evaluating the question, *what is in the best interest of the child*, there continues to be a lack of adequate substance abuse histories of the parents. When ambiguous cases of child neglect and abuse are seen, for example, a thorough screening for substance abuse, including routine urine checks from the parents, may save a child's life.

For children from lower socioeconomic families, the exposure to illicit drugs tends to be commonplace. These children are also the victims of the grosser forms of abuse and neglect, and they tend to show such severe problems in self-regulation that they are often misdiagnosed as "mentally retarded" or "hyperactive" and placed on a drug such as Ritalin, only to begin the cycle of continuing drug use. These children may be removed from their seriously disturbed family environments temporarily, only to be placed again within the same family, where the problems tend to be repeated. A lack of ongoing, sustained recovery efforts for the parents and the children perpetuates the cycle of addiction and child abuse. When a parent does come into contact with some legal agency as a result of child abuse or neglect, often it is the symptom of incest or physical abuse which receives the primary focus. The parents will be ordered to participate in a series of programs to increase their parenting skills or communication skills; however, the requirement that the parent needs *first* to complete a program of treatment for substance abuse is only a token one. A few counseling sessions or a few months of alleged abstinence will constitute the basis of substance abuse "recovery."

Is it any wonder that there is a high recidivism rate among substance-abusing, child-abusing families?

RESPECTABLE DRUGS AT HOME

> It is not unheard of for a mother to give her year-old baby Valium so he will sleep soundly if she wants to go out in the evening. . . . If Valium becomes the means of insuring the child's sleep, a natural balance will be undermined at a very early age. . . . The Valium not only undermines the child's natural ability to fall asleep but also interferes with the development of his perceptive faculties. At this early age the child is not supposed to know that he has been left alone, is not supposed to be afraid, and perhaps later (as an) adult will be unable to perceive inner danger signals as a result. (Alice Miller, 1983, p. 132)

Physician-prescribed medications may result in a chemically dependent family structure where addiction to the "respectable drug" is not even discussed as a problem. Yet, ongoing use of tranquilizers, pain killers, sedatives, and other classes of mood-altering chemicals accounts for parents who are not only unaware of their own inner processes but also insensitive to their children's imbalances.

Our cultural tradition of granting to physicians the status of guardianship over questions of mental health has led to our unquestioning acceptance of their prescriptions for our lives. The powerful authority invested in "the doctor," along with the power of the pill, has filled in that missing part of the self that lacked inner strength. Physician-prescribed drugs hold a source of magic which imparts soothing to the troubled spirit. No spiritual resolve is needed. Comfort, tranquility, well-being, and serenity are each available in capsule form, tablets, pills, or elixirs — available at any time and with instantaneous results.

The likelihood that a parent is abusing prescription drugs should be considered in every case of familial alcoholism. Until a thorough history and screening have been completed for the use of these medications, recovery for the parents and children will be thwarted. Parents typically will not volunteer information about addiction to prescription drugs. They remain guarded and secretive about their use, particularly when the drug is being used for the purposes of self-regulation.

A parent who turns to socially approved chemicals is usually as dysfunctional as the parent who turns to daily alcohol. The name of the game in this parenting relationship is CONTROL. Parents who require regular prescriptions of drugs to control their own feelings rarely have empathic attunement to their child's emotional life. Indeed, there is a lack of tolerance for the child's emotions. Children come to learn early on that feelings — spontaneity, gaiety, exuberance, enthusiasm, anger, sadness, loneliness — are unacceptable to the disapproving parent. Therefore, feelings are BAD!

A child who is unable to integrate his emotional life into his self-experience develops essential problems in self-regulation. This child, like the parent before him, becomes predisposed to look outside himself for a chemical solution to his inner turmoil. These children become controlled, over-adapted, good little boys and girls who grow up to be bitter, controlling men and women who are perplexed by their own and their children's feelings. An emphasis on doing, on performing, on looking *good* overshadows the right to feel, to emote, to simply *be* in the world. As adult children, these individuals have the most resilient denial about having been reared in a chemically dependent family environment. Behind the false-self façade of intactness, there is the despair and longing of the lonely unmirrored child, the lost self. But, because these adults cannot permit the intrusion of their emotional pain, they are constantly shielding themselves from the pain of others.

Nicotine is one of the "respectable" addictive drugs commonly found in alcoholic/addictive families. Yet, cigarette smoking continues to be defended as the right of the individual. Despite the 1964 U.S. Surgeon General's finding linking smoking with lung cancer, Americans continue to smoke. Today the evidence is much less equivocal: Nicotine is an *addiction* as difficult to break as that to other mind-altering drugs. Among the most staunchly defiant about their addiction to nicotine are certain recovering alcoholics and addicts, who insist, "We can't be expected to give up everything!"

Another blind argument, which ignores the physical damage of secondhand smoke to others, especially children, goes something like this, "I'm not hurting anyone but myself." However, reports issued by the National Research Council and the U.S. Surgeon General in 1986 indicated that "environmental tobacco smoke" inhaled by unsuspecting smokers can cause lung cancer and other serious illnesses (Ticer and King, 1987).

Research completed on a matched sample of recovered alcoholics, relapsed alcoholics, and community controls found the heaviest smokers among relapsed alcoholics. However, the recovered alcoholics were more likely to smoke — and to smoke heavily — and to complain of one or more physical symptoms due to smoking than community controls (Moos, Finney, and Chan, 1981).

Children of smokers have been found to suffer more bronchitis, pneumonia, and other respiratory illnesses than children of non-smokers (Gibbs, 1988). In many instances of recovery work with the families of alcoholism and addiction, I have found that, when a parent smokes, one or more of the children tend to suffer allergies. Headaches; red, watery, itchy eyes; sneezing, wheezing, coughing — these are the physical side effects suffered by children who must live in smoke-filled environments.

Also, children are far more likely to become smokers when their parents smoke. Research supported by the National Institute of Health indicated that the "modeling effect" of parents' smoking increases the likelihood that a young person will smoke by his teen years. When the parents plus an older sibling smoke, there is a four-times greater likelihood that the teenager will smoke (Evans, 1988).

But what about the psychological maltreatment which children suffer as a result of parental nicotine addiction?

Numerous children in recovery speak to me privately about their parents' smoking. These children know about the physical consequences of smoking and suffer inner turmoil about the likelihood of abandonment if the parent becomes seriously ill. Their feelings must be taken seriously. More dramatically and cruelly, recovering parents have been known to threaten to start drinking again when their children confront them about their smoking.

Case Illustration — Emily

Emily was a thoughtful third grader of eight years, the youngest in a family of four, who was emotionally attached to her recovering alcoholic mother. This family had been in recovery work during the three years that the mother was recovering from alcoholism; meanwhile she continued to smoke.

At one individual child therapy session, Emily spotted a book on a shelf in my office by Adele Faber and Elaine Mazlish, *How To Talk So Kids Will Listen and Listen So Kids Will Talk* . . .

"I wish you could teach me how to talk so my mother will listen to me," Emily said, lowering her face. When she looked up, her eyes were brimming with tears. " . . . because I'm afraid my mother is going to die . . . she won't stop smoking and she won't listen to me when I try to tell her how scared I am about that."

As customary, I suggested to Emily that we could discuss her concern for her mother in a family session with her parents and her other three siblings. The rapport with this family had been built up over many weeks and months, and the mother's capacity for empathy with her children had been strengthened, I thought, so that she would respond appropriately to Emily's feelings.

However, in the family session, as Emily shared her fears, puckering her face to hold back more tears, her mother began to stiffen and to tap her foot nervously. Her face flushed by the time Emily had stopped speaking.

"Well now, what have we here?" The mother asked looking around the room accusingly. "My little Emily is plotting with the doctor to stop Mommy from smoking! Really! Well, darling, if you think Mommy is going to quit smoking just because *you* say so, you can think again. I have a right to do what *I* want to do in my own home. I'm not hurting you, or your sisters. So I don't want any of your pressure."

Then, slumping back in her chair in a regressive posture, Emily's mother changed her voice to a child-like plea, "Besides, darling, if you don't let up on Mommy about this smoking, you could make me start thinking about drinking again. . . . "

As of this writing, few chemical dependency treatment programs provide for the care of the nicotine-addicted alcoholic. Although there are some notable exceptions, smoking cessation programs and ongoing support are not provided routinely.

Caffeine is another mood-altering drug which has earned a highly respected place among folks who are recovering from alcoholism and addictions. The self-help program of Alcoholics Anonymous has among its unwritten traditions the saying, "The only thing needed to start an A.A. meeting is a couple of drunks and a coffee pot." Caffeinated beverages — whether coffee, tea, or carbonated drinks — become a part of the sober alcoholic's new way of life. However, caffeine is highly addicting and can interfere with the emotional life of a parent. Symptoms of irritability, anxiety, fear, and panic may be present in a recovering alcoholic parent who is consuming several cups of coffee and cola drinks each day. These negative feelings are bound to affect the parent-child interaction.

Caffeine is a drug we take for granted. I do not mean to suggest that the recovering parent should encounter yet another deprivation; however, it is important to educate the family about the stimulating effects of caffeine on physiological mechanisms. This education is the first step in enabling the parent to exercise sound decision-making for the child. Most recovering parents are extremely grateful for this education as a way of assisting their youngsters who may be drinking caffeinated soft drinks in huge quantities.

FOOD ADDICTIONS AND EATING DISORDERS

Eating disorders within the families of alcoholism and addiction affect not only adults but also children. As we have seen in the preceding case illustrations of Buff and Claudine, a food substance is used in the same way that other substances are used — as a source of soothing, stimulation and self-regulation.

The average kitchen cupboard in the families of alcoholism and addiction is a testimony to the value placed on sugar. Although a teaspoon of sugar may have only a short-range effect, to an addiction-prone individual one dose of sugar usually calls for another, which calls for yet another, and so on. . . .

Our historical tradition equates sugar availability with abundance and its lack with deprivation. When sugar rationing was discontinued after World War II, sweet treats became associated with the new image of the stable American family. A cultural stereotype of the nurturing mother was one who lovingly greeted her children with fresh-baked cookies. While the alcoholic mother may not be able to provide home-baked goods, she may supply the cash and instruct her youngster to trot off to the nearest pastry shop in search of satisfaction. Food as a substitute for the missing relationship with a parent is behind many a compulsive need to eat. In the absence of reliable, person-centered relationships, members of alcoholic/addictive families look for comfort outside themselves — in the refrigerator, the local deli, or the closest vending machine.

As many alcoholics withdraw from alcohol they begin to eat compulsively, ravenously. Small wonder. For, masked by alcoholism is a primary addiction to food substances. Many of the most addicting foods — sugar, corn products, white flour products — are also the essential ingredients in the various types of liquors — beer, whiskey, scotch, etc. — which have been used addictively in the past.

The authors of *Eating Right to Live Sober*, Dr. Ann Mueller and Katherine Ketcham, indicate that the mood swings and other serious symptoms of "the dry drunk syndrome" in a recovering alcoholic are nutritionally based.

> Most recovering alcoholics have no idea that their diet can contribute to a relapse. The most common mistake they make is to load up on sweets, which work quickly and effectively to get rid of fatigue, depression, the mid-morning blahs, and even the cravings for alcohol; but sweets contain a hidden time bomb that can transform the immediate relief into long-term discomfort and even agony. For alcoholics, sweets can actually be deadly, weakening sobriety to the point where the alcoholic is no longer able to fight the urge to drink — no matter how much he may want to stay sober. (1983, p. 18)

These authors identify "hypoglycemia," a condition of erratically fluctuating blood sugar commonly known as "low blood sugar," as prevalent among recovering alcoholics. This condition is responsible, they say, for over 30 sobriety-based symptoms: exhaustion, depression, insomnia, anxiety, irritability, headaches, tremor, and, even more severely, fainting, convulsions, and suicidal tendencies.

Nutritional disorders are prevalent among parents who have been affected by alcoholism and addictions. A parent may be in "recovery" for years but continue to show destructive food habits, leading to such physical consequences as obesity and hypertension. Rather than drinking away feelings, the parent uses food to escape. Children of these parents learn that food can be used to soothe, to calm, to entertain, to stimulate, to relieve boredom.

The self-experience of the child in the throes of nutritional disor-ganization will seem every bit as fragmenting and psychologically disruptive as other forms of serious mental disorders (Jesse, 1985). Yet, the problems of children of alcoholics are rarely linked to their nutritional status. In a recent exhaustive survey of the literature on younger children of alcoholics, I found not one reference which discussed or investigated the important relationship between these children's emotional and behavioral problems and their dietary prac-tices. It is likely that younger COAs suffer from the same type of cellular malnourishment that affects their parents. For example, a strong association between hyperactivity and attention deficit disor-der (ADD) in children of alcoholics has been reported frequently in the literature (see Chapter 6). Lipsitt (1987) reports a well-controlled study which links hyperactivity and ADD to elevated sugar levels in the child. Children aged eight to thirteen who were hyperactive were found to have higher than normal blood sugar levels. When these children were given a high-carbohydrate-with-sugar diet, their con-dition worsened, producing severe problems in attention and memory.

Another study of hyperactive children aged six to twelve suggests that these youngsters do not outgrow their disorder. "For most, their hyperactivity continues, and then becomes compounded by lower thresholds for abusing drugs, and getting into aggressive, delinquent modes of behavior" (Lipsitt, 1988b, p. 7).

During an informal retrospective survey of the children of alcohol-ic and addictive families whom I had treated over the past 15 years, I ascertained that roughly one-fourth suffered from problems in obesi-ty. Another 65% appeared to suffer from nutritional inadequacies. Children's conflicts over body image and the tendency to worry about their weight have been reported (Feldman, 1988), suggesting that the presence of eating disorders in these younger COAs further compounds their already low self-esteem.

The exposure of younger COAs to sweets and junk foods would appear to be greater than for children in the general population. Due to the erratic nature of mealtimes and parenting schedules in the home of practicing alcoholics and addicts, children may have no supervision of their diets. Often, they are simply given money by the parent and expected to fend for themselves. The lack of monitoring of nutrition by the parents is a problem which I see clinically demon-strated during early recovery. This does not appear to be the case for COAs who have been adopted into "normal," non-addictive families.

Case Illustration — Franky

Franky was the ten-year-old youngest son of a newly recovering alcoholic father. The boy had been having severe problems in the classroom and was described as "hyperactive" by some of his previous teachers. He was also said to be aggressive and hostile on the playground. A short attention span and distractibility interfered with his ability to retain information.

A nutritional evaluation at the beginning of recovery indicated that Franky usually made his own breakfast of sugared cereal and chocolate milk. He used his school lunch money on candy bars and sugared drinks from the vending machines. His father was so often dysfunctional and his mother so preoccupied with his father that no one ever questioned Franky about his meals. Afterschool snacks were more sugared specialties.

Frank was rarely hungry at supper when his mother rushed home from work to shove a heated TV dinner in front of him. He would turn up his nose and retreat to his room, where he had hoarded goodies, both to enjoy when he became hungry and to soothe himself during his parents' nightly arguing.

During child recovery work, after Franky's father had begun outpatient treatment for alcoholism, the information about Franky's poor nutrition came to light. His pediatrician expressed concern to the mother about her son's nutritional status when the boy sustained a fracture after falling at school.

Franky was withdrawn from his all-sugar menu by his mother, who now implemented a healthier diet, rich in vitamins and minerals. Whole grains, cheese, hard boiled eggs, potatoes, and fresh vegetables and fruits were included on Franky's home and school menus.

By the end of the first month, Franky had shown marked improvement in his school performance, both academically and socially. His pediatrician indicated that he no longer suffered from the previously diagnosed nutritional inadequacies. Most important of all, Franky's peer relationships improved as his aggressiveness decreased.

Children in recovery need the benefit of a careful nutritional assessment, as well as nutritional education and counseling. Often their problem behaviors are directly linked to dietary imbalances. Moreover, their food addictions and eating disorders may be precursors of later alcohol and drug problems.

CHAPTER 2

Prisoners of the Family War

Thus, it may well be that the plight of a little child who is abused is even worse and has more serious consequences for society than the plight of an adult in a concentration camp.

—Alice Miller, 1983, p. 116

On April 25, 1988, President Ronald Reagan signed into law legislation extending and revising programs on child abuse and family violence. In particular, this measure called for a two-year study by the National Center on Child Abuse and Neglect of "the incidence of child abuse in alcoholic families and the relationship between child abuse and familial alcoholism" (Lipsitt, 1988a).

Do children from alcoholic and addictive families suffer more abuse than children in other families?

The answer is an overwhelming, "Yes!" Recent statistics from one metropolitan Child Protective Services Bureau (Willingham, 1988) indicated that as many as 70–80% of children who suffer abuse and neglect are from substance-abusing households. Incest behavior has been associated historically with parental alcoholism. Indeed, one of the leading experts in the treatment of incest (Herman, 1987) has commented that incest families tend to follow the same pattern of family dynamics and compulsive styles as chemically dependent families. In all of these instances of alcoholism and addiction, as well as child abuse and incest, the family members are not valued as autonomous individuals, separate and distinct from one another. Rather, children come to be valued only for the functions they provide or the roles they fulfill. In the classic abusing family, the child is father to the man in the literal sense. In an instant of emotional regression, the abusive parent strikes out at the little child, whose misbehavior recreates for the parent his own childish feelings of frustration, helplessness, and failure. These are intergenerational abuse dynamics.

Children from alcoholic/addictive homes may be, and often are, abused or molested by the very parent who provides succorance. Although sibling abuse is common in these chemically dependent families, the children also huddle together during times of family crises. At other times, children show a callous, unfeeling attitude when a sibling is being abused: "Better you than me."

In this chapter, we will be considering the major categories of child abuse: physical abuse and neglect; incest/sexual abuse; and psychological/emotional abuse. In each of the categories, we will be discussing not only how the parent inflicts injury on a child, but also how siblings abuse each other. Sibling abuse, a regular occurrence in the families of alcoholism and addiction (Jesse 1977, 1988), has received almost no attention in the literature on children of alcoholics. Parental violence and its effects on the observing child are considered in the section on physical abuse and neglect.

PHYSICAL ABUSE AND NEGLECT

The role of alcohol in aggravating aggression and violence has been reported in the alcoholism literature over the years. Also, there is a great deal of literature on the physical abuse and neglect of children. While substance abuse is indicated as one of the influences upon parents who physically abuse their children, we find very few explicit links in the literature between alcoholism and child physical abuse. Yet clinical experience tells us that children of alcoholism and addiction experience exceptional physical cruelty, inflicted not only by parents but also by siblings.

Physical neglect, which tends to be chronic in nature, is the inattention of the child's caretakers to the child's basic needs for nurturance, food, clothing, shelter, medical care, safety and education. Of special importance to our discussion of the children of alcoholism and addiction are the behavioral signs of neglect (JAMA, 1985, p. 6):

- Lack of appropriate adult supervision
- Repeated ingestions of harmful substances
- Poor school attendance
- Exploitation
- Excessive child care and housework responsibilities
- "Role Reversal," in which the child becomes a parental caretaker
- Drug or alcohol use.

One or more of these signs are commonly found among children whose parents are actively abusing alcohol and drugs. I have found the persistence of three of these signs in various children when the parent enters recovery:

- Lack of appropriate supervision
- Excessive child care and housework
- Role reversal.

Sometimes a parent simply will not know that it is neglectful to leave a child of six or seven unattended. The parent is behaving in accordance with an internal script derived from the period of her own childhood when she was left without parental care. One recovering alcoholic mother had spent her childhood as caretaker to the other four children in her family, who lived alone with her in a trailer. Her parents, who resided in the same trailer park, lived several trailers away and were often unavailable to the children. The mother, in recovery, was genuinely surprised to learn that she must not leave her ten-year-old child to spend nights and weekends alone while she was out of town working. Other times, a parent may express misgivings about leaving a child alone, but, because of the lack of available support, she will claim no other choice.

This milieu of abandonment becomes a classic feature of the poly-addicted family, particularly when there is only one parent in the household. Since it is predicted that by the year 1990 one-half of all families will be headed by single parents (Morrison, 1986), we cannot ignore the issue of abandonment for these children.

Long into a parent's recovery, a child may continue to be given responsibility for excessive housework and care of siblings during the parent's absence. For example, one 11-year-old caretaker functioned in the role of family homemaker, foregoing her own childhood, because of her recovering mother's demand that she come home after school to prepare the family's evening meal, clean the house, and do the laundry. (Recovering alcoholic parents often have a fastidious attitude about household chores during their increased awareness in recovery.)

Similarly, role reversal, where the child functions as the caretaker to the parents, typically persists into recovery. Family dynamics during early recovery remain the same as they were during the drinking period; during this shaky time the role reversal helps the family maintain the status quo.

Case Illustration — Gabe and Gale

Gabe and Gale were eleven-year-old identical twins whose successful parents were never home. Their mother was a professional woman who worked inordinately long hours, and their self-employed father came home to end his business day with an evening of loneliness, frustration, and scotch. He rarely missed Gabe and Gale after their homework hours, believing that they were in bed asleep, as he drifted off into an alcoholic stupor. Neither was he aware that his twin sons were addicted to a variety of drugs and that they were hustling a steady business among teenagers selling crystal methamphetamine. The boys socialized with friends who were heavily into drugs and often visited an upper echelon drug dealer who lived within a heavily guarded compound overlooking the Pacific ocean.

When Gabe's life was threatened by the drug dealer's son, the boys became panic-stricken. They went to their attorney mother for assistance, fully disclosing their addiction. The mother placed both boys in an out-of-state hospital program for drug rehabilitation and quickly pointed the finger of blame at her alcoholic husband. An immediate disruption of the family occurred, with the mother filing for divorce as a way of assuaging her own guilt, while maintaining a façade of social respectability. Gabe and Gale, when they were discharged from acute care, returned home to an unsupervised family setting. With the father out of the home, and the mother continuing to work long hours, the pre-teen recovering addicts were thrust back into the milieu of abandonment.

Exploitation of a child involves having a child steal, beg, panhandle, push drugs, pimp for the parent, or engage in other forms of unlawful activity. Chemically dependent parents also sometimes involve a

Table 1 A Summary of Characteristics of Neglecting Parents

Anger is expressed through indirect stratagems (such as leaving the child alone), pouting, or withholding from the child.

Ambivalence about parenthood which was begun in adolescence leads to an escape from responsibilities through neglectful behavior toward the child.

Overburdened and overwhelmed by the responsibilities of parenthood, they abandon the child through neglect.

Feeling "burned out" on parenting as a result of acting in a parentified role during childhood leads to the subsequent neglect of one's own offspring.

Role reversal begins with the child who is expected to fulfill the parent's affectional, nurturance, and self-esteem needs.

The parent's low frustration tolerance leads to impatience and hostility towards the child, expressed as neglect.

---

child in procuring various street drugs or make drugs available to the child.

One child of an alcoholic, ten years of age, told me how she had been caught stealing after having been coaxed by her father: "I did pretty good shop lifting a few little things here and there for myself, and never got caught. One day my Dad found out, but instead of getting mad, he just made out a list of what *he* wanted, and said, 'Don't come back empty handed!' But that's when I got caught." After the child was apprehended, the father denied any involvement in her crime. However, the child's mother confided to me that her husband was guilty of encouraging the child to steal for him.

Physical abuse of a child may result from willful cruelty or unjustifiable punishment, to include corporal punishment, where the child suffers physical trauma through other than accidental means. The nonaccidental injury to a child known as child abuse often results in the child's being seen by a physician. The parents provide vague explanations, such as stories about accidents. The signs of *physical trauma* include bruises and welts over the body, burns, fractures, lacerations or abrasions, abdominal injuries, and central nervous system injuries. The behavioral symptoms of abuse in a child may either provoke or be a result of physical abuse (JAMA, 1985).

We may suspect physical abuse in a child who is

- less compliant than average
- negative and hostile
- unhappy
- angry, isolated, destructive
- abusive towards others
- showing problems in forming relationships
- showing an excessive amount or complete lack of anxiety about separating from parents
- inappropriate in caretaking behavior towards parents
- constantly in search of attention, favors, food, etc.
- showing developmental delays (cognitive, language, fine and gross motor).

Other than the disinhibiting effects of alcohol on the brain centers which affect reasoning and judgment, what leads the alcoholic/addictive parent to harm a child? Why do siblings in these families tend towards abuse of each other?

Of the families who have been found to be at high risk for child abuse, there are certain distinguishing characteristics (JAMA, 1985):

- Socially isolated families are more abusive.
- Stressors, such as drug and alcohol abuse, are associated with child abuse.
- Child abuse is more prevalent in families where there are abusive interactions between the parents.
- Parental expectations do not coincide with the child's developmental capabilities.
- Parents who were maltreated as children are more likely to abuse their children.
- Child abuse and neglect are reported more often in lower income families.

From the above list, we recognize many of these characteristics found in the families of alcoholism and addiction:

- Social isolation
- The presence of alcohol and drug addictions
- Abusive parental interactions
- Excessive parental expectations and demands on children.

Several studies have documented the degree of conflict and disturbed communication patterns in families of alcoholics (Billings, Kessler, Gomberg, and Weiner, 1979; Jacob, Favorini, Meisel, and Anderson, 1978; Moos and Moos, 1984). Other studies have reasoned that family functioning will continue to be marginal even if the alcoholic member ceases to use alcohol (Orford, 1975; Paolino and McCrady, 1977). One view of the alcoholic family (Steinglass et al., 1987) postulates that alcohol is the glue which actually holds the family together in a type of adaptive functioning and that family life will deteriorate when the alcoholic commences sobriety.

When we consider different theories to explain the child-abusing parent, we find that there is no one personality type or character trait model. Rather, the abusive parent suffers a particular personality *deficit*:

> An inability to nurture their own children results from the parent being reared in a way that precluded the experience of being mothered. It is combined with a lack of trust in others, a tendency towards isolation, a non-supportive marital relationship, and excessive expectations from the child. (Smith and Kunjukrishnan, 1985, p. 49)

Addictive parents generally have aggressive and hostile tendencies while under the influence of the substance. Certain substances are known for increasing the aggressive potential, particularly amphetamines and synthetic amphetamines, cocaine, crack, PCP, ecstacy, and so on. Alcohol, as dependence and tolerance increase, begins to affect the deeper brain centers which render a person aggressive, even violent.

Periods of acute withdrawal are also risky. The severe physiological and psychological symptoms which accompany detoxification are likely to leave the individual edgy, irritable, and ready to lash out. Unfortunately, a child in the home may be the target of assault.

Other, more "respectable drugs" are associated with hostile, even aggressive reactions of a parent. One such drug is caffeine. When a parent has consumed several cups of coffee, for example, he may be more prone than usual to overreact to minor annoyances. Similarly, a parent withdrawing from a high-sugar diet may be angry, hostile, hypersensitive, and even paranoid.

Three other factors have been identified as contributing to physical child abuse. The relevance of these to the families of alcoholism and addiction are as follows:

1. *Constitutional features of the child:* If a child of an alcoholic is genetically predisposed towards states of hyperarousal, an abusive
   parent may single out this temperamental child as the target of
   abuse.

   One recovering alcoholic father told me about his rage when his
   wife had to walk the floor with their colicky infant in the middle
   of the night. Once, under the influence of alcohol, he grabbed
   the child from his wife and threatened to smother him with a
   pillow until his wife freed the child.

2. *Role reversal:* This prominent feature of alcoholic/addictive families has been found to be highly correlated with child abuse.
   When a child is used to fulfill a parent's needs to feel loved and
   protected, and that child fails, he is seen as depriving and
   incurs the parent's rage.

   An alcoholic mother became belligerent with her son and then
   regressed to clinging, whiny, childlike behavior. She expected
   her ten-year-old boy to comfort her. Once, when the child
   expressed disgust with the mother's drunkenness, she lunged at
   him with full force, pushing him backwards down the stairs.

3. *Environmental stress:* The ongoing stress in the lives of children of
   alcoholics has been reported in the literature (Cermak, 1988;
   Jesse, 1977; Nylander, 1960). This stress factor is also associated with child-abusing families. Environmental stress does
   not disappear when the parent stops drinking. Life for the
   recovering parent, as well as for the child, remains stressful
   throughout the parent's acute and post-acute withdrawal phase
   of recovery (see Chapter 8). Consequently, the likelihood of
   child physical abuse during a parent's recovery must be assessed during the acute care phase of early recovery.

When we ask how children are affected by their parents' *recovery* or
relapse from addictive practices, the data are confusing. First, there
are problems in reliable definitions of "recovery" and "relapse." Moos
and Billings' study (1982) is often cited as evidence of the positive
effects of a parent's recovery from alcoholism on the mental and
physical health of children; however, they surveyed only mothers'
perceptions. Further, among the criteria used to define the "recovering" group was one which more appropriately belonged in the "relapsed" category — at least, as the terms "recovery" and "relapse" are

being used in this discussion. In the Moos and Billings study, a parent was considered "recovered" if he had "consumed less than five ounces of 100% ethanol on a typical drinking day the month prior to follow-up" (which occurred at six-month and two-year intervals). The "relapsed" category was defined by the criterion of hospital readmission.

As I will argue, *recovery* of a parent involves more than controlled drinking or abstinence. Recovery involves an improved way of life on several planes of human existence: biological, psychological, social, and spiritual. New attitudes and patterns must supplant the previous addictive way of life.

Similarly, *relapse* involves resumption of former attitudes and behaviors in one or more of the biopsychosocial and spiritual planes, that is, a return to the old, addictive way of life. A person could be observed by an outsider to be in relapse *before* he ever resumed alcohol and/or drug use. Accordingly, relapse prevention begins in early recovery with the education of the recovering parent about the need to implement and maintain a variety of positive self-care functions. Otherwise, stressful family interactions, particularly those between recovering parent and child, tend to deteriorate into conflict.

In earlier research with children of alcoholics (Jesse, 1977), I found indications that, during the parents' recovery process, the lives of these children involved a high incidence of physical abuse. The following are examples of the responses children provided when asked to describe the time they experienced *"the most trouble with your parents"* during the parents' recovery.

- "One time when we woke up from our nap and my Dad got mad at us and started spanking us all with his belt."
- "When my Mom pushed me so hard that I fell back and hit my head on the rocking chair rocker."
- "When I came home late from riding my horse and my Dad grabbed the riding crop and started beating me with it."
- One time when we were swimming in our pool and my Dad was trying to drown me. We got in a fight, but he wouldn't stop. He kept on trying to drown me."
- "Last night when I was taking my shower, and my Dad started slapping me around and held my head under the water and said, 'Boys aren't supposed to stay in a shower all night.'"
- "When my Dad smacked me in the lip and cut it."
- "When my Mom grabbed my hair and kept on pulling it and made knots come out on my head."

What can explain the obliviousness of these recovering parents to their children's pain and suffering? Alice Miller writes:

> Lack of empathy for the suffering of one's own childhood can result in an astonishing lack of sensitivity to other children's suffering. This kind of insensitivity has its roots in the abuse a person suffered as a child. He or she may be able to remember what happened, but in most cases the *emotional content* of being beaten and humiliated has been completely repressed. This is where the difference lies between treating an adult and a child cruelly. The *self* has not yet sufficiently developed for a child to retain the memory of it or of the feelings it arouses. (1983, p. 115; italics mine)

The *disavowal* of the emotional content of being abused as a child leads abusive parents to do to their children what was done to them. Unable to contact their own emotional pain, they have no empathy for their children's pain or degradation. These parents reenact the crime of their own childhood family battlegrounds by victimizing their helpless offspring.

Parental Violence

Addicted or alcoholic parents tend to be violent, even in recovery. While a child may not be the target of violent actions, he may witness attacks on other family members, for example, his mother or siblings. Or the parents may launch an all-out physical war while their bewildered children watch.

Most commonly children in recovery tell me of occasions when an enraged parent commences to destroy the family possessions, even the child's belongings.

Case Illustration — Howard

Howard was a seven-year-old boy whose practicing alcoholic father was prone to drunken outbursts of violence. Howard had become brutally aggressive himself, his mother stated, since a few weeks earlier when he had witnessed his Dad smashing his Christmas toys, which had been displayed under the tree during the holidays.

Numerous times I have listened to a child describe watching a drunken parent break furniture. Seeing the family television set demolished by a father swinging a baseball bat is a memory that is *not denied* by a child. That child recalls with horror the very vivid memory of the act. What is later *disavowed* is the child's *fear* and *rage* at seeing the adult caretaker behave so viciously. What we must be concerned about in working with these children in recovery is the blocked emotional content of the memory. Otherwise these stored emotional memories are likely to be released and reenacted when that child has matured, and if the child should begin to use substances in later life, they are likely to be released uncontrollably. The vicious cycle of abuse continues.

The modeling effect of parental violence leaves a child in a most unfortunate position when he starts to explore adult heterosexual conduct, man-wife, and parent-child relationships. He draws upon a limited repertoire of complex behavior patterns, many of which are irrational and violent.

The children of alcoholics, I believe, learn complex patterns of behavior from their parents that provide a preset series of responses that may be readily available in their own adult life when faced with stress. . . . relatively complex behaviors, such as moral judgmental orientations, linguistics structures, teaching styles, self-imposed delay-of-gratification patterns, and pro-social frustration reactions, have been demonstrated to be elicited through observational learning. Simpler behaviors — such as distinctive aggressive behavior, as already noted, and dramatic play patterns — are also easily learned and modeled. (Burk, 1972, p. 195)

Rarely does a child have an adult available to provide empathic attunement when he has witnessed his caretakers at war. All of the child's fear, doubt, confusion, and outrage are held deep within the self, never to be reflected upon in the light of an adult's reality, only to be reexperienced as a sense of inner dread, shame, and worthlessness. Those children who internalize the secrets of family violence rarely share these fears.

What we know about the effects of childhood trauma when a group of so-called normal children are victimized and unassisted by adult support during the trauma has been reported by Terr (1979, 1981, 1983a, b, 1984), who examined the child victims of a school bus kidnapping. At the time of the traumatic event, these previously normal children were believed to suffer a disruption of ego functioning so intense that they were fearful of a repetition of the kidnapping. Thus, a condition of "traumatophobia" developed, rendering the children susceptible to states of hypervigilance and hyperalertness.

Unexpectedly, the kidnapping victims did not employ the psychological defenses of repression and denial to block out the trauma of what had happened to them.

> Each child interviewed was able to tell a fully detailed story of what had happened. None exhibited the repression, amnesia, memory lapses, emotional numbing or blurring of consciousness described in adults after extreme stress. (Terr, 1979, p. 564)

Terr questioned why the psychological defense of denial, which had heretofore been associated with immature functioning, had not been present in these children.

> Why do adults exhibit massive use of a primitive immature defense (denial) whereas children do not?
> Is denial truly an immature defense? (Terr, 1979, p. 565)

I believe that traumatized children are able to recall with vivid memories what they have experienced and witnessed because of the defense of *disavowal*. The traumatic incident is stored in memory, but emotions and affective meanings associated with the incident are disavowed. According to Terr, a fear of further trauma in the kidnapping victims was generalized to a "fear of the mundane." The children of alcoholism and addiction also exhibit numerous mundane fears, including the fear of interpersonal closeness.

When children have been traumatized together in a small group, such as siblings, they may be expected to follow the pattern observed by Terr (1984), who noted the lack of post-traumatic group cohesion. This is not unlike the alternate patterns of sibling clinging and disbanding which I have described as affecting younger children of alcoholics (Jesse, 1988).

Sibling Abuse

From the time of my earliest research, when I first observed the secret war of siblings among the children of alcoholics (Jesse, 1977), there has been a glaring lack of attention to sibling issues in the literature on children of alcoholics. The question arises: Are siblings in poly-addicted families any more violent with each other than siblings in so-called normal families?

When Straus (1980) examined acts of sibling violence among the general population by surveying over 2,000 American families, he found a high incidence of child-child acts of violence generally. These occurred in about 80% of the families studied. (However, there was no attempt in this study to tease out those families that were chemically dependent. Latest statistics indicate that this would be one out of every three to four families.) The study disclosed that these violent acts among siblings decrease as the children grow older. Among the violent families 75% included children three to four years of age; 64% included children between the ages of five and nine; and 47% included pre-adolescents (10–14 years of age).

One point that Straus makes to explain violence among siblings is the tendency for family members to accept as "normal" or inevitable that which would not be tolerated outside the family. If, as I have suggested, violence is a natural part of alcoholic/addictive family life, there is every reason to believe that sibling abuse in these homes may occur with greater frequency and more violence than in other families. As the children recreate with each other what they observe, the effect of parental modeling intensifies their bitter sibling altercations. The motives for sibling abuse in alcoholic/addictive families include:

1. Parental modeling of negative, hostile interactions.
2. Displacement of anger and rage towards parents onto a "safe" sibling target.
3. Resentment of sibling responsibilities by child caretakers who are overburdened and overwhelmed.
4. Resentment of older siblings who have been abusive to a younger brother or sister.
5. Resentment of a sibling who maintains a favored place with a parent or threatens the child's favored place.

Each of these situations creates environmental stress in the life of a child who already has been overstressed by parental alcoholism.

The following are some examples of sibling abuse which were described to me by children in recovery asked about times when they encountered *"the most problems with a brother or sister."*

- "One time Jerry (oldest brother) threw a rock and hit me in the eye and it bled and I had to have stitches."
- "One time Patty (youngest sister) tore up all my homework, so I whipped her with the dog chain, and then I got in trouble with my Dad. He blistered my butt."

- "One time Chuck (oldest brother) was punching me in the stomach so hard that I doubled up on the ground."
- "One time when Susan (middle sister) pinched me all over my arms and left scars, and I was ashamed to go to school."
- "One time when Judy (oldest sister) tied me to the bed when I was asleep, and she and her friend painted lipstick all over me, and then they woke me up and laughed at me. I tried to get loose but I couldn't. I screamed."
- "One time when all of us kids started hitting each other with curtain rods. We were so mad."
- "One time my brother knocked a hole in the wall of our room, and he lied and said I did it, and I got spanked with a belt."

Sibling abuse can have a lasting, deleterious effect on the life of a child. Although the tendency is usually to discount the importance of cruelty between children, as we will learn in Chapter 6 a child's primary attachment figure in the alcoholic/addictive family may be not a parent, but a sibling. If a child is primarily bonded to a sibling, and this sibling turns against the child with vindictiveness, the child's sense of self is devastated. The rejecting sibling may have been only tenuously bonded to the other. Other times, a rejecting sibling may be influenced in his behavior by seeing a parent reject and abuse the brother or sister.

Case Illustration — Irene

Irene was a child of eleven years, a runaway whose mother had died from alcoholism when the child was seven. During the early part of Irene's life, there were violent parental fights provoked by the mother. The children had witnessed the mother's rageful attacks on the father, and sometimes had been caught in the crossfire of flying dishes, lamps, and other assorted household items. They had never been the victims of direct physical abuse, nor had they suffered physical trauma. Neglect was apparent, since the mother increasingly left the children home alone when she was out bar hopping.

Sibling clinging continued to characterize the children's interactions when the mother died from alcoholic cirrhosis. Irene's attachment to her older brother, Joe, was the stabilizing fact of her life. Joe was her champion and protector, caring for her during the many long hours their father was away at work.

The father remarried when Irene was nine and Joe was twelve.

The new stepmother, also a drinking woman and somewhat seductive, quickly formed an attachment to Joe, who readily entered a type of role reversal with her. Because he was made the center of attention by his stepmother, Joe readily catered to her. Pleased with Joe's compliant, responsible behavior, the stepmother was nevertheless resentful of needy little Irene's attention-gaining misbehavior. Under the influence of alcohol, the stepmother could be quite verbally abusive to Irene.

A rift in the relationship between Joe and Irene soon developed. To maintain his special position with his new stepmother, Joe — maturing into puberty — began to push Irene away. Within a short time, he became physically abusive, slapping her, shoving her, locking her in the cellar, and eventually giving her a black eye. It was at this point that Irene began to run away from home. When she eventually was taken into foster placement, she was suffering from a severe depression.

Sibling abuse among the children of alcoholic/addictive families must be taken as a given when the family enters treatment. An assessment of these abusive dynamics is important. Although the siblings will not usually discuss the severity of their fighting and abuse of one another, they will offer the clues, particularly focusing on this topic during the post-acute phase of therapy (see Chapter 6). The emphasis in sibling intervention is to extend care to *all* children within an alcoholic/addictive family system. This means that, anytime a child is referred for any reason from these families, an assessment of the siblings and sibling subsystem functioning is essential. Children in recovery require ongoing attention to the healing of their troubled sibling relationships (Jesse, 1988).

INCEST/CHILD SEXUAL ABUSE

Alcoholism has been linked historically to incest, not as causative, but as one factor which may contribute to or accompany reported incest. It has been suggested that alcohol is used to allay guilt and anxiety over incestuous relating. Estimates for the coexistence of alcoholism and incest range from 10% to 50% of the cases reported (Black, 1981; Courtois, 1988; Shepherd-Look, 1987). However, I would suggest that these figures grossly underestimate the present-day statistics for alcoholism and incest. These lowered statistics may be due to the retrospective nature of the studies, where the research subjects were adult women looking back in time. Their own denial of the parent's alcoholic behavior or their lack of awareness of the criteria for an alcoholic diagnosis may account for the low estimates. Herman (1981) reports that approximately one-half of incarcerated sex offenders have been given an alcoholic diagnosis; she found a similar proportion of alcoholics in her studies of father-daughter incest. Herman (1987) also reports that the family dynamics of incest resemble the dynamics in families with other addictive disorders.

Approximately one-half of all cases of child sexual abuse involve *incest, the sexual contact between two individuals who are legally excluded from marriage through kinship ties*. This includes intercourse, mutual masturbation, hand-genital or oral-genital contact, sexual fondling, exhibition, and sexual propositioning (Finkelhor, 1979). Of these contacts, approximately 80% are father-daughter or father-stepdaughter. However, in the families of alcoholism and addiction, we also note frequent reports of brother-sister incest. In our discussion we also will include cases of emotional incest or an incestuous bond between mothers and sons, which, while not illegal, sets up a bewildering and traumatic situation for the child. Excerpts from a case of actual mother-son incest will be reported to demonstrate these dynamics.

While an alcoholic/addict or spouse may not violate the child sexually, that parent, through neglectful behavior, may place the child in a situation which leads to the child's abuse by another trusted adult close to the family. Close to 80% of all cases of child sexual abuse are committed by individuals close to the child (Finkelhor, 1979).

Finally, an aspect of child sexual victimization which seems to occur with regularity in the families of alcoholism and addiction is the overstimulation of a child sexually by either parent's promiscuity, nudity, pornography, or exhibitionism. For example, a single parent who has lovers in and out of the home may engage in sexual behavior without respecting the child's need for privacy. In this context, it is important to review a definition of child sexual abuse offered by Brant and Tisza (1977, p. 81): "the exposure of a child to sexual stimulation inappropriate for the child's age, level of psychosexual development, or role in the family."

Sexual overstimulation of a child by an alcoholic parent may not always be legally reportable as an actual sexual offense, even though the parent's behavior represents a blatant disregard for the child's vulnerability. Take the case of an alcoholic mother with a live-in boyfriend, where both profess a liberal attitude about nudity and walk about in the presence of her daughters, eight and nine. Does the boyfriend's nudity constitute a reportable offense of exhibition-ism? Group sex among intoxicated, cocaine-snorting adults may occur under the watchful gaze of a child who cannot fall asleep. Does the fact that the child stumbles onto the drunken orgy indicate that the parents have failed to protect the child?

Another type of sexual overstimulation occurs when there is pro-fessional denial of a child's vulnerable developmental position. A child of an alcoholic, for example, whose father merely "invites" her to sleep with him is required to participate in group child sexual abuse treatment with victims of sodomy, forceable rape, and inter-course. Does the exposure of the less severely affected child to sexual-ly provocative group treatment constitute a type of re-traumatiza-tion? What can be the rationale for this type of *treatment* when alcohol-specific treatment for the family is not recommended?

Among the different explanations for why children are sexually abused or victimized, Finkelhor (1979) reports three factors asso-ciated with their *family context*. These are particularly relevant to our understanding of incest as arising from the *unstable family constellation* of alcoholic/addictive families. Although this constellation will be discussed in more detail in Chapter 5, let me point out here the three factors which coincide with Finkelhor's findings, specifically as they relate to the families of alcoholism and addiction:

1. *The milieu of abandonment:* Individuals in alcoholic/addictive fam-ilies seek a primary relationship with a substance or activity rather than with members of the family. These addictive prac-tices lead members in the family system to feel abandoned, interfering with the need for *belonging*. A lack of attachment to others in the family sets the stage for incestuous relating.
2. *Role confusion:* Parent-child role reversal interferes with effective family *leadership* and the *control* mechanisms necessary for sys-tems maintenance. With a daughter in the role of family care-taker and the mother or father in a sibling-type relationship with his/her own children, the family context fosters incestuous relating.
3. *Social isolation:* The families of alcoholism and addiction become increasingly isolated socially as substance abuse progresses. Substance abuse actually increases *personal isolation* or narcissis-tic self-absorption. Despite ongoing social contacts, such as through employment or school or peer relationships, the de-gree of personal isolation, or narcissistic withdrawal increases and interferes with *intimacy*.

Belonging, control, and *intimacy* (or affection) are essential family processes. They will be explored more fully in Chapter 9 as they pertain
to the family in recovery. For now let us look at these themes as
depicted in the mapping* of a nine-year-old incest victim's mental
representations of her interpersonal (object) ties (Figure 1). The
child (Self*) was the daughter of an alcoholic father. We can see
displayed the *milieu of abandonment* (child isolated from all other role
figures). *Role confusion* is apparent (mother is grouped in a parent/sib-
ling arrangement; father is alone and isolated). *Social isolation* is seen

*Derived from the statistical procedure known as iterative intercolumnar cluster
analysis (Jesse, 1977).

Figure 1 Milieu of Abandonment

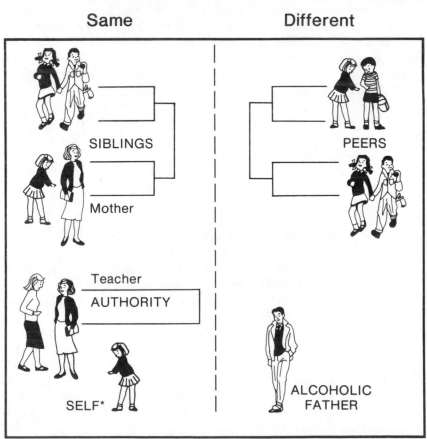

with both the child and her father separated from all other people. (See Chapter 5 for an explanation of the mapping procedure.)

The *interpersonal isolation* which is depicted above as affecting both the child and her father actually sets the stage for incest. The illusionary emotional "bond" is an artifact of incestuous relating, not unlike sibling "clinging." The interpersonal distance actually obscures kinship ties as the parent looks to the child for love, using her for the functions provided and the role fulfilled. A child who is viewed so narcissistically by a parent is experienced by that parent as an object to be controlled, to be used, to provide pleasure. Warmth, nurturance, and pleasurable interactions may be sought from a child when the spouse is cold and withdrawing. Thus a lonely, love-starved child in a practicing alcoholic/addictive family becomes vulnerable to the parent's sexual advances.

Finkelhor (1979) has indicated two themes which seem to characterize incest families. These also are apparent in the families of alcoholism and addiction: (1) there is a family history of *abandonment* (either to alcoholism, addiction, or physical separation); (2) family *membership is constantly shifting.* Children move in and out of the family circle, or a parent or stepparent comes and goes. "The family boundary is diffuse and poorly maintained" (Finkelhor, 1979, p. 27). Thus, incest often becomes a sexualized solution to a nonsexual problem, an attempt to establish permanency and belonging (Shepherd-Look, 1987).

In a case of mother-son incest reported in some detail in the literature (Margolis, 1977), the son's adult demands for sexual intercourse with his mother may be understood by examining the childhood *unstable family constellation.* The patient, John, was the son of a brutal alcoholic father who beat the mother. The mother became alcoholic during John's adulthood. During childhood,

> John remembered taking showers with his father and baths with his mother at ages three to four. He remembered sitting between her legs as she soaped his body. He recalled being sexually aroused by looking at her breasts and vagina. During the same period, the patient recalled one Sunday morning when the inebriated father insisted on having sexual relations just before the family went off to church. The mother submitted in resignation as he and his brother watched. (p. 271)

In the preceding vignette, the child, John, appears to have been overstimulated by the violence and sexual exhibitionism of the parents. In the face of the father's physical abuse, which involved expressions of rage and loathing towards the child and mother, sexual contact with the mother came to be misunderstood by the boy. Needs for affection and succorance from the mother were confused with the early erotic interactions, later leading the patient to feel an air of sexual entitlement towards his mother.

Although other cases of *incestuous-type relating* between alcoholic mothers and their sons are not as dramatic as the one just described, seductive interactions are common. While these do not conform to the legal description of "incest," they constitute a trauma for the son. The mother, under the influence of alcohol and/or drugs, may make erotic, flirtatious gestures towards the child. She then has little recall of these interactions when she is sober. She will not understand the cool, hostile distance or rageful demands which her son makes upon her, nor will she understand his confusion. The mother may revert to blaming the son, accusing him of not loving her. These boys typically carry a tremendous amount of rage towards the seductive mother. Often their rage is expressed through acting-out behavior, which may involve stealing money or possessions from the mother and others. This incestuous pattern may persist, and generally does, through the parent's recovery, although in a much more disguised form.

Although cases of parent-child incest usually do not involve sadistic force, brother-sister incest frequently does (see the case illustration of Quinnella in Chapter 6). Most of the time, it is the middle or youngest sister who is dominated by an older brother and forced to engage in sexual contact. This pattern of relating also generally persists into the parents' recovery. Sometimes a child is forced by an older sibling to engage in sexualized contact with another younger sibling, peer, or relative.

The following examples of incest among siblings from alcoholic/addictive families were reported as times when they encountered *"the most trouble with a brother or sister."*

- "One time when Ted (oldest brother) told me and my next door neighbor to 'hump' and he held us down and laughed at us."
- "One time when Carl (oldest brother) called me into the bathroom and when I came in, he held out his penis and squirted pee on me."
- "One time when my sisters and me had our clothes off and we were measuring boobs, and my brother came in and grabbed at us."

- "When Chuck (middle brother) jumped on top of me from the top bunk bed. He wouldn't get off and started feeling me all over."
- "One time when Sissy and I were sleeping together and we took our clothes off and started messing around, and the next day she told Mom."

In their distracted state, alcoholic/addictive parents may expose a child to sexual abuse by trusted friends or relatives. When the child is allowed to mingle with adults who have been drinking heavily, that child is placed in a compromising, often life-threatening situation. The parent, however, will completely deny the harmful effects of this type of exposure for the child. When the child is sexually molested, the parent who has compromised the child may express outrage about the behavior of the trusted adult. However, the parent's blaming attitude interferes with an honest recognition of personal responsibility for the child's protection.

Case Illustration — Jake

Jake was the six-year-old youngest son of an alcoholic mother, who left him in the care of a neighbor teenage babysitter. The older boy had been suspected of drug and alcohol involvement, but Jake's mother claimed that she did not think he was a "problem child." Besides, she stated, she often partied with the family and observed the teenager to be "a pretty easygoing kid" who seemed to take care of his two younger sisters during the parents' absence. She thought Jake would be "safe" with him.

On one babysitting occasion Jake was forced into sex play with the teenage boy's younger sisters, as the boy threatened the children, "I'll kill you if you don't do it." The younger children were forced to orally copulate each other while the older boy masturbated and then sodomized Jake.

During the recovery of Jake and his mother, the key signs of negligence were brought into focus. Jake's mother admitted that she had been too preoccupied with her own needs to date, drink, and have fun to adequately check out his care during the babysitting arrangement. During sobriety, she had a retrospective vision of the teenager as "a hostile kid, now that I think about it. His Mom was always teasing him when she got drunk, and I could tell he almost hated her . . . plus, her boyfriend roughed him up sometimes."

Children will continue to be sexually traumatized in the families of alcoholism and addiction. Until such times as the parents in these families develop the ability to see their children through sober eyes, they will make the often tragic mistakes which we have been discussing. The effects of these mistakes on the child victim will depend upon the type and frequency of sexual abuse, the type of relationship the child has with the abusing person, the child's developmental position, and the implications for the family system.

PSYCHOLOGICAL/EMOTIONAL ABUSE

In his discussion of psychological maltreatment, Garbarino (1987) stresses that this topic should not be considered as ancillary to other forms of abuse and neglect. Rather, "we should place it as the centerpiece of efforts to understand family functioning and to protect children. In almost all cases, the psychological consequences of an act define that act as abusive" (p. 7).

Interferences with the child's sense of self result from a parent's emotional or verbal abuse, threatened assault, irritable scolding, disparaging remarks, comparisons with another child or sibling, withholding love and affection, threats or actual abandonment, character assassination such as name calling, or more subtle insults.

In most of our case illustrations there are vivid examples of psychological abuse to children. Summarizing from Garbarino (1987), we note that psychological maltreatment usually takes five forms:

1. *Rejecting:* The parent refuses to acknowledge the child's worth and the legitimacy of the child's needs. (See case illustration of Irene, p. 42.)
2. *Isolating:* The child is removed from important social experiences, leading the child to experience himself as alone, without friends. (See case illustration of Martin, p. 71.)
3. *Ignoring:* The adult is physically present, but is absent emotionally and psychologically, ignoring the child's needs. This is the "parent who is there but not *really* there." (See case illustrations of Buff, p. 15, Franky, p. 27, Gabe and Gale, p. 32.)
4. *Terrorizing:* The parent assaults a child with words, instilling fear, and bullies or frightens the child, leading the child to experience the world as a hostile place. (See case illustration of Quinnella, p. 103.)
5. *Corrupting:* The adult "mis-socializes" the child, or over-stimulates the child, or leads the child to engage in destructive

behavior, and reaffirms the child's deviance, creating an individual who is unfit for normal social experiences. (See case illustrations of Buff, p. 15, and Dirk, p. 18.)

Children in early recovery typically reveal the negative programming of their emotional and psychological maltreatment. Almost akin to brainwashing, the parent's failures ("You're selfish, spoiled, not as good as, lazy, bad, ugly . . . ") are projected onto the child and then lead to severe interferences in the child's self-worth and, ultimately, in the child's self-identification.

SUMMARY

Alcoholism and addiction establish a family context for ongoing, repetitive psychological maltreatment of a child. However, these inconsistent parent-child interactions are in contrast to those regimented, pedagogical types described by Alice Miller (1981, 1983). Miller does contrast pedagogy to *inconsistent parenting*, which I believe more accurately describes the families of alcoholism and addiction.

> It is different for children whose fathers have outbursts of rage and can then, inbetween times, play good-naturedly with their children. In this case, the child's hatred cannot be cultivated on such a pure form. These children experience the difficulties of another sort as adults; they seek out partners with a personality structure that, like their fathers', tends towards extremes. They are bound to these partners by a thousand chains and cannot bring themselves to leave them, always living with the hope that the other person's good side will finally win out; yet at every fresh outburst they are plunged into new despair. These sadomasochistic bonds, which go back to the equivocal and unpredictable nature of a parent, are stronger than a genuine love relationship; they are impossible to break, and signal permanent destruction of the *self.*" (p. 163, italics mine)

And so begins a new alcoholic/addictive family system which, as we can see, has had its genesis in the psychological, physical and/or sexual maltreatment of a little child.

PART II

The Child Versus The System

Children have been carrying banners to proclaim their families' pathology for a long, long time. These banners, often illegible to adult onlookers, were crudely spelled out with the symptoms of various childhood disorders.

Only in the past few decades have these cries for help been translated into valid statements of family dysfunction. Psychotherapists working with children began to shift their focus from the affected child to the entire family. Looking at the interrelationships between family members, this *systems* approach was a major innovation in treating mental health problems.

The shift from individual to family treatment was championed by such family theorists as Nathan Ackerman in New York, Murray Bowen in Washington, and the Palo Alto group of Gregory Bateson, Jay Haley, Don Jackson, Virginia Satir, and others. The popularization of the family therapy movement has been attributed to Virginia Satir, whose charismatic style and clear, nontechnical language attracted a large following during the 1960s and 1970s. Certainly, Satir influenced those who began to work with alcoholic families (Lawson, Peterson, and Lawson, 1983). This emphasis on working with the family system rather than a single child within the system has prevailed in family work with alcoholics.

Influenced by Satir's work (for I, too, had spent a training session with her during the 1970s), I began my work with alcoholic families using a conjoint therapy modality, seeing the parents together with their children. Elsewhere (Jesse, 1988), I have reported on the difficulties of maintaining an exclusive systems approach when attempting to address the problems of school-aged children of alcoholics. As I was to learn, this approach can imitate a process that runs parallel to the alcoholic family's pathology, ignoring, de-individualizing, and glossing over the inner self of a troubled child. Even when employed by the most seasoned of family therapists, an exclusive systems approach will only stir up the longings of the damaged child-self, which silently screams for individual attention through symptomatic behavior.

The children taught me: Again and again, with each new family therapy "success" (when the alcoholic parent had maintained several months of sobriety), a formerly quiescent child would in some way begin to demand attention. Often, these demands were made in the form of increased behavioral and psychological problems. (A systems explanation would claim that the child was simply carrying the banner to proclaim the family's pathology. But this was *sobriety!* The alleged pathological family member had completed a successful period of inpatient treatment and had remained abstinent for several months.)

Despite the parents' ongoing participation in Alcoholics Anonymous and the Al-Anon family programs, the life of the child sometimes appeared to worsen during recovery. Although the parents were being assisted, the children's problems continued to broadcast the message that they often felt invisible, not only within the family milieu, but also in the family therapy.

Abrupt changes in a child would lead to increased acting-out behavior. Other, more subtle changes occurred over time, which nonetheless led to dramatic, self-destructive acts (running away from home, drug and alcohol use, promiscuous sex, stealing, shoplifting, etc.). The baffled parents turned their attention to the child's problems and, in so doing, *momentarily forgot their own.* This should have provided the clue (although I did not *see* it at the time) about the delicate therapeutic balance which must be maintained between individual child and systems level work with alcoholic and addictive families when school-aged children are involved.

If our interventions with these families are to be effective, addiction must be addressed not only as a family process dynamic but also as a disorder of the self which affects individual children within the system. This working model of addiction will naturally guide us to approach the small group culture of the family, as well as the parents and children, in a more holistic manner. Understanding the dynamics of addiction, we soon begin to recognize that symptomatic treatment of a child's overt problems may be necessary, but not sufficient, treatment. Similarly, a child embedded within the addictive family system who does not appear overtly symptomatic must not be denied our attention. Both symptomatic and asymptomatic children require ongoing recovery from the effects of parental alcoholism and addictive practices.

This section is concerned with how children are constrained by the *system* from living effective, chemical-free lives. Then we focus more specifically on the reciprocal effects of the system upon the individual *child-self*. This will lead us to maintain a simultaneous focus on the larger processes of the family group and on the inner processes of the developing child-self.

As our focus broadens to the overall workings of the alcoholic/addictive family system in Chapter 3, we momentarily lose sight of the individual. Then, when we emphasize the effect of parental interactions upon a child (Chapter 4), we narrow our concerns to the individual self within a systems context. This figure-ground relationship between the individual and the system will continue to affect our vision of what is relevant at any given point in time.

Bridging the gap between the individual and the systems views is the presentation of the *unstable family constellation* in Chapter 5. Chapter 6 will examine a system-within-a-system, the sibling subgroup of the alcoholic/addictive family.

Now, we begin our discussion by examining the evolution of the alcoholic/addictive family system from its inception.

CHAPTER 3

The Alcoholic/Addictive Family System

. . . alcoholism in the great majority of cases is not so much the result of immediate stress as of early predisposition underlying some environmental stress. I have come to believe that the chief environmental stress for many of the parents in my study, as well as for their parents, was marriage and family life.

—*R. Margaret Cork, 1969, p. 79*

Through her analogy of a hologram Schaef (1987) provides an excellent glimpse of the alcoholic/addictive family system. The hologram, Schaef explains, is a structure in which each piece not only is a part of the whole but also has the entire pattern and way of functioning of the whole embedded in it:

> This is a useful way to look at the Addictive System. The system is like the individual and the individual is like the system. In other words, the Addictive System has all the characteristics of the individual alcoholic/addict. And because we live in this system, every one of us, unless recovering by means of a systems shift, exhibits many of these same characteristics. (p. 37)

Family systems theory espouses the belief that the family's disease or dysfunction will always be expressed in some concealed manner, that is, through symptoms such as alcoholism. Indeed, Steinglass et al. (1987) propose that the drinking of alcohol has adaptive consequences for the alcoholic family, which in sobriety runs the risk of disintegration. Family rules are believed to govern a type of systems logic. Although not always understandable to the outside observer, this logic (or illogic) explains symptomatic behavior. Key concepts, such as *homeostasis* (how the family regulates itself and maintains a balanced state) and *accommodation* (those shifts within the family structure which are required to maintain that steady state), distinguish systems thinking. The notion of *dynamism* explains the intergenerational transmission of family pathology, as, for example, when an alcoholic family system becomes dynamic and self-perpetuating (Jesse, 1975).

As family theorists have concentrated on these family processes they have ignored the individual child-self embedded within the family matrix. The social context, rather than the intrapsychic or intersubjective experiences of an individual, commands the attention of the family therapist.

THE TWO-PERSON SYSTEM

The alcoholic/addictive family system begins when two individuals come together to form a couple. In all probability, one or both of the partners are either practicing an addiction or recovering from an addiction or were once a part of an addictive family of origin. The perpetuation of alcoholic/addictive family systems across generations is profound. It is likely that psychological and social influences combine with genetic predisposition to maintain the system. We are left with the evolutionary puzzle. Was there an original genetic accident which occurred through random events? When was the *first* two-person addictive family system? How did all of this begin?

We may surmise that the first two-person addictive family system actually began at the *beginning*, with Adam and Eve. With all due respect to religious interpretations of the story of Creation, from which we now depart, how can we be sure that Adam was not the original addict and Eve his chief enabler? Since the natural world yields an abundance of consciousness-altering substances, how do we know what the "forbidden fruit" contained? Mind-altering substances are found in various types of plants all over the globe—from desert cacti (peyote) to tropical vines (psychedelic-type seeds of the Hawaiian woodrose vine.) Now, as the story of Creation goes,

> The Lord God placed the man in the Garden of Eden as its gardener,
> to tend and care for it. But then the Lord God gave this warning, "You

may eat any fruit in the garden except the fruit from the Tree of Knowledge—for its fruit will open your eyes to make you aware of right and wrong, good and bad." (Genesis, 2:15–17, from *The Living Bible*)

Did the fruit contain a psychedelic substance, or a hallucinogenic, such as are found in the seeds of various exotic plants?

The story of the original co-dependent, Eve, continues:

And the Lord God said, "It isn't good for man to be alone; I will make a companion for him, a helper suited to *his* needs." (Genesis 2:18, italics added)

As we are told, Eve was not created as a fully autonomous self, but derived part of her physical being from her husband, Adam.

"This is it!" exclaimed Adam. "She is part of my own bone and flesh! Her name is '*woman*' because she was taken out of a man. . . . " Now although the man and his wife were both naked, neither of them was embarrassed or ashamed. (Genesis 2:23, 25)

The serpent (perhaps the original drug pusher) was said to be the craftiest of all the creatures which the Lord God had made. The serpent begins to push the forbidden fruit on Eve.

"Really?" he asked. "*None* of the fruit in the garden? God says you mustn't eat *any* of it?"

"Of course we may eat it," the woman told him. "It's only the fruit from the tree at the *center* of the garden that we are not to eat. . . . God says that we mustn't eat it or even touch it, or we will die."

The woman was convinced. How lovely and fresh looking it was! And it would make her so wise! So she ate some of the fruit and gave some to her husband, and he ate it too. And as they ate it, suddenly they became *aware* of their nakedness and were embarrassed. (Genesis 3:1–3, 6–7, italics added)

And so, we see that Adam and Eve were the original narcissists. For narcissism is not healthy self-love, but rather *self*-absorption, *self*-preoccupation, *self*-consciousness. (Of course, if we accept this account, we see that Cain and Abel were the original children of addiction. Even by today's standards, they would be typical of COAs, with their intense sibling rivalry, manipulation, strife, and violence.)

While husband and wife in the two-person alcoholic/addictive family system have not been joined at the rib since the time of Adam and Eve, there is the tendency for them to proceed *as if* one has filled in the missing part of the other. The joining of a couple actually establishes the parental *selfobject* unit. This concept of *selfobject* (Kohut 1971, 1977) refers to the psychological as well as the social experience of the individual whereby *the other person is experienced as a part of the self.* Indeed, the other person is looked to as substitute for the missing part of the self—which is actually the capacity for self-esteem regulation, i.e., the ability to feel "whole."

There is a *legitimate* need for these selfobject experiences to affirm one's sense of self. This need begins in earliest infancy with the need for the parents to affirm the child's developing self. It continues throughout life with the need for important others to provide acknowledgment and affirmation of the self. Siblings, friends, lovers, marital partners, and eventually one's own offspring will be expected to provide self-affirming responses. When these are not forthcoming—when selfobject failures occur on the part of one or both spouses in an alcoholic/addictive family system—the effect is potentiated by a resurgence of feelings from the past. Hurts and disappointments from earlier *selfobject* (parenting) failures in the family of origin are reexperienced, but now these failures are projected onto the mate.

A wife who is critical of her husband's lack of attention may actually undermine his ability to provide positive affirmation, for he begins to experience her as the critical, nagging parent of his youth. A husband who disappoints through an empathic failure (such as failing to remember his wife's birthday) comes to be experienced by the wife as the depriving, inconsiderate alcoholic father of her childhood. Although this type of reenactment is largely unconscious, it contributes to overreactions in the present. These overreactions involve a flooding of past feelings of disappointment, shame and rage without a conscious memory to relate them to the past. To the partner who has suffered a massive disappointment in the selfobject relationship, there is an inner disruption to the sense of self. Feelings of unworthiness and unimportance lead to shame and rage.

To wake up one day as an adult and find that one's prince charming has metamorphosed into one's drunken, alcoholic father is a cruel twist of fate. Here, the experience of shame has to do with one's worst secret being confirmed—that one is, after all, unworthy and unloveable. To be treated in the present as one was treated during childhood—with abuse and neglect—is to become flooded with the original disavowed feeling of childish rage.

The flip side of the affective state of shame is "rage," and it is the mobilization of this self-centered rage which actually triggers compulsive efforts to bolster self-esteem. Shame is a passive emotion; rage stimulates the kind of blind, driven activity that is seen in the addictions. The husband who "drinks at" his wife, after she has told him how inconsiderate he is, has found the perfect antidote to his wife's callous criticism. He can retaliate (passively) at the same time that he soothes his rage and diminishes his shame. Indeed, alcohol is an effective antidote for the poison of shame. Shame threatens the individual's primitively held view of his own perfection; however, the underlying force leading the individual to addictive behavior is not shame. Rather, "it is the disorganized mixture of massive discharge (tension decrease) and blockage (tension increase) in the area of unneutralized aggression as the experience of narcissistic *rage*" (Kohut, 1972, p. 158).

The desire to turn a passive experience of shame (childhood memories of shame, humiliation) into an active one occurs in those individuals who as children were treated insensitively by their parents.

> All these factors help explain the readiness of the shame-prone individual to respond to a potentially shame-provoking situation by the employment of a simple remedy: the active (often anticipatory) inflicting on others of those narcissistic injuries which he is most afraid of suffering himself. (Kohut, 1972, p. 144)

Sarcasm, ridicule, criticism, fault-finding, and sadistic teasing are all variants of the type of negativism which characterizes marital and family transactions in the alcoholic/addictive family system. Often this negativism may be so subtle that an outside observer would not recognize the ongoing undermining of self-esteem. The blending of hostility and affection into a mildly sarcastic form of joking not only relieves tension but also provides relief from the illusion of intimacy. As each mate becomes progressively more dysfunctional in his or her ability to recognize and meet the needs of the other, addictive patterns become more firmly entrenched as regular family transactions.

ENTER THE CHILDREN

Children born into a psychological milieu distorted by hostile, negative interactions between the parents cannot remain unaffected. Parents who are experiencing disappointment in each other will have difficulty shielding the children from these negative transactions.

What had been a stressful dyadic relationship now comes to be triangulated. That is, a child is used to buffer the emotional turmoil of the marital relationship. With the addition of each child to the system, stress on the parental relationship increases, as does addictive behavior. Parents who are preoccupied with their own hurt, disappointment, and defensiveness have difficulty relinquishing self-absorption in order to be concerned about the self needs of the child.

Case Illustration — Kyle

Kyle was a seven-year-old boy with red hair and freckles and two missing front teeth. According to the parents, Kyle had been affected adversely during the last part of his mother's alcoholism. Now four months sober, the mother declared that her husband had a drinking problem, too. Although Kyle's father staunchly denied that he was alcoholic, he admitted that he drank a few beers to "calm down" when his wife became incorrigible.

During the initial session, as Kyle attempted to describe a particularly brutal parental altercation, he fidgeted in his seat and nervously kicked the rungs on the chair. He used his hands to gesture wildly as he explained, " . . . and one night when I was in bed, I couldn't go to sleep because I could hear my Dad breaking all the windows upstairs, and my Mom kept yelling for him to stop. . . . I hid in the closet."

"But *why* was I doing it?" Kyle's father broke in defensively. "Tell the doctor *why* I was doing it! Your drunken mother was trying to climb out the windows naked, and I couldn't think of any other way to bring her to her senses."

Parents who are experiencing massive disappointments in their selfobject relationship have difficulty yielding to a concern for the child during their negative transactions. Often the child may be used as a sounding board, a confidante, or an advisor. Although this type of role reversal is associated with the various forms of abuse, there is no existing law in our culture to shield a child from this form of exploitation by the parent.

Most often, as in the case of Kyle, the parents' obsessive preoccupation with each other interferes with their ability to clearly *see* their child and his needs. Children suffer interferences in self development when parents are so consumed by their own needs that they lose sight of the child's needs.

The basis of self pathology in the child is the parents' pervasive lack of empathic attunement to the child's needs. Recent research (Farber and Egeland, 1987) on the maltreatment of children, which encompassed physical abuse, hostility/verbal abuse, psychological unavailability and neglect, indicates that psychological unavailability or abuse can be as devastating as physical abuse and neglect. While all maltreatment groups in this study functioned poorly, children whose caretakers were *psychologically unavailable* exhibited the largest number of pathological behaviors. Further, these youngsters displayed progressively more maladaptive development at each period of assessment. The authors concluded, "the caretaker's lack of emotional responsiveness is a devastating form of abuse" (p. 266).

Such parental failures are rampant in the alcoholic/addictive family when the parent's own self-centeredness or narcissism interferes with a child's developmental requirements. Not only do these parents fail to provide the necessary self-validating responses to the child, but they often encourage tasks which are not appropriate to the child's needs at that level of development. A daughter or son may function in the role of head of household, taking on emotional and caretaking responsibilities for siblings and parents which are in advance of their developmental capabilities. For example, it is apparent that Kyle's father expected him to comprehend the bizarre window-breaking as a form of "shock treatment" for Kyle's intoxicated mother. Not only did the father's self-centered or narcissistic requirement stipulate that Kyle should comprehend the logic of this violent act, but there also was the most chilling requirement of all—that Kyle put aside his own feelings (of fear, terror, rage, and confusion) and empathize with his father, allying himself with the father against the mother. Three months after this session Kyle's father was able to accept that he, too, was alcoholic; however, he was almost ten months into his own recovery work before he was able to see outside himself to the bewilderment of his son.

The strain which the alcoholic parent places upon family relationships has been described by Bill Wilson, the co-founder of Alcoholics Anonymous. Wilson was an astute observer of his own psychological processes, and he was able to translate these observations into generalizations which applied to other alcoholics. In the literature of A.A. (Alcoholics Anonymous, 1976), Wilson discusses these "twisted relationships" with family members, stating that the alcoholic parent either insists upon dominating family members or depends on them too heavily. He reasons that such "self-centered behavior" interferes with the "partnership" (selfobject) relating of family members.

We cannot overemphasize this major feature of the alcoholic/addictive family system interfering with childhood development: *In the alcoholic/addictive family system, the selfhood of the individual is neither acknowledged nor validated. This means that persons are not viewed as having independent centers of initiative — as whole, autonomous beings — but are experienced as parts of one another in terms of the functions they provide or the roles they fulfill.*

Because parents in the alcoholic/addictive family system typically do not see each other as separate selves, they tend to experience the child as the partial self of a family role. Social roles in these families are often indicative of a false-self adaptation which has been born out of response to the parents' needs (Winnicott, 1965).

Children who adopt social roles to survive an alcoholic/addictive family situation often come to be valued solely in terms of their role behavior. While family systems theory would posit that the child's role begins in response to the dysfunction of the system, the parents (often unwittingly) contribute to the maintenance of a particular role. A child who is lauded for being "Mommy's little helper" will come to experience herself as valuable, worthwhile, and important when carrying out the role. A child who has been valued in terms of what she can *do* for the parent (rather than for who she *is*) will experience herself as empty and lacking when not performing her designated function. Such individuals tend to pursue external sources of comfort and stimulation, not only during childhood but throughout their lives. During adulthood they typically join with another who they believe can provide a bolstering of the tentatively formed self. This is usually the beginning of another alcoholic/addictive family system.

CHAPTER 4

The Child-Self within the System

The child that is to survive psychologically is born into an empathic-responsive human milieu . . . just as he is born into an atmosphere that contains an optimal amount of oxygen if he is to survive physically.

— Heinz Kohut, 1977, p. 85

The development of a healthy self begins with what may be referred to as the "caretaking surround" — that is, the optimal responsiveness of the caretakers (in most instances, the parents) to the child's basic biologic needs. When the child is responded to in a perfunctory manner devoid of the caretaker's delight in the child's emerging self, he is deprived of the important function of the relationship in need fulfillment. Parental acknowledgment of this unique child-self is crucial in the consolidation of a real self (as opposed to a false self adaptation expressed through rigid social role behavior to please the parent).

According to Masterson (1985):

This mirroring or matching process seems vital to the development of the real self. It is important to keep in mind that I do not mean physical caretaking such as feeding, clothing, etc., but rather the capacity of the parents to perceive the *unique characteristics* of the child's emerging self and to respond to these in a positive, supportive manner, to identify, acknowledge, and treat with respect his or her unique temperament, to encourage the unique style or manner in which the child's individuation is expressed in his exploring, experimenting, self-assertive adventures with reality. Failures in this parental function make an important contribution to the failures of the self's development. (p. 29)

When the parent repeatedly fails to meet the child's needs for self development, the young child will begin to adapt the self to that which pleases the parent. This forms the basis of a false-self façade.

THE SELF AS SYSTEM

But what is the *self*? Can we plot the course of the developing self in the young child? Can we see or touch that part of the child where the self resides? Yes, if we are talking specifically about the *body self*. But surely this is not *the* self which is said to be the locus of addictive problems and the keystone of developmental problems in children.

Is self not that part of us which each of us intuitively knows? Or are we talking about some elusive psychological construct, *self*? Or, does the notion of *self* apply to one's moral dilemma when personal interests supersede the needs and rights of others? Webster considers all these definitions of *self*: "One's individual person; one's personal interest, ego." And here we are offered even another confounding term, *ego*. Can we say that ego and self are synonymous, as in ego-centered and self-centered? (This distinction will be made in Chapter 7.)

The expanded concept of *self* most relevant to our understanding of the children from alcoholic and addictive families has been provided by Kohut (1971, 1977). Here, the *self* is that independent center of initiative which organizes our *experience* of our separate body parts and physiological and psychological functions into a unified mind-body-self. This notion is consistent with the laws of general systems theory governing the regulation of physical systems. This "self as system" is concerned with *homeostasis*, or maintaining an inner sense of equilibrium, as well as *accommodation*, or those internal and external shifts which are required to maintain a steady state.

The relevance of the "self as system" to alcoholism and addiction work is readily apparent. When we focus on the efforts of the newly recovering alcoholic parent, for example, we recognize the presence of physiological and psychological factors *as well* as family interactions which have a bearing on how this person behaves. Few will deny that there is a reciprocal relationship between these internal processes and external, or family, processes. However, from our models of family theory we proceed as though internal factors do not exist. (At least, if we are purists, this is how we will proceed. In the real world of alcoholism and addiction treatment, we know that we simply cannot ignore these inner self processes of recovery.)

> Common sense tells us that, though we are joined together with others, we are still separate persons. The self is a center of initiative, not independent of others, but not determined by them either. This is not just an abstract point. If we do not give heed to the selves that make up families, we miss the reality of those we seek to help and we lose the leverage necessary to make them partners in a joint endeavor. (Nichols, 1987, p. 9)

As we begin to recognize that it is the "self as system" which integrates our separate mental and physical functions into a unified whole, we will begin to understand how other systems concepts apply. Like other systems, the self is concerned with homeostasis, the kind of self-regulation which achieves balanced functioning. Both inner regulation and exchanges with the environment are required to sustain the self. And, as with all systems, there are four important laws which pertain to the functioning of the self as system:

1. All aspects of self functioning are equally important—physical, mental, social, spiritual. (We are "bio-psycho-social-spiritual" organisms.)
2. Imbalances in any one aspect of self functioning will seek expression through symptoms (a disguise), which may not be understandable to the outside observer but are an entirely "reasonable" compromise. (The self has a "logic" of its own . . . as when a spiritual malady becomes manifest through an addiction.)
3. Because the self has its own internal logic, it tends to maintain dysfunctional behavior until a system shift has occurred. (A child who has been neglected will use problem behavior to express lack of inner soothing and difficulties in self-regulation.)
4. Self-regulation disorders tend to increase when one problem is used to conceal another. (A child who uses problem behavior to express lack of nurturance tends to push away potential caregivers, thereby increasing lack of nurturance.)

A child begins life with the basic organizing capacity of a whole-some self system. Despite genetic variations, this budding self will organize sensory and physical experiences. To maintain a calm internal state, the self seeks exchanges with the environment in the form of nurturance, safety, and empathic attunement from the caregivers. In order to achieve optimal functioning the developing child-self will continue to require different variations of these same exchanges — nurturance, safety, and empathic attunement — at different phases of development. When nurturance, safety, and empathic attunement have been provided in an expectable way, the child will be able to move successfully to the next developmental phase. When any of the needs for nurturance, safety, and empathic attunement have not been met in an optimal way, the child will experience interferences in the capacity for self-regulation.

EARLY CHILDHOOD

From the earliest period of development during infancy, the care-taking surround must provide the child with the necessary responses for self-regulation. An emphasis on *doing for*, rather than simply *being with*, the child interferes with the child's need to realize a calm, internal state. It is the caretaker's confirming *attitude* towards the infant which contributes to the child's *inner experiences* of being valu-able, worthwhile, and loved.

The *enthusiasm and delight* which the caretaker shows in the child's *total self* must accompany caretaking functions. A caretaker's scorn, lack of interest, or preoccupation signals for the child internal states of being unacceptable, unworthy, and unloved. Lack of external approval comes to be absorbed by the child as an internal sense of unworthiness. A child in and of himself is helpless to overcome these vague, negative disruptions to his inner self experience. He will feel empty and depleted. Such a child tends to display unrest or agita-tion, signaling a lack of inner soothing. These young children are particularly vulnerable in a family where active alcoholism and chemical dependency are practiced. When parents are functioning under the influence of a potent substance, they will be either over-reactive or insensitive to the child's attempts for self-regulation. In-fants and toddlers in the poly-addicted family often suffer abuse and neglect in attempting to make their needs known.

A lack of inner soothing mechanisms is apparent in young chil-dren who turn to external forms of self-stimulation. Thumb sucking, self-rocking, and masturbation are but a few of the more common ways that young children attempt to provide self-soothing or stimulation.

MIDDLE CHILDHOOD

The elementary school years, from the ages of about six or seven to twelve years, are referred to as the *latency* period of development. This period of development, as we have been told by one of the most prominent clinicians and theorists in this area (Sarnoff, 1987), is both an age period and a *psychological state*. These middle years of childhood are *normally* characterized by a calm, pliable, educable personality organization, in contrast to early childhood, which is marked by rapidly fluctuating changes in development, as well as corresponding dramatic emotional and psychological shifts. The development of the school-aged child is slower, steadier and marked by an outward composure. Puberty will usher in another tumultuous period of personality changes, with the adolescent sometimes seeming to shift almost daily. These are normal, expected features of the periods of early, middle, and late childhood.

The naturally calm internal state of latency does not seem to apply to children from alcoholic and addictive families. Self-regulation problems in these youngsters indicate that their inner experience is not one of tranquility. Rather, interferences in self development which have been occurring throughout the earlier years of childhood render these latency-aged children vulnerable, particularly to the effects of stress.

Cermak (1988) suggests that sensitivity to stress in children of alcoholics arises from the traumatic family environments of their childhood years. Although Cermak concentrates his discussion on adult children of alcoholics, his observation of a likely post-traumatic stress disorder in these individuals has been a valuable contribution to our work with children. Describing the dynamics of human reactions to stress, he states: "PTSD develops when a person's normal coping mechanisms are confronted with abnormal levels of stress, overwhelming the person's ability to break the stress down into digestible bites" (p. 77).

During the latency years of childhood, the tendency to be overwhelmed by stress arises from the developmentally vulnerable position of the child. Sarnoff (1976) advises that, for all practical purposes, the latency-aged child and his parents are considered two parts of one unit. This corresponds to the notion of *selfobject* functioning introduced earlier. The emotional resources of the school-aged child are not sufficiently developed to effectively cope with severe stress. To achieve calm and reassurance the child turns to the parents. When the child experiences very intense stimulation from the parents, such as hitting or yelling or even sexual overstimulation, he or she may become disorganized and behaviorally excited. This child has no one upon whom to rely in reestablishing inner equilibrium. A child who comes to school fidgety and restless may be encountering overwhelming levels of stress in the home. Frustrated by his parents' manipulation or arbitrary behavior, the child is unable to actualize his needs for calm, effective problem-solving.

Stress sensitivity in children from alcoholic and addictive families can be observed through behavioral signs and symptoms. External stress not only contributes to problems in self-regulation in these youngsters, but also interferes with their ability to draw upon mechanisms for effective coping. For example, a child with good intellectual ability and sound common sense reasoning will often show poor judgment when placed in a stressful family situation. For instance, recently a six-year-old girl in an alcoholic family divulged to me how she was being terrorized by her oldest sibling when her parents were out drinking. The eleven-year-old sister, functioning in a parentified role, was outwardly conscientious. However, a devious side to her personality emerged when she felt overwhelmed by the care of her younger siblings. To achieve compliance from them during her parents' absence, she had taken to threatening them with a large hammer which she swung over their heads, chanting, "Three raps on the head, and then you'll be dead, so you better stay in bed!" When she heard a disturbance from inside their rooms, she would tap the hammer three times on their door, again chanting, "Three raps on the head . . . " The little children were terrified.

In the majority of school-aged children from alcoholic and addictive families whom I have seen, there are problems in self-regulation. Even the compliant, high-achieving child will demonstrate some problems in self cohesion. It is misleading and erroneous to advance the notion that these youngsters as a group are problem free because many of them are successful academically.

Case Illustration — Louise

Louise was the pretty little seven-year-old daughter of an alcoholic father who had abandoned the family when Louise was barely a year old. Consequently, the mother had returned to work for most of Louise's second year of life. The father, a violent man who physically abused the mother, then returned briefly, until the mother became pregnant again; then he disappeared for good. When I first saw Louise, it was because her five-year-old sister had been molested by an uncle. The mother wanted Louise evaluated, too, "just in case. . . . "

When the mother and her two daughters arrived for their sessions, they gave the impression of having groomed for hours, as though they were all ready to sit for a family portrait. Louise wore frilly, ruffled dresses and patent leather slippers; her hair was a wreath of blonde curls and satin ribbons. To outward observers she would certainly seem an attractive child who had no problems in self development. Indeed, Louise was described by her mother as being "a good little girl," a compliant child who excelled academically and was very helpful at home with her younger sister.

However, as psychological assessment proceeded, Louise began to show an unexpected symptom. In the midst of striving to succeed and win praise from the therapist, she seemed to have difficulty regulating inner tensions. As the stressful nature of the evaluation increased, Louise sat with her thumb in her mouth making loud, sucking noises. She seemed to lose sight of the examiner, withdrawing into herself in a lonely kind of autistic reverie. This type of extreme self-absorption is typical of self-regulation problems seen in children from alcoholic/addictive families.

When this impression was shared with Louise's mother and the question was raised about ongoing addiction, the mother began to sob. She admitted that she had a serious problem with Valium addiction and often potentiated its tranquilizing effect with a six-pack of beer. Using this means of escape since early in her marriage to Louise's father, she often relied on Louise to perform parenting functions for the younger sibling.

Bright, competent children in alcoholic/addictive families both assume and are delegated tasks beyond their developmental capabilities. The overfunctioning of one segment of the personality is usually accompanied by underfunctioning in another area. The child pays the price of uneven self development.

Case Illustration — Martin

Martin was an eight-year-old with dark eyes, jet black hair, and a mischievous grin. Although he had not lived with his alcoholic father since his parents' divorce the previous year, Martin still recalled his father's emotional and physical abuse of him. He also talked about how his father had taken a baseball bat and smashed the television set and destroyed the rest of the family furniture in a drunken rage. At times, Martin had engaged in post-traumatic play where he used his own baseball bat to wreck the toys of his peers. This play had been stopped through the therapist's clear directive early in Martin's therapy.

Martin's mother was concerned because his third grade teacher claimed that Martin was unruly and disruptive in the classroom, and that this was interfering with his academic progress. The psychological assessment revealed that Martin was a bright little boy who was able to excel when given individualized attention. Indeed, he seemed to thrive on the positive feedback he received at the completion of the assessment. When the mother conferred with the teacher, she learned that Martin had been assigned to a peculiar classroom seating arrangement for that entire first quarter of the year. The teacher had "isolated" Martin in a seat in the back of the room, with his chair outside the circle of other children. She insisted that she would keep Martin "in isolation" until he "learned" to settle down.

An intervention was required with the school to provide the principal with confidential information about Martin's background and about the results of the psychological evaluation. The principal, a sensitive listener and seasoned administrator, admitted that Martin's teacher was a rather rigid woman who would make no exceptions once she had determined a certain course of action for a child. When the principal was advised that Martin's acting-out was compounded by the deprivation from social contacts, she volunteered to move the boy to another classroom.

Martin's transfer to a new classroom with a less controlling and more compassionate teacher had a positive outcome. The warm, supportive learning environment greatly facilitated the boy's superior ability to learn, and he began to improve academically. Involved and interested in learning, Martin's academic success improved his self-esteem and peer relationships. His acting-out behavior decreased proportionately.

School-aged children who show problems in self-regulation are often mislabeled as "hyperactive" or "conduct disordered" in the learning environment of a classroom. Unfortunately, this type of child tends to be viewed in terms of surface acting-out behavior and then punished rather than assisted. A punitive approach simply compounds the problem in self-regulation. Or, a child may be pre-scribed Ritalin, beginning or continuing a pattern of relying on drugs for self-regulation.

Children who show problems in self-regulation tend to gravitate towards seemingly more reliable and gratifying pastimes with an addictive substance or activity as a way of bolstering the empty self. Problems with junk food consumption are seen in these youngsters during the childhood years. These problems are often precursors to later abuse of alcohol and other drugs and should be met with con-cern by caretakers and helping professionals.

Case Illustration — Nedra

When Nedra first began family meetings during her father's inpa-tient treatment for alcoholism she was a chubby six-year-old who entered the play therapy room carrying an iced "Big Gulp" drink and a sticky assortment of candies. Her rumpled dress wore the stains of a day filled with sugared goodies. When the parents were advised that Nedra's moodiness and temper tantrums might be related, in part, to sugar consumption, they seemed not to hear. Nedra's mother simply stated, "Oh, that's silly! She's just nasty like her Daddy."

Although I did not see Nedra after her father completed his treat-ment, her problems in eating behavior continued throughout her elementary school years. As a sulky, obese, prepubertal child, she returned to therapy briefly when her parents complained that she was "never happy." Nedra admitted that she hated herself because she was "a fat slob." However, her mother didn't want to deprive Nedra of sweets because that would make her feel "mean." This time the family dropped out of treatment after only two sessions.

My next contact with Nedra was during her first year in high school. Her father, now seven years sober, demanded that she come to therapy. He stated that he had "completely lost control" of his daughter. Nedra had lost a great deal of weight, but, her parents explained, this was "part of the problem." She had begun using street drugs, including the synthetic amphetamine crystal, in order to lose weight. Now addicted, Nedra was verbally and even physically abusive with her mother. Inpatient treatment for her chemical dependency was required.

In the previous case illustrations, three different children used three different external resources to bring about self-regulation:

Louise used thumb sucking and withdrawal; Martin used acting-out; and Nedra used food and later drugs. In much the same way, other children from alcoholic/addictive families engage in rigid role behavior to bolster the empty self. The child who is an academic high achiever, for example, is often driven to seek the external reward of good grades and praise from teachers. This is as much an example of uneven self development as Martin's clownish behavior or Nedra's drug use.

When we relate to a child in terms of his or her role behavior, we are perpetuating the major failing of the addictive family system. When we become preoccupied with the role or façade, we are doing a disservice to the developing child-self, which has never known full expression. By focusing on a child in terms of the role he or she fulfills, we are failing to translate—for the child, the parents, and ourselves—the deeper meaning of that role behavior. Indeed, this translation becomes the heart of effective psychotherapy with the child and the parents.

Our translation must take place as an empathic response that mirrors the child's inner experience. Through this *process of empathy* we can come to know the child's experience as if it were our own. *Empathy*, in this context, is more than a sympathetic feeling toward the child. It is, rather, that *process* whereby we relinquish our ego needs long enough to perceive as the child perceives, reason as the child reasons, and then *feel* as the child feels. We will then articulate back our empathic reflection to the child in the language of emotions. In child-centered therapy, we refrain from asking a child, "How did you feel?" about this or that. We empathize and then *reflect back* to the child the feeling state that we now share through the process of our attunement to the child's inner state. For example:

> "That must have been very *frightening* for you, Kyle, when you heard the upstairs windows breaking—and no one was even there to comfort you. You must have felt very lonely and afraid."

If we are correct in our empathic reflection, we will experience an immediate connection with the child. If we are incorrect, the child will simply look puzzled, or frown, or stare blankly. At such times, we merely try again. A child is usually not injured by our mistakes, except the mistake of giving up prematurely.

All children have difficulty integrating their emotions until empathic reflection has been provided by the adult. However, parent-child interactions in the alcoholic/addictive family system are characterized by a pervasive lack of empathy. It becomes the task of child-centered work to establish an empathic milieu for both the child and the parent. Unlike group therapy with children in the years of middle childhood, individual child-centered work is primarily for the purpose of facilitating cohesion of the child's self system.

What is it about the alcoholic/addictive family system that leads to failures in empathy?

First, the parents' own lack of self cohesion interferes with their ability to acknowledge each other or their children as separate, autonomous beings. In fact, the presence of alcoholism or addiction in a parent can be viewed as evidence of a disordered self (Kohut, 1977). While the presence of a chaotic or unstable self is most obvious in the parent who is actively practicing alcoholism or addiction, a disordered self is often present in the nonalcoholic parent as well. In the same way that this parent's co-dependence is far more subtle (and, therefore, often more resistant to change), his/her lack of self cohesion may also be less obvious. As long as this parent functions within a rigid external structure, the sense of self will appear intact. A loss of external structure threatens an impending loss of inner control, which is experienced as disruptive anxiety; hence, there is an emphasis on maintaining control.

The aim of external control encompasses other people, places and things, or situations. Other persons or objects external to the self, including one's children, are actually experienced as parts of the self. Any action on the part of an external other—even though it may be in the interest of self development and autonomy for the other—threatens separateness and therefore is experienced as damaging to the inner self experience of the parent. A parent *experiences* this need for control of the child in the same way that he experiences the need for control over his own arms, legs, or other body parts.

The aim of control, then, is always in the interest of maintaining an integrity to the sense of self. If we keep this in mind, we will be empathic with the feeling behind this need for control, which is tremendous fear. The abiding fear in the alcoholic/addictive family system is the fear of loss of self. This in turn results in rigid mechanisms of self-protection which interfere with the ability to be empathically attuned to others, especially one's children.

Children require structure and consistent, predictable guidelines for behavior. In the normal course of development, children of about eight to ten years show mild obsessive or compulsive symptoms as they attempt to regulate themselves with the standards for behavior which they have internalized from their parents. We can observe these compulsive struggles through the games and activities of the latency period.

When parental standards are imposed rigidly or fluctuate inconsistently, children have difficulty internalizing their own standards for behavior. Consequently, many compulsive symptoms commonly seen in children during the middle years of childhood are intensified in addictive families. Through internalizing their parents' rigid expectations, certain children may come to have an unrelenting conscience, which drives them compulsively. "You are not good enough," is the echo of low self-worth pushing them towards perfection. Interferences during this period of development are associated with ongoing struggles with compulsive patterns.

Often children will fluctuate between compulsive symptoms and total noncompliance. This is not unlike the behavior within the alcoholic/addictive family, which runs from overcontrol to chaos. Not only is the alcoholic parent inconsistent between drinking and sober periods, but divisiveness between the parents often results in one parent using a rigid model of control and the other being overindulgent and permissive. *Leadership* conflicts within the alcoholic/addictive family characterize these parental interactions. The result is difficulty for the child in achieving internal self-regulation.

When a value is placed on external standards for behavior rather than on the inner development of the unique child, a youngster will experience himself as incomplete and lacking. A vague sense of inner emptiness will lead such a child in constant pursuit of external people, places, or things to achieve a sense of wholeness and aliveness. While more intellectually able children may seek academic rewards through good grades and recognition, other children may use toys or food or constant activity of some type or another. The need for external stimulation is required to relieve the vague tension states that children cannot overcome on their own and usually cannot even articulate.

Case Illustration — Oscar

Oscar was the nine-year-old son of an alcoholic father with several years' sobriety and an overweight, food-addicted mother from an alcoholic family of origin. The family maintained an extremely authoritarian structure when the father, a traveling businessman, was at home. Oscar's father not only set standards for the care of

Oscar's room, but also chose Oscar's clothes, hairstyle, playmates, and food. Oscar's mother tried to compensate for her husband's rigidity by offering her son a totally lax home environment during her husband's absences.

When the father was out of town on business, Oscar would complain to me about feeling lonely. This "loneliness" was not attached to his father as a person; rather, it was a vague sense of emptiness which pervaded his life. He stated that he simply could not think of any way to entertain himself to make himself happy. There was no activity that seemed interesting. He had no hobbies and no peer activities such as scouting or Little League. His mother used the father-absent times to socialize with her friends; hence, there was little interaction between mother and son.

The drawings in Figure 2 were provided on one of the father-absent times when Oscar was attempting to describe his loneliness. He drew a bland, imposing figure with no hands or feet. The self seems to have retreated into the large, oversized body. When asked to provide a resolution, i.e., what would be his ideal way of realizing happiness and enthusiasm, Oscar drew the second figure, which suddenly has come alive with stimulating details and groundedness. The second figure is playing with a "remote control car," holding the remote control device in his hand as the car moves on command. The emphasis on harmony and aliveness of the inner state is achieved according to Oscar, by being able to control an external object.

It is not unreasonable to suspect that Oscar is going to have a lifetime of conflicts surrounding issues of control.

As we proceed with our discussion of the child-self, it becomes necessary to expand our focus to the context of the overall family system. The following chapter will examine this family context — not as it is seen by adult onlookers — but as it is experienced and perceived by each individual child.

Figure 2 Oscar's Drawings during Father's Business Trips

CHAPTER 5

The Unstable Family Constellation

All of us are only too eager to deny our effect on our children and others around us — just as we have little hesitation in blaming the other guy. It is small wonder that parents are more intrigued by hereditary and chemical explanations of their child's emotional problems. . . .

— *Virginia Satir, 1967, p. 32*

When we ask little children to tell us about their inner turmoil, they usually cannot or will not. Indeed, *this* becomes the central task of child-centered therapy. For, unlike the work which we do with adults, where we rely on the data of their recollections to guide us, therapy with children requires that we supply the information about their confusing, disorganizing internal states. This is not an easy task.

When we are trying to learn about these children and to keep our learning as free as possible from our own subjective biases and interpretations, the goal is to devise a method for examining the child's mind at work without increasing that child's self-consciousness or interrupting the child's spontaneous elaborations. Within a developmental framework, this assessment must flow from a determination of the major issues of the years of middle childhood. For example, we know that one of the most conspicuous features of the middle years of childhood is the psychological separateness of the world of children and the world of adults. We simply cannot reach a child's inner psychological realm by using the methods that we use with adults. An adult, reflecting back on childhood experiences, will provide us with a flow of introspections. A child will not do this. As Anna Ornstein (1985) notes, the method of play therapy is used with the young child who is not developmentally able spontaneously to elaborate inner conflicts. To access the world of school-aged children, we must build a bridge which is consistent with their age and cognitive development.

Children of the years of middle childhood employ cognitive skills that are built upon the consolidation of the self-image and the manipulation of symbols. By "cognitive" I am referring to the children's mental ordering of their perceptions of the external world. Through this ordering process, children build up an "internal world" of cognitions (or how they *think* about what they *see*) which governs outward behavior.

The importance of validating a child's perceptions of the external world has been emphasized by Virginia Satir (1967), who quotes Theodore Lidz on the irrational denial in families of schizophrenics where, "The world as the child should come to perceive it is denied." Another type of denial of the child's perceptions is observed in the families of alcoholism and addiction. Here, the child's perceptions of family functioning are not even acknowledged. Since the child is not seen as an independent center of initiative — a separate self — there is no value placed on the child's reality. This is a most insidious form of denial.

Alice Miller (1981, 1983) emphasizes the effects of "pedagogy," the systematic conditioning of a child "at an early age not to become aware of what is really being done to him or her." While Miller's views have been influenced by child-rearing practices in the historically more rigid culture of Germany, we respect her sensitivity to these child victims. However, children of alcoholics are not often victims of pedagogy, for they receive little in the way of consistent, systematic attention from anyone. Also, children of alcoholics *are aware* of the horrors of alcoholic family life (Jesse, 1987); there simply is no credence placed on their perceptions. Perhaps one reason adult children of alcoholics find it so liberating to speak out about their traumatic childhood family situations is that they are finally being heard and acknowledged.

The tendency to disregard a child's perceptions has constrained alcoholism family therapy work, particularly when school-aged children are involved. However, as I have reported elsewhere (Jesse 1977, 1988), children of the years of middle childhood can lead us

through their inner personal world to an improved understanding of
the system. Virginia Satir (1967) has explained the child's ability to
cognitively structure his or her world:

> A child needs to learn how to structure the world. With the help of
> language, he learns how to differentiate and classify beyond the world
> of self, father, and mother. He learns to classify cats and dogs, adults
> and children, males and females, family and not-family.
> From his parents he learns not only how to classify but how to evalu-
> ate and predict. . . . (p. 45)

A school-aged child has the ability to tell us about the important
people in his life according to whether he *perceives* them as the same
or different from him. He can then provide a *construct* which explains
these same/different categories. For example, when a seven-year-old
boy is asked to tell us about his relationship to his parents, he may
tell us that he is most like his father because they are "both boys" and
that he is most different from his mother who is "a girl." This will
inform us about that child's process of *identification*, and more specifically about his *sexual identification*, which is proceeding as we would
expect, i.e. with the same-sex parent. However, when we ask the
same boy to compare himself to his mother and his nine-year-old
sister, he may say that he is most like his mother because they both
"have red hair" and unlike his sister who "has brown hair." Although
the superficial construct of *hair* does not tell us very much, we do
know that this child is expressing an *identification* (a process of relatedness) with his mother over his sister.

We can continue with this type of classification process until we
have arrived at a fairly sophisticated clustering of a child's interpersonal relations. Using this method to group interpersonal ties, we
can obtain an analysis of object relations (intrapsychic constructs)
for several children.

Indeed, this is a research method I used with school-aged children of
recovering alcoholics during the 1970s when I first recognized their
intrapsychic view of the *unstable family constellation*. Before turning to a
discussion of this type of relationship analysis, we need to understand
the literature that had provided the context for this study.

ALCOHOLIC PARENT-CHILD RELATIONSHIPS

One of the first attempts to gain a deeper understanding of children of alcoholics and their family relationships was made by a
Canadian social worker, Margaret Cork (1969). Cork has not been

properly acknowledged by those who have since written about younger children of alcoholics; she is, in my opinion, *the* pioneer in this field. She was the first to call attention to the plight of younger children of alcoholic parentage in her seminal work, *The Forgotten Children*.

Although Cork's study was not empirically based, she was very careful to report data from her unstructured interviews with 115 Toronto school children between the ages of ten and sixteen years. One of the themes that emerged was *a clear separation in the parent-child relationships*. While some of these children reported being divided in their loyalties, and often took the side of one parent against the other, most children felt a lack of attachment to either parent. A dramatic finding was that the child's life did not improve significantly with parental abstinence. There was little difference in the lives of children whose parents were still drinking and those whose parents were abstinent. Personal relationships between the abstaining parents and their children were still far from positive.

One of the earliest and most comprehensive studies of children of alcoholics (Nylander, 1960) was conducted in Sweden primarily for the purpose of determining the effects of prolonged emotional stress on children. The environment of the chronic alcoholic was chosen as the only one where it could be said with any high degree of certainty that children had undergone such stress. This study also examined the effects of parental abstinence on 229 children, ages four to twelve, whose fathers were chronic alcoholics undergoing treatment. Findings indicated that a child's difficulties were not alleviated by the parent's abstinence. In terms of the frequency of their emotional symptoms, there was no difference between children whose fathers had abstained for at least six months and those whose fathers had not. Even when a finer discrimination was made according to the father's drinking history, i.e. the length and duration of the drinking, there was no difference in the frequency of emotional symptoms in the children. This provides evidence contradicting the arguments of parents who maintain that their drinking was "not that bad" and, therefore, did not affect their children. Research shows that there *are* deleterious effects upon the child *regardless* of whether the parents' alcoholism is mild, moderate, or severe during the child's growing-up years.

Another remarkable finding of the Stockholm study was that *alcoholism as a single factor* had a disturbing influence on the life of the child. When the fathers in the study were grouped according to whether they had another psychiatric diagnosis ("mentally abnormal," "socially maladapted") or were "mentally normal," there was no difference in the extent and frequency of emotional problems in the children.

A second phase of Nylander's (1960) study is important because it provides information about the disturbed relationship between the child and the non-alcoholic parent. Records were examined in the case of 121 children who had been admitted to a psychiatric clinic in Stockholm and whose fathers were known alcoholics. Among the families, 55% were separated, with the mother assuming custody of the children. In *all* of these children, there appeared to be a disturbed relationship with the non-alcoholic mother. The lives of these children had not been improved by separation from the alcoholic parent. Rather, the converse was true. This finding has direct implications for alcoholism specialists and mental health workers who provide services to the alcoholic family.

While it must be kept in mind that Nylander's study was conducted several decades ago in a Scandinavian country, there is every reason to believe that the findings are applicable to children of alcoholics today. In different settings where I have worked with children of alcoholics over the years, including publicly funded community mental health facilities, alcoholism inpatient and outpatient treatment centers, and private practice, I have found clinical corroboration for Nylander's findings. Indeed, my earlier research with children of recovering alcoholics established, *"The mere fact of parental abstinence does not seem to improve the life of the child"* (Jesse, 1977). We will now return to this research for a discussion of the *unstable family constellation*.

THE UNSTABLE FAMILY CONSTELLATION

The twelve children of this project were studied intensively over a three-month period of time (Jesse, 1977). Each child, seven to twelve years of age, had lived with an actively alcoholic parent for at least two years prior to the parent's treatment for alcoholism. The impact of the final stages of parental alcoholism was the critical feature of the research. At the time of the study, each alcoholic parent had completed a six-to-eight-week inpatient treatment program for alcoholism and was continuing to maintain sobriety. The average period of sobriety was eight months.

A systems influence was acknowledged as generating a special type of alcoholic family system which was both dynamic and self-perpetuating. Even after the alcoholic parent had gained sobriety, the child was believed to view this parent as deviant. A child's-eye view of the world established during the period of active alcoholism was believed to tightly govern a child's perceptions (what she/he saw) and cognitions (what she/he thought). The guiding theory for this belief had been derived from George Kelly (1955), whose most basic notion was that a person's psychological processes are governed by his expectations.

On the basis of interpretations of past events in the family, the child develops a set of predictions about how he and others will behave in the future. These expectations might have little to do with the way the alcoholic parent is actually behaving during recovery; instead, the child's perceptions of this parent will be colored by the parent's past behavior. The child continues to act in accordance with the set of expectations derived from the period of active alcoholism.

Perceptions of interpersonal functioning derived from the chaotic period of active drinking are extremely resistant to change. Even though the perceptions are sometimes minimal, fragmentary, or misguided, a child uses this inner world view to anticipate and defend against the crises of alcoholic family life. A child will not suddenly shift his internal belief system because a parent professes a new way of life. Intrapsychic change comes about slowly. Assessment of a child's responses to alcoholic family life thus becomes an assessment of the ways in which a child anticipates events and construes relationships.

Over the three-month period of time that a particular child participated in this research, the parents and siblings were interviewed. Psychometric data were obtained on each child, including projective personality measures, tests of intellectual functioning, group process observations, interview data, and family relationship analyses. The method for conducting the family relationship analyses used both empirical and projective procedures. A statistical process* allowed for a conversion of these analyses to a schematic map, or actual picture, of each child's intrapsychic framework of interpersonal attachments.

When an aggregate data analysis was performed on the clusterings of all twelve children, two important features of an unstable family constellation were demonstrated:

1. The child displayed a faulty self-identification (negative or no attachments to other people).

*Iterative intercolumnar cluster analysis.

2. The child was either isolated from or in opposition to his parents.

The unstable family constellation is consistent with the earlier observations of Cork (1969) about a clear separation in the parent-child relationship. The child's lack of attachment to either parent is also consistent with the research of both Cork (1969) and Nylander (1960).

The third, unexpected finding of the unstable family constellation suggests:

3. The child perceived attachment among siblings.

Figure 3 shows an unstable family constellation derived from a child's intrapsychic (cognitive) mapping of interpersonal attachments. In this example, the child (Self*) is isolated from both parents and from all of the other role figures. (The child perceives himself as "alienated" from all these other people, i.e., *faulty self-identification*.) Also, the child is in direct opposition (most different from) the alcoholic parent. There is a clustering of siblings and peers, where the perceived similarity is identical (strength of association = 100%) for two of the siblings, and very similar in the remaining cluster of three siblings. The alcoholic father is different and isolated from all others. Finally, the mother and a teacher are viewed as quite similar and as "authority" figures.

Faulty Self-Identification

Faulty identification was evident in ten out of twelve children in this study. The self-profile clusters of these children included a large number of constructs based on negativity, immaturity, gender role confusion, and self-ambivalence (grouped with role figures described as "mean," "bad," etc.), as well as marked isolation from others in their interpersonal world. Whether a child would fall into one or more of these categories associated with faulty self-identification was independent of ordinal position, sex, age, or intellectual potential. An individual analysis of each child's conceptual structure for ordering relationships provided the key that unlocked that particular child's problems in attaining a positive self-identification. Overall, this finding supported the observations of numerous other writers that the child of the alcoholic exhibits gender role confusion and emotional immaturity, as well as feelings of shame, personal inade-

Figure 3 The Unstable Family Constellation

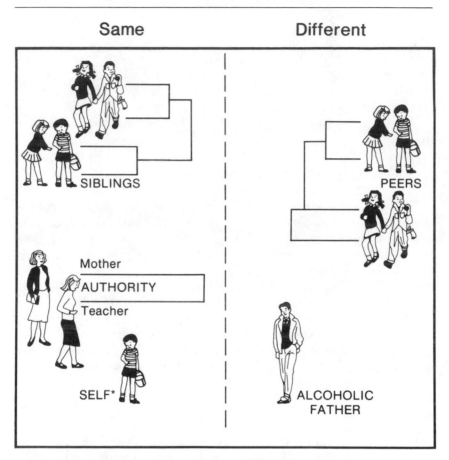

quacy, and alienation (Cork, 1969; Fox, 1962, 1968; McCord, 1972; McKay, 1960).

The two children who showed a positive self-identification shared no common features other than their above average intellectual ability and high academic achievement *together* with a positive feminine identification. The interdependence of intellectual ability, positive sex-role identification, and self-concept is suggested.

In children who showed sex-role confusion, this did not seem to be explained by early separation from the same-sex parent. Rather, there appeared to be more subtle factors operating in the parent-child relationship.

Parent-Child Relationships

An overwhelming proportion (eleven of twelve) of the children in the study experienced themselves as isolated from or in direct opposition to their parents. In children from the most disturbed families of the study, the ability of the child to cognitively isolate the alcoholic parent from all other role figures was profound. This attests to the stability of a child's perceptions of parental deviance long after that parent has gained sobriety. This finding emphasizes the need for children to become involved in a program of their own recovery as soon as the parent enters treatment, if not before.

The child's relationship with the non-alcoholic parent also showed evidence of disturbance. Either both parents were clustered together and isolated from the child, or, if the parents were not together, there was no alignment of the child with the non-alcoholic parent. In families where the parents had separated, none of the children was aligned with the parent remaining in the home.

The disturbed relationship with the alcoholic parent did not seem to bear any relationship to whether the mother was alcoholic or the father was alcoholic. Such a finding lends credence to the notion of environmental influences which favorably shape or distort parent-child relationships. As this study demonstrated, the subtleties and nuances of the parent-child relationship create for the child a repertoire of perceptions and cognitive meanings. These findings also support the warning that parental abstinence as a single factor does not strengthen the child's relatedness to either the recovering alcoholic or non-alcoholic parent.

Desire for Parental Support

When the children of alcoholism and addiction fail to realize an attachment to their parents, how do they cope? To whom do they turn for nurturance and support? Particularly in times of stress, how do these youngsters receive assistance in solving the crises of everyday life?

To answer these questions, a second portion of the previous research with the twelve children of recovering alcoholics was concerned with the perceived *actual* and *preferred* support these children had experienced in their lives. A Stress Situation Test was devised using the children's actual life experiences. For example, each child was asked to identify common life experiences when he or she had experienced stress. The child was not asked specifically about any event associated with the parent's alcoholism. However, if a child wanted to discuss these events, he/she was able to do so. The common stressors of middle childhood, which *all* children experience at one time or another, were the primary topics of the interviews.

All school-aged children encounter trials which they experience as stressful at one time or another. These various life stressors are usually seen as minor or even overlooked by the parent or other adult caretaker. However, the assistance of a caring adult can often make the difference as to whether the child experiences a stressor as traumatic. For example, severe loneliness when in the care of a baby-sitter sometimes troubles a child. Or, when away at school, a child sometimes misses one or both of his parents. Other commonly experienced stressful themes for all school-aged children are various worries associated with the compulsive defense system of this age group. Feeling misunderstood, angry, jealous, guilty, ashamed, or excluded is typical of childhood. Most children also experience problems in their relationships with their parents and siblings at one time or another. Finally, childhood illness or injury can be very stressful. When these stressful life events occur for latency-aged children who are already alienated from their parents, to whom do they turn for assistance or guidance?

To answer this question, each of the various stressful life events was presented in a card sorting procedure to each child. A child was presented with 16 cards, each of which indicated the name of a potential societal helper, beginning with the "self," then each of the parents and siblings, other adult relatives and neighbors, peers, clergy, teachers, physician, police, counselors, favorite pet or toy, and "no one." As each stressful life event was discussed, the child was asked to sort through the array of helpers and to identify who had *actually* provided help and support during that situation. Then, using the same stressful situation, the child was asked to choose again, selecting the ideal helper of his *preference*.

The child was expected to have derived some support from other societal helpers outside the family. Indeed, these twelve youngsters did express dependency needs in times of stress that had not been met by their parents. However, the children did not report receiving any support from other societal helpers except the siblings. In the majority of cases, there was a basic lack of human support — the "no one" card was most frequently selected by the children.

An analysis of the stressful situations revealed the types of conflicts most difficult for these youngsters. Despite the fact of parental abstinence, the children continued to describe stressful family relationships and interactions. In fact, while there were only occasional references to stressful situations during the time of the parents' drinking, there were common themes of serious, ongoing conflicts in the home. One prevalent theme was the child's perceived abandonment. Being left alone by parents or being left in the care of siblings or baby-sitters seemed very troubling for these children. Their reports indicated that the parents often were completely unaware of the effect of this abandonment, however temporary or necessary, on the child. Failures in parental empathy were reported frequently. These took the form of punitive tactics with the child or sadistic teasing or actual physical punishment that bordered on abuse. As reported by the child, the parent was usually totally unaware of the traumatic impact of his or her behavior on the child. While the punitive tactics most often had been delivered by the non-alcoholic parent, the alcoholic parent was usually the one to use sadistic teasing and physical punishment. Conflict between the parents, including separation and divorce, was a source of stress to these children. Reports of bitter sibling interactions and sibling abuse seemed to exceed the type of dissension which is considered normal among siblings.

A most unexpected finding was the *preference* for support which these children indicated. Overall, they preferred much more assistance than they had received. However, of all available societal helpers, *only the parents were desired to provide support*. Although parental abstinence did not seem to have improved the parent-child relationships, the children seemed to experience longings for parental support and assistance. This would appear to shed light on the child's awareness of the potential for the parent to serve as a source of calm and strength during times of stress. Despite all their reported difficulties with their parents, the children continued to express a strong need for an improved relationship with them. During this period of middle childhood, the youngsters appeared to retain hope of realizing a type of relationship with their parents that they had never known.

The implication for treatment is clear. Any path towards recovery for the children of alcoholism and addiction must include a program of therapy which seeks to restore or build anew a workable parent-child relationship.

Child-Sibling Relatedness

An unexpected feature of the unstable family constellation was attachment among siblings, according to the child's intrapsychic ordering of relationships. In short, the findings of this study indicated that children of alcoholics perceive a commonality among sibling relationships during the years of middle childhood.

Although the child might display the "self" as interpersonally isolated and apart from the sibling subsystem, the remaining brothers and sisters were strongly associated as a "like" cluster. At other times, a parent might be grouped among the sibling cluster, suggesting a type of parent/sib arrangement.

During times of stress, children who experience deprivation in the parental relationship tend to seek out their siblings for protection and guidance. The sibling subsystem in the families of alcoholism and addiction comes to have a powerful influence upon family life. Yet, most recovery efforts with these families typically proceed without assistance to the troubled or distorted sibling relationships.

Family treatment which simply includes the sibling group without first uncovering the covert sibling power dynamics is likely to fail. The parents will have difficulty developing an effective, congruent style of leadership until the dynamics of the sibling subsystem have been made manifest and are gradually changed. The interested reader is referred to Coleman's excellent discussion of "The Surreptitious Power of the Sibling Cohort: An Echo of Sin and Death" in *Failures in Family Therapy* for an account of the problems which siblings bring to bear on the treatment of the alcoholic family.

CHAPTER 6

The Secret War of Siblings

The bad effects, upon the individual child, of alcoholism, of various emotional disorders, of child abuse, and of deprivation of parental care have been the subject of numerous clinical studies; but rarely have these traumas' effects on the sibling relationship been noticed.

— Stephen P. Bank and Michael D. Kahn, 1982, p. 15

The lives of children during the years of middle childhood are in many respects secret from adult onlookers. When we see a group of third grade girls, for example, we may observe various aspects of their social development. We can even guess as to the social role each plays within the peer group — who is the leader and who is the follower. However, we must admit that we will continue to be mystified by the giggling, secretive nature of their childhood bond.

The clandestine nature of the middle years of childhood is a prominent feature of this developmental phase and one which many adults deny. Cryptic codes and secret languages, diaries and treasure maps reveal children's special need to have a world which is private from adult onlookers. This need appears to be consistent with the striving for selfhood which is separate and autonomous, distinct from the parents. Moving into the world of same-sex peers, boys and girls go their separate ways to pursue the developmental tasks of sex-role identification and socialization.

Generally, no other period of development is marked by so many freedoms and so few responsibilities for a child. However, in the families of alcoholism and addiction, children are often pushed towards a pseudo-maturity and burdened with family responsibilities. One of the most obvious manifestations of the overwhelming nature of these responsibilities is the child's tendency to complain about sibling care or chores.

Rarely do these siblings from alcoholic/addictive family systems have the cognitive ability to verbally elaborate the conflict of their precocious development, their robbed childhood experiences. Rarely do they divulge the full impact of being used inappropriately as a confidante to one parent in the war against another. Rarely do they come forward even in their own best interest when they are being victimized sexually by a parent. Yet, when one child is maltreated from a family system, the other siblings linger in the background, untreated, ignored by societal agencies which purport to help.

In most normal families where there are siblings of latency age, these children will show a typical, natural tendency toward covert functioning at certain times. Secrets will be traded and shared. Attempts to keep the parents off guard will strengthen the sibling bond. However, young children from alcoholic and addictive families function as a secretive group of prisoners in the family war. They will give name, rank, and serial number, but they will not discuss the dreaded family secret. If you ask one of these children who accompanies a sib to therapy how he or she is doing, the answer will be, "Fine!" The child may even *look* fine. And the conclusion by the observing professional helper usually is that, yes, indeed, the sibling is unaffected, even though the abused child is black and blue from yesterday's belting.

Case Illustration — Perry

Perry was the eleven-year-old son of a practicing alcoholic who had been abusing the boy steadily during his middle childhood years. The beltings usually occurred just after the father had sobered up from binge drinking. The bruises to the boy's buttocks, concealed from public view, had never attracted attention; however, the child was becoming increasingly fearful of his father's verbal assault. The motive for the beatings, the father said, was Perry's constant noncompliance. Unlike his nine-year-old sibling, Pete, who was described by the Dad as "the best kid on the block," Perry was said to be a klutz, a slouch, a bum. When I insisted that Pete would have to come in also for therapy, the parents were aghast. "But why would you want to see Pete? He's such a good little kid. It's Perry who's got the problem."

However, when little Pete finally showed up for therapy, it didn't take more than five minutes to see that he was the instigator of endless family dissension, which was then adeptly shifted onto Perry as culprit. With Perry absorbing the family blame, the mother did not have to discuss her disappointment with her husband's drinking, the father was home free, and little Pete was the center of praise. Perry, who resembled his father physically, was the receptacle for his father's self-hatred and disgust. He hurled expletive after expletive: "You're worthless, an idiot, a slouch." Meanwhile little Pete served as his father's catalytic agent for these family dynamics of abuse.

It was Perry who first began to talk to me about his father's excessive drinking. When this came up in a family session, the dynamics shifted rapidly. Perry's mother expressed her despair, and the father soon entered treatment. Several months into the father's recovery, little Pete began to act out viciously in the home environment. . . .

Blackmail, manipulation, and physical threats are all ways of ensuring that family secrets are kept. Although these secrets usually exist, rarely do the children of alcoholic/addictive parents betray them, for fear of retribution. One child may know or suspect that another is being sexually molested, for example; however, these children may reach adulthood before sharing the secret openly.

SIBLING RELATIONSHIPS DURING MIDDLE CHILDHOOD

As we examine some of the latest research on sibling relationships during middle childhood, we find that this developmental period is a transitional phase for siblings.

Vandell, Minnett, and Santrock (1987) studied 73 sibling pairs between the ages of four and eleven. Although they considered the effect of birth order, all of the children were from two-child families, thus eliminating any possible understanding of middle-child dynamics. Based on their observations, they described sibling interactions in terms of six dimensions: *power/status, teaching/helping, conflict, companionship, positive tone*, and *self-praise*. Their findings indicated that, "with age, siblings became more equal in power and status, whereas sibling help/instruction decreased and sibling companionship and positive emotional tone increased." Then, as these normal siblings

entered adolescence, their conflict increased. These authors concluded that the years of middle childhood constitute a "mid-way point"
between the open bickering observed among toddlers, teenage conflict, and the supportiveness which appears in adult sibling relationships.

Do the children of alcoholism and addiction follow this same
trend, with a decrease in power differences and an increase in positive emotional expressions? My ongoing work with this population
of youngsters indicates that the answer is "no." A sibling hierarchy is
maintained, largely determined by birth order. *Teaching/helping* occurs
among siblings, but is often accompanied by resentment and conflict. Sibling conflict appears to increase with age but is not offset by
positive expressions of praise. Nevertheless, there is a tenacious sibling bond which persists through the years of middle childhood.

SIBLING RELATIONSHIPS IN
ALCOHOLIC/ADDICTIVE FAMILIES

What is the special nature of the sibling subsystem in the families
of alcoholism and addiction? What accounts for the tenacity of the
bond, despite lack of trust and bitter dissension? What can we learn
about these sibling relationships to improve our understanding of
children in recovery?

While my initial understanding of these childhood sibling relationships in alcoholic families was fostered by my early research
(Jesse, 1977), I have continued to learn from these and other siblings
whom I have followed over the years during their recovery. It has
now been twelve years since I completed my original study of children of recovering alcoholics. As those children have moved into
adulthood, I have been able to receive feedback about certain of
them. What has distressed me has been the high incidence of serious
addictions affecting the children who were seen for only brief intervention. Others, who have been followed off and on through normal
family developmental crises, are living rather adaptive lives. What I
learned from this population about the secret war of siblings in
alcoholic/addictive families has withstood the test of time.

Time and again I have seen siblings during middle childhood
alternately cling and disband as a way of surviving. As more and
more leadership functions in the family system of alcoholic/addictive
parents need to be fulfilled by the dominant sibling, the family
constellation becomes increasingly unstable. Siblings group together
during times of family crises until, during interludes of abstinence, a
parent wrests control again of family leadership. Then siblings seem

to disband and revert to bitter, conflictual relating and divisiveness. A new parental crisis will then lead to renewed sibling clinging, until the cycle repeats itself.

Unless the covert power in the sibling subsystem of the alcoholic/ addictive family is recognized, any family therapy effort is likely to fail. Particularly during recovery, it is unlikely that a system which is based on the survival needs of children will relinquish its power easily. Developing an effective leadership model for the parents is an essential task of therapy when the family begins recovery. Without some guarantee that the new family leadership offers a superior way of life, the siblings will not readily fall in line.

A particular problem in working with these sibling groups in recovery involves a family leadership pattern where one or both parents form a sibling-type relationship with their own children. (This "parent/sib" arrangement has been depicted graphically in Chapter 2, Figure 1. See also, Jesse, 1988.) This role reversal is subtle and difficult to resolve in family therapy work. Because the parent/sib dynamic results from the parent's unconscious mechanisms, the parent is often extremely resistant to change. Parental overidentification with a sibling group is regressive in nature and based on powerful intrapsychic motives arising from the dysfunctional (usually addictive) family of origin of the parent. A birth order effect is usually apparent, with the parent/sib being a middle child or youngest child who grew up being cared for primarily by siblings. Although the original sibling relationships were marked by ambivalence, they also provided comfort and contact. The parent/sib now comes to recreate these sibling relationships with her children, splitting them into positive and negative components. Nurturance and emotional support may be sought from one child, while the other(s) will be experienced as frustrating.

A parent/sib dynamic becomes apparent soon after the family arrives for the first session. Bickering between the parent(s) and children may commence in the waiting room. Or, in family therapy sessions one of the siblings may take a dominant leadership role, as the parent/sib shrugs or makes other gestures of helplessness.

Interventions to facilitate the parent/sib's rightful assumption of a family leadership role will be discussed in Chapter 11.

THE SIBLING HIERARCHY

A definite pecking order or distribution of power among siblings occurs in the families of alcoholism and addiction. I have referred to this as "the sibling hierarchy."

The ordinal position of a child in any family will influence that child's experience of the self, the parents, and the siblings. However, children in an alcoholic family system are valued less for their uniqueness as individuals and more for the functions they fulfill or the social roles which they come to play within the family. For this reason, there is a pronounced birth order effect operating in the families of alcoholism and addiction. Where a firstborn child may be characterized as dominant and controlling generally, this will be extreme in the alcoholic family. Likewise, with a lastborn child, often described as "the baby of the family," there is an exaggeration of immaturity in addictive families. The members of an alcoholic/addictive family system force on one another the types of role behaviors which are needed for system maintenance. The underfunctioning of one family member will typically lead to exaggerated role behavior on the part of another family member.

Often, we may be tempted to simplify the enormous complexity of the task before us with children in recovery by dividing the family camp into social roles. However, when we categorize a child in terms of a social role, we are engaging in a process which is parallel to that of the alcoholic/addictive family. I have never found it helpful to find out which child is playing which role. This type of reductionism obscures rather than clarifies the task before us, which is to reach the inner child. When we look at a child through the clouded lens of a social role, we will often see a projection of our own inner world and childhood experiences.

With this word of caution, let us proceed to look at some of the influences of birth order upon children from alcoholic and addictive families. In their comprehensive work on sibling relationships, Bank and Kahn (1982) have noted the differing scientific views on birth order effects. Statistical studies have been quite inconsistent, and no researchers have dealt extensively with birth order effects among children of alcoholics. What is being reported is drawn from clinical observations of what occurs most frequently in the children I have treated.

The Firstborn

The oldest child in the alcoholic/addictive family may have escaped an infancy marked by the parent's destructive, final stage alcoholism; however, heavy drinking and partying have usually encompassed this child's early family life. The parents, in their disappointment with the selfobject functioning of each other, may have begun to use this child narcissistically to meet their own emotional needs. Most often this child serves as selfobject for the mother, satisfying her emotionally and actually interfering with the marital relationship. Because of the closeness between the firstborn and the mother, the child comes to internalize many of the mother's values and attitudes. This child also will be the one to absorb the mother's anxieties and hostilities.

If the father is alcoholic, the child will have an inner, unspoken dread about the father's drinking. If the mother is alcoholic, the firstborn will internalize the mother's turmoil and tension. These difficult feeling states will become part of the inner self experience of firstborn children. The ideal source of calm and serenity missing in the maternal relationship will be sought by this child throughout life. A vague, underlying resentment towards the mother may never be fully conscious for the child until adulthood and participation in some type of uncovering psychotherapy. More often, the child will use reaction formation, seeing the mother as perfect and without blame. Other people, including the siblings, the father, and later the spouse, will become targets for the displaced maternal resentment.

Typically the firstborn suffers a serious narcissistic injury upon the birth of the second child in the family. As the mother pursues all-involving closeness with her new baby, the firstborn watches, confused and isolated. The mother may not be empathically attuned to the hurt and bewilderment of her firstborn, who is attempting to cope with loss. The caretaker's lack of sensitive responsiveness to the emotional state of the firstborn interferes with this child's ability to integrate the threatening emotions into the self experience. Dissociation or disavowal of these negative feeling states leads to a fragmentation of the self experience. The brittle structure of a false-self façade is erected. In later years, when these firstborns enter psychotherapy as adults, they typically recall as some of their earliest memories vague, depressive emotional states. They may spend a lifetime trying to run away from these feelings through addictive behaviors.

The firstborn who also lacks an empathic relationship with the father becomes a self-reliant, pseudo-independent toddler. The child's attempts to cope by being self-sufficient are strongly reinforced by the parents. "Look at Mommy's little MAN! What a good little helper you are! Here comes Daddy's *big boy*!" Such comments force the child into a precocious social role that, with the progression of alcoholism and addiction, tends to become increasingly parentified. Seeking the external rewards of parental attention and approval, the child learns early on that he must *earn* this acknowledgment through work and achievement.

The firstborn soon learns that he can feel important and special by functioning precociously or fulfilling a helping role. Eventually this little child becomes compulsively driven to achieve. During the years of middle childhood, this youngster may be viewed by well meaning adults as having "no problems." Seen as "a good little boy" or "a helpful little girl," this child continues to receive social reinforcement for wearing the façade of a social role. An elementary school teacher may remark unwittingly, "Wish we could have a hundred kids just like you!" The child will continue to equate his value and worth with compliant, achieving behavior. Self development is uneven, however. The rigid set of compulsive defenses of the false-self façade will lead this child into difficulties during adulthood. Never feeling quite real, the adult-child senses that he or she is "an imposter." While these youngsters are quite adept at obtaining recognition for themselves, they will never be quite satisfied or quite believe their success.

Grandiose, narcissistic visions permeate this child's fantasy life. Fantasies of becoming president or a benevolent queen conceal the deep hurt about early parental rejection. Becoming "world famous" or "internationally renowned" is a way of compensating for the opposite feelings that one is, at a most basic level, unloveable. To have an audience of spellbound admirers is to have evidence of one's specialness and greatness. These need-fulfilling fantasies also relieve the oppression of alcoholic family life.

Middle Children

The secondborn and subsequent children arrive in the alcoholic/addictive family and begin to fulfill special functions and roles for their parents. How a particular child is designated to carry out a family function is a result of a complex interaction between intrapsychic and social influences on the parent. Williams (1981) notes a striking similarity between the descriptions of family experiences of young children of alcoholics and their alcoholic parents' recollections of their own childhood experiences in their families of origin.

On the basis of influences from the family of origin, one parent may form an overidentification with a particular offspring, independent of the child's sex, but based prominently on a birth order factor. For example, a mother who was a middle child in her family of origin may have been dominated and abused by her oldest siblings. Through her identification with her own middle son, she may form an unconscious resentment of her own firstborn. However, she does not identify empathically with the middle son; rather, her emotional reactions are a product of her own projective processes.

The development of middle children from alcoholic/addictive families is usually complicated by a self experience which is highly subject to rupture or regression under stress. Since the family environment becomes increasingly stressful and chaotic with the arrival of each subsequent child, these middle children show a high incidence of self-regulation disorders. Problems with temper outbursts, anxiety, fearfulness, shyness, agitation, and other symptoms of "hyper"reactivity are all indicators of problems in self cohesion. Failures in empathy are more profound from the increasingly dysfunctional parents. Also, failures in empathy result from interactions with the parentified child, usually the firstborn. While this firstborn may be quite efficient and reliable in the caretaking of siblings, he or she is also basically unempathic and often abusive. A naturally egocentric latency-aged child becomes even more so with resented siblings, performing caretaking but without a depth of caring.

A secondborn who is scolded, spanked, discounted, or shamed for problems in self-regulation experiences the *self* as essentially bad and unloveable. Now there are two children in the family, each dealing with the inner experience of being unacceptable, unloved. The secondborn faces a powerfully rivalrous relationship with his firstborn sibling. The firstborn, now skilled in bossiness and pseudo-adult functioning, is dominant and unyielding with the later born, same-sex sibling. However, when firstborn and secondborn children in the alcoholic/addictive family system are not of the same sex, there is no clear pattern to their sibling relating. An older brother may be dominant and harsh with the secondborn sister, or he may form a buddy-type relationship with her. Similarly, an older sister with a younger brother may follow the typical firstborn pattern of dominance or protect her brother during parental conflicts. On the other hand, the secondborn son may actually form an alliance with the non-alcoholic mother, moving into the role of male "head of household" during the father's drinking and using episodes. During these instances, the secondborn brother may function in a protective manner with his older sister.

Later born middle children in the alcoholic/addictive family system are not unlike those in most other families who have difficulty accepting societal limits and following rules. Since later borns generally are found to be defiant and rebellious towards authority, these are the children in recovery who most often will be identified as "conduct disordered" in the classroom. The acting-out behavior of these middle children seems to be due to several factors. First, by the time of each successive child's birth, the parents are less enthusiastic. A child's infancy may be colored by caretaking interactions which are perfunctory and filled with tension. The child comes to internalize a basic attitude of being unloveable. Second, parental role models have become increasingly dysfunctional. The parents set poor examples about how to follow rules and accept limits. Third, as family disorganization increases, there are no consistent guidelines for behavior. Neither is there any value placed on respect for authority or societal institutions. Finally, the sibling leaders are inconsistent, abusive role models. Being subjugated within the family, these middle children displace their aggression onto the youngest sib, peers, or external authority figures.

The difficulties these middle children show in school have less to do with ability than with problems in self-esteem and self-regulation. Within the family, these children have not been rewarded for achievement. Their problems in self-regulation usually interfere with success in the classroom.

Youngest Children

The youngest sibling in the alcoholic/addictive family system often begins life when the parent is in the final stage of alcoholism or addiction. Early infancy is thus marked by caretaking interactions which either are filled with parental distress or are assumed by the oldest sibling. An older sibling actually may come to experience this child as if he were her own. Attempts to protect the child from the parents' destructive interactions further intensify the oldest–youngest sibling bond. An overidentification with the smallness and weakness of the youngest may lead the oldest to fiercely shield this child from the other siblings.

The youngest child often is kept immature and dependent in his functioning by a symbiotic attachment to one of the parents. The triangulation of this child maintains the precarious systems balance, offsetting the now totally dysfunctional relationship between the parents. This is the child who will still be sleeping with a parent into the middle childhood years. For instance, one mother would typically leave her husband's bed in the middle of the night to sleep with her six-year-old youngest son. A careful history of parental interactions with this child will often disclose other dysfunctional patterns.

Youngest children from alcoholic/addictive families often have serious problems in adjustment when they begin school. These problems become labeled as "hyperactive" and "attention deficit disorder (ADD)". Learning disabilities also seem to affect a large percentage of these youngsters. Symptoms of aggression, immaturity, poor impulse control, and difficulties with attention and concentration all complicate the child's ability to learn.

Research has shown that later born sons of alcoholic fathers tend to be at greater risk than firstborns for the development of adolescent adjustment problems (Michalik, 1981).

Although youngest daughters of alcoholics tend to use a variety of attention-gaining behaviors, they are generally better behaved than youngest sons — until their teenage years. Then youngest daughters also begin to show a variety of adolescent adjustment problems.

The Only Child

The plight of only children in alcoholic/addictive families is especially poignant. Lacking even the fragmentary emotional support of siblings, these children have no human support in times of parental crises. Cork (1969) has noted how the uncertainty of family life for these children is followed by peer relationships limited by fear and distrust.

An only child may be alternately indulged and isolated by ambivalent interactions with each parent. Because of the greater availability of financial resources in the one-child family, this child tends to be "bought off," receiving material evidence of parental caring rather than the parents' time, interest or attention. Triangulated in the bittersweet relationship between the parents and used narcissistically for the parents' needs, this only child develops serious problems in self-worth. These range from having no clear sense of self to having an overinflated sense of his own importance. This is the youngster who seeks to feel special. In many of the alcoholic families I have treated over the years, the only child will have been placed by the parents in an addictive-type relationship with lessons and activities. Music, ballet, gymnastics, swimming, or Little League feed this child's grandiose longings to be the center of attention. Most often, the parents' own narcissistic needs fuel the child's grandiosity. The child absorbs the intensity of the parents' need to become "a star." Attention is demanded from peers and teammates with an almost ruthless air of entitlement. For these confused, lonely youngsters, activities rather than sibling interactions are sought as sources of comfort during family upheaval. In the absence of soothing interactions with the parents, the child has an emptiness and inner restlessness. He will seek the stimulation and excitement of thrilling activities to infuse the lonely, unmirrored self with a sense of aliveness.

Deep hurt and bewilderment affect these only children at an unspoken level. They cannot resolve the reason for the parent's alcoholism and abandonment. The child is left with the question: If he is so special, why he has not been able to claim the parents' *full* attention? Seeing a parent choose an addiction as the primary relationship is a deep narcissistic wound for all children, but especially for the only child. Hence, this child's drive to become important to others outside the family hides a deep injury.

Both Kyle (p. 62) and Oscar (p. 76) were only children from addictive families. Each shared the common dilemma of being used in the war between the parents, and in both cases, this pattern persisted into the parents' recovery.

Stepsiblings

Conflict typically permeates the home where children from two different family cultures blend. Often loyalties to parents outside the newly blended family will be tenaciously defended, creating serious problems in the relationships with the new stepparents. Problems between stepchildren and a stepparent are then absorbed by the other siblings in the home. Fierce coalitions and family camps develop. When these blended families practice an addictive lifestyle, the tensions and rivalries are rarely dealt with adaptively through direct problem-solving. Blaming and counter-blaming occur among siblings as well as between parents and parents and children. The scapegoating of a particular child in the family is a way for others to obtain love and attention. By casting someone else in an unfavorable light, one can feel included among the in-crowd. Problems in belonging may never be corrected in these blended families.

Another serious problem is the displacing of a child from a certain birth order position by a stepsibling. This can have a devastating effect on a child in the alcoholic/addictive family system. When, for example, a child's sense of self has been maintained through functioning in a parentified role, she will not easily relinquish this position to the new intruder. If the stepsibling is older and more competent to fulfill the parentified role, the younger child may suddenly revert to severe problem behavior as the sense of self is fragmented. Only children have a particularly tough time when they must suddenly share the family spotlight with one or more stepsiblings. This

necessity will rarely be buffered by parental empathy for the displaced child's hurt and bewilderment. Rather, the "only" will typically be subjected to chastisement and humiliation by a parental evaluation that he is spoiled and selfish. These pejoratives are then taken
up by the new stepsiblings, who mock and tease unmercifully,
"Spoiled brat. Sissy. Scum-bag."

In remarried alcoholic/addictive families there is rarely sufficient
family identity to provide the siblings with bondedness or closeness.
This becomes the therapeutic focus with these recovering families.
Unless there is recovery of the family above and beyond chemical
dependency treatment, chances are that the family will not stay
together as an intact unit. Family therapy combined with sibling
group and individual therapy for the children is crucial. Otherwise,
the instability of these family groups is profound. Children come
and go from the home to their other parent, and eventually to the
homes of relatives, foster placement, or institutions. In the most
unstable of these families, imminent separation of the parents and
even divorce always poses a threat of abandonment to the children.

Within the family unit, one child may be singled out by a stepparent in a war against an extrafamilial parent. The custodial parent's
projection process is unleashed on both the child and the ex-spouse.
Typically the result is a cruel, hostile attack on the extrafamilial
parent, which is accomplished through belittling that parent to the
child. This amounts to psychological abuse of the child.

Case Illustration — Quinnella

Quinnella was a tall, pretty 11-year-old girl who covered her good
looks with eyeglasses and shyness. Academically successful and
verbally articulate, Quinnella was quite intense about achievement. The older of two daughters, she and her younger sister had
resumed long summer vacations with their father after his four-
year recovery from alcoholism. These out-of-state visits were cor-
dially received by the Dad's new wife, although there was some
friction between her 13-year-old son, Claude, and Quinnella.

On one of the summer visits, Quinnella told her Dad that she
was not happy living with her mother because of the mother's
apparent neglect. Outraged, Quinnella's father sought and obtained physical custody of his daughters, with the full support of
his new wife. Eagerly, this new blended family moved into a new
home that had enough bedrooms for each child and was close to
good schools.

Within a few short weeks, the tension between Claude and Quinnella was overwhelming for everyone in the family. Claude, as an only child, had not been used to sharing attention with anyone. Now he became a constant competitor with Quinnella, putting her down every chance he got. When Quinnella's father tried to intervene, his new wife came to Claude's defense. The younger sister tried to cling to Quinnella in confusion and desperation.

By the time I began seeing the family, open warfare was occurring between Claude and his mother and Quinnella, her father and sister. The stepmother, who refused to work an Al-Anon program, became verbally abusive to Quinnella, calling her "slob," "skinny," and other pejoratives. Quinnella complained that, if she were to maintain her excellent academic record in the new school, she could not perform meticulous housekeeping chores every afternoon for her stepmother. The stepmother held Claude out as an example of good behavior. He was involved in a heavy athletic schedule, she claimed, but *he* still managed to do *his* chores. Quinnella's father argued with his wife that *her* son was only expected to do chores on weekends. A rift in the parental relationship divided the family.

Harsh sibling interactions ensued. Tattling, teasing, fighting, and belitting increased. This led Quinnella's stepmother to call the natural mother on the telephone, threatening to send Quinnella back to the mother, denigrating, insulting, blaming. "I can understand why you wanted to get rid of your daughter. She's a slob! I may have to send her to a foster home. . . . "

After only three months this family dropped out of treatment, and within a short time the father had relapsed. Soon, Quinnella's stepmother and Claude had moved out of the home.

One day I received an emotional telephone call from Quinnella while her father was still in treatment. Encouraged by a friend to call me, Quinnella was brought to the office by her friend's parent. Shaking, sobbing uncontrollably, Quinnella disclosed to me how — just before the separation of the family — she had been forcibly raped by her stepbrother, Claude.

The war that goes on in the sibling subsystem in alcoholic/addictive families is but a reflection of the larger war. The secret nature of this war is sometimes not even known to the participants, the siblings themselves. Parents with disturbed relationships towards each other and ambivalent attitudes towards interpersonal relationships in gen-

eral tend to create similar disturbances in their children. The ensu-
ing projective processes are largely unconscious. When a parent
begins to split off unwanted, disowned parts of himself onto a child,
he begins to see that child exactly as his own hated mirror image.
The remaining "good self," which is attributed to another child,
represents to the parent all that he likes about himself. This ambivalent splitting is most clearly demonstrated in the case illustration of
Perry and Pete in this chapter. Additionally, in the case illustration of
Quinnella, her stepmother began to split off negative, unacceptable
aspects of her own worse self-image onto the child.

Siblings will often treat each other in accordance with a parent's
wishes. To gain favor with a parent, one sibling will war against
another without really knowing why. The heightened sibling rivalry
which results will be experienced by the child as *real*, for a child will
really come to hate a brother or sister who is judged by the parent to
be stupid, lazy, no good, worthless, and so on.

Finally, it is the quality of the marital relationship which actually
provides the most influential model for sibling interactions. When
the parents are at war, the siblings will take up their weapons and
begin to fight each other, often without knowing the full reason for
their bellicose actions.

PART III

The Process of Child Development

Child development is concerned with learning about an individual child so that we can better comprehend and know that child. By applying what is gathered from systematic observations of groups of children, we can see whether our particular child is proceeding according to what is usual for most children of his or her age.

The study of child development also provides us with a background for understanding adult behavior. When we attempt to communicate about the adult child of alcoholics (ACA) syndrome, for example, we need to know something about normal child development. Adult retrospections may give us clues, but we are better prepared to speak with accuracy when we are grounded in the data of childhood.

Another reason to be concerned about the process of childhood development, as well as the implications of its disruption for school-aged children from alcoholic/addictive families, is that some of our most pressing social problems both arise from and affect this period of development. Child sexual abuse, physical abuse, and psychological maltreatment traumatically disrupt the years of middle childhood. By the teen years children are already involved in destructive patterns of drug and alcohol abuse.

Chapter 7 explicates the developmental process of the total, integrated child-self by isolating each segment of the various functional units. The reader should bear in mind that this abstraction is merely for the purpose of convenience; in reality, the child-self as system is an interrelated whole.

Developmental Consequences of the Poly-Addicted Family Environment

Although children have been scurrying under the watchful eyes of interested and intelligent adults for a very long time, we have a less satisfying explanation of human development than of the life cycle of the fruit fly, which has been an object of study for less than one hundred years.

—Jerome Kagan, 1984, p. xi

In this chapter we consider how certain features of the expected developmental sequence become distorted when a child has lived within a poly-addicted family environment. Do these distortions persist into adulthood? Indeed, do they later form the basis of what has been called the "adult child" syndrome?

Commentaries on children from alcoholic/addictive families contain implicit assumptions about the manner in which human beings grow and develop. Even when an author does not state a set of theoretical assumptions explicitly, we know that she cannot divorce herself from a general philosophical model on which her theory is built. When we examine the model, we glimpse the author's beliefs about the nature of child development. We can see, for example, whether the child is viewed to be a passive, reactive, and empty organism — such as in those models based solely on behavioral explanations. Or we note that the child is presented as an organized, participating entity, as in models based on cognitive explanations

(Piaget, Kagan) or psychoanalytic principles (A. Freud, Erikson, Kohut).

Theories of cognitive development are associated with the maturing central nervous system. Piaget (1952) has identified three major stages of cognitive development:

1. A *sensory-motor stage* during the first two years of life.
2. A *pre-operational stage* from ages two to seven when the child uses words and images to represent objects.
3. The *concrete operations* stage during the preschool and elementary school years. Here, the child is largely concerned with organizing his world into classes, relations, and numbers.
4. The *formal operations* stage during adolescence, which involves the growth of logical thought.

Jerome Kagan, researcher and professor of developmental psychology at Harvard, is renowned for his pioneering work in cognitive development. Kagan (1984) notes that an emphasis on family experiences has dominated writings about the child since the second decade of this century. However, Kagan reminds us that a child's thoughts, fears, actions, and even his sense of self are all constrained by the way his brain functions. This applies with no less certainty to children from alcoholic and addictive families.

While the theoretical basis for the present view of child development is influenced by Piaget and Kagan, much of the theory integrates these views with the self psychology of Kohut. Although self psychology has its roots in psychoanalytic theory, it departs from the classical drive-defense model proposed by Freud. Sigmund Freud viewed development as proceeding through a series of psychosexual stages during childhood. From infancy on, an individual is subject to inner conflicts arising from the sexual and aggressive drives. A concentration of innate body energy (libido) was believed to be associated with the different body zones during each of the psychosexual stages of development. Characteristic defenses were developed at each of these stages, permitting an individual to mature psychologically and advance to the next psychosexual stage. Although Freud developed his theory from the analyses of adult patients, his basic notions later were extended by Anna Freud to her work with children.

Anna Freud viewed development as a process which involved an interaction between a child's constitutional endowment and environmental conditions. She believed that overstimulation of or deficiency in libido resulted in anxiety and regression in the child. Her concept of developmental lines explicated the sequence of maturation through five stages from infancy through adolescence.

Another psychoanalytic theorist and student of Anna Freud's was Erik Erikson, who formulated eight developmental stages from infancy through the life span. Much of Erikson's work is based on Freud, including his acceptance of the drive-defense model. According to Erikson, conflict results from two opposing drives manifested in the personality throughout the eight stages of development. Although Erikson stressed that the first two years of life formed the basis of personality, he also saw that environment played a role in development. However, the ongoing struggles between opposing drives accounted for personality change and growth.

Beginning with Freud and continuing with Anna Freud and Erikson, human development has been understood largely in terms of the child's conflicts with instinctual drives. Although Erikson's legacy has to do with his emphasis on ego development across the eight stages of the lifespan, his concept of identity is still based on the notion of fixation points and regressions in drive development. Accordingly, his view of identity is very different from the concept of "the self" described by Kohut (Cohler, 1980).

Kohut did not believe that there was a scientifically demonstrable aggressive drive or instinct. He saw aggressive behavior as a response to frustration. Although he accepted the notion of a reproductive sexual instinct, he believed that sexual behavior was not necessarily related to a drive, since it might also be tension-reducing.

Self psychology was begun to correct the notion that the therapist knows what is wrong with the patient because of the predetermined theory of sexual and aggressive drives. Kohut introduced the "empathic approach," in which the therapist seeks to view the patient's difficulties through the patient's eyes rather than through a theory superimposed on the person by an outside observer.

The present theory of child development blends this self psychological perspective with a recognition of the child as a developing psychophysiological organism. COA observations and interventions must commence with a regard for a child's biologic maturation. For example, even the most articulate of our verbal interventions will fall on the seemingly deaf ears of a child who has an auditory processing deficit. A conceptual framework of child development is crucially important when we attempt to provide services to young COAs and their families. This framework broadens our understanding of a child's functioning while directing our goals and interventions.

Children in recovery must be understood in terms not only of how particular children function within the family but also of how their development and behavior are influenced by their family experiences. However, in the discussion to follow we will narrow our scope from family functioning to the development of the individual child.

Perceptual, motor, cognitive, emotional, motivational, and social developments are each aspects of ego functioning and contribute to the core experience of the self. Here, the term "ego" describes that psychological modality which coordinates and integrates the various functions of the self experience. This is to say that it is the ego which mediates between the self and the external world and which makes sense of and attributes meaning to the subjective experiences of the self.

Although the ego, like the self, is an abstraction, we can infer and, indeed, observe differential evidence of ego and self functioning. Knowing how the words "ego" and "self" are used in child psychology will prepare us for the discussion which follows about the failures of the "developing self" and the compromises of the "maturing ego." Our discussion does not cover ego development per se; rather, we will emphasize the observable functions which are constantly being orchestrated by the maturing ego.

It also is important here to distinguish the terms "self development" and "ego development" from "personality development." In the latter instance we would be concerned with "traits" or character "types." But the personality of a child is still forming, unfolding, open to change during the years of middle childhood and on into adolescence, so that personality is not always a relevant concept. For this reason, we will be more precise in our understanding of a child if we do not superimpose constructs of types, traits, labels, or roles. We will find that we already have a wealth of information with which to concern ourselves when we simply focus on the observable features of the developing child-self and the inner logic of this development as it is organized by the ego.

Figure 4 is a schematic representation of the coordinated functions of the ego as they make up the self experience. Functional boundaries overlap and intersect to integrate the various aspects of the self experience in a cohesive arrangement.

As we discuss the different functions of perception, cognition, affect, motor development, social behavior, motivation, stress, and self-regulation, we will be considering the normal developmental picture for the years of middle childhood. We will then examine research findings for school-aged children of alcoholics and drug-addicted parents.

Figure 4 Schematic Representation of the Coordinated Functions of the Ego as they Comprise the Self-experience

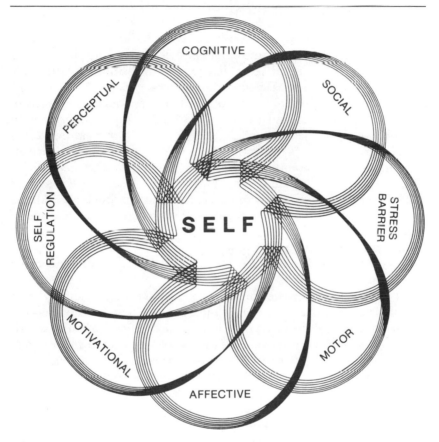

PERCEPTUAL DEVELOPMENT

Perception involves the raw data of sensation devoid of meaning or judgment. A child receives sensory impressions from the world around him through his five sense organs. From birth onward, these impressions become more refined with the child's increasing ability to discriminate and differentiate. The process of maturity links increasingly complex cognitions (or thoughts) and affects (or emotions) to these sensory inputs. For example, a blinking yellow light may simply be perceived by a very young child. To a school-aged child, the light comes to have a meaning attached, "traffic light." And, to a teenager learning to drive an automobile, the light also is tinged with emotion, "Slow down, caution, proceed carefully. . . . "

An infant's earliest perceptions of the caretaking milieu are combined with primitive affective meanings. A child *perceives love and affection* as feeling experiences when the parents' caretaking gestures are sensitive and soothing. Indeed, the internalization of these calming interactions appears to form the basis of the child's ability to self-soothe. When the family environment is one of discord and violence, the child comes to perceive the outside world as a hostile place. He or she then develops a mind set (cognitive predisposition or "attitude") of mistrust, with a defensive style of wariness.

The perceptual ability of school-aged children forms the basis of their ability to learn and to achieve academically. Impairment in auditory or visual perceptual channels results in a condition often referred to as a specific "learning disability." Perceptual disturbances sometimes suggest emotional problems rather than a brain dysfunction. High-stress situations which result in strong affective reactions of fear and anger interfere with perceptual functioning by blocking a child's ability to perceive accurately. For school-aged children of alcoholics and addicted parents who have been exposed to turbulent family environments, interferences in visual or auditory perception pose an academic hardship. A child learns to "tune out" incoming stimulation.

In order to read, write, or follow instructions in school, a child needs to be receptive to incoming information. The keen perception of shapes and sounds forms the basis of successful academic experience. Since children rarely know how to talk about their problems in perception, these deficits may not be picked up in the school for many years. This can be a devastating form of perceptual as well as social impairment for children of alcoholics, whose feelings of shame and personal inadequacy are already profound. These failures in self-esteem run a parallel course to problems in peer relationships. A child who is unable to perform at the level of same-age peers suffers inwardly. Outwardly, his/her defensive posture might be one of aggression or playing the clown. Problems in perception are associated with problems in self-esteem, academic achievement, peer relationships, and emotional development.

Attention and Perception

In addition to the adequacy of a child's perceptions, which is dependent on visual and auditory acuity and discrimination, there is also a *selectivity* of the perceptual process, which is dependent on *attention*. Sometimes children will listen attentively to a set of instructions, and other times they will appear simply to turn a deaf ear to all incoming information. Children from alcoholic/addictive families who are being constantly exposed to a barrage of noxious family interactions seem to feel a need to withdraw into themselves. Perceptual overload involves the need to protect the self from feeling overwhelmed.

A condition known as Attention Deficit Disorder (ADD) has been found to be a relatively common disorder among children from alcoholic/addictive families.

Learning and Perception

Perceptions can be influenced by previous experience. A child tends to organize what he sees or hears in line with his previous experience. He will organize his current perceptions on the basis of past events, regardless of changes in the current situation. This perceptual process is selective. In Chapter 5 I described how children of alcoholics organize their interpersonal relationships based on perceptual and cognitive selection.

Research in Perception

Few studies have examined the likelihood of perceptual problems in children from alcoholic/addicted families. Here we will review briefly those which are relevant to children in the years of middle childhood.

An important study was done by Hennecke (1984) who investigated boys and girls, aged ten to twelve, whose fathers were alcoholic. This study was for the purpose of exploring perceptual problems in children considered at risk for alcoholism and thereby inferring a genetic basis for the development of alcoholism. A perceptual test of tactile-kinesthetic perception was administered to test stimulus augmenting in these children. The theory of stimulus augmenting holds that what is perceived is sensed to be of greater magnitude than it is. Augmenters are highly sensitive to discomfort since any form of stimulation tends to be experienced more acutely. Earlier research had found alcoholics to be stimulus augmenters on this same test of tactile-kinesthetic perception. Indeed, Hennecke's study found this same augmenting tendency in the children of alcoholics. This particular perceptual disorder is believed to be antecedent to the development of alcoholism in COAs.

Using a standard psychological test of visual perception (Frostig), Aronson et al. (1985) examined the visual perception of children of alcoholic mothers. While all controls were normal, there was a perceptual delay exceeding one year in one-half of the school-aged children of alcoholics. Short attention span was found in over one-half of the study group, but not among controls. Members of the study group with traits of the fetal alcohol syndrome showed pronounced perceptual delay.

These studies point out the importance of assessing the perceptual functioning of children in early recovery. Until research has provided more information about perceptual modes which may be affected in COAs, our ongoing evaluations are required to supply the missing data.

When a child is not perceiving accurately, that child will experience problems in self-regulation. Over the years, school personnel with whom I have consulted have shared the observation that children from practicing alcoholic and addictive homes do demonstrate a type of "perceptual overload" in the classroom. Although there may be no measurable visual or auditory deficit, a child will complain of not being able to see or hear accurately. A little girl may cover her ears with her hands, for example, and complain that she is being bothered by noise. Another child may appear not to see figures on the blackboard, even though he has no problems in visual acuity.

COGNITIVE DEVELOPMENT

Our concern for children in recovery is based not only on children's view of the world—their perceptions, or what they *see*—but also on what they *think* about what they see, that is, their cognitions. Children's cognitions form the basis of the way they come to think about themselves in relation to others.

Cognitive development is associated with the mastery of language and the ability to manipulate symbols. Piaget has identified the stage of *concrete operations* as the time during middle childhood when children classify and organize their experiences. According to Piaget, a child's ethical growth commences during this period with the child's "unilateral respect" for his parents and their ethical standards. The child's identification with these standards leads to his "moral realism." What can we say about children from alcoholic/addictive families whose identification process with the parents is disturbed? How does the child's ethical development become established?

All children in the years of middle childhood engage in "scapegoating." Venting one's frustrations and resentments on another person is anxiety-reducing. While this occurs with regularity, normally parents help the child accept more socially adaptive cause-effect relationships. The child is taught not to blame, but to accept personal responsibility for his actions. However, the tendency to *blame* is a common feature of alcoholic/addictive parents. Indeed, this parental tendency makes it all the more likely that children from alcoholic/addictive families will persist in "scapegoating" into adulthood.

The development of a child's linguistic abilities cannot be separated from the family context. When parents do not talk with a child, that child will show a lack of verbal interaction in certain areas of his cognitive functioning. If a child's family environment consists of enriching verbal communications, that child will usually display linguistic strengths which support him through his school years. Parent-child interactions which are tension-filled or contain mixed messages or hidden meanings are likely to be associated with linguistic deficits in a child.

A child's increasing socialization is reflected in his speech. Piaget studied the functions of language in a child's life and determined that speech follows a pattern from "egocentric" to more "sociocentric." In egocentric speech, the child is not concerned with having an interaction as much as she is in speaking for herself for her own pleasure. She is not even concerned with the point of view of her listener. However, as the child becomes more socialized, her speech considers the other person, her point of view, and the exchange of ideas and information.

Intellectual Development

With the growth of language, a child's abilities in cognitive functioning can be measured on standard psychological tests called "intelligence tests." Two major modes of cognition can be measured on these tests: A *verbal* mode relies on the use of words, or language, for communicating and understanding ideas; a *performance* (nonverbal) mode relies on visual-perceptual or visual-motor functioning independent of verbal abilities. A child's perceptions, therefore, have a direct bearing on his cognitive functioning.

The assessment of intellectual development usually involves the notion of I.Q. or intelligence quotient. Actually, the I.Q. is the score a child has attained on any one of the standardized psychological tests which measure different aspects of verbal and performance capacities. To say that a child has "a high IQ" is to speak in oversimplified terms about complex functioning in a variety of cognitive and perceptual-motor (*performance*) modalities.

Several studies have looked at the intellectual development of children of alcoholics during the years of middle childhood. One of the most relevant was that conducted in Sweden by Nylander (1960). When he examined the psychiatric clinic records of 108 children of alcoholic parentage, he found that their obtained scores on the intelligence tests (Terman-Merril, Wechsler-Bellevue) were normally distributed. However, Herjanic et al. (1978), studying 26 children of alcoholic parentage and 14 children of heroin-addicted men, found a tendency for the children to show lower IQs than their parents.

In a more recent Scandinavian study from Denmark, Gabrielli and Mednick (1983) compared WISC-R scores of 27 children of alcoholic fathers with 114 children of non-alcoholic parents. The COAs were found to have lower full scale and verbal I.Q.s, but similar performance I.Q. scores. Aronson et al. (1985) conducted a study in Sweden using Wechsler scores for children to examine the difference between 21 children of alcoholic mothers and 21 control children of non-alcoholic mothers. Results showed that the COAs scored 15–19 I.Q. points lower than the controls.

Another study (Ervin et al. 1984), conducted in the United States, examined the full scale I.Q.s of 41 children of alcoholic fathers, finding these scores to be significantly lower than those of 41 children of non-alcoholic parentage.

Black (1985) makes some claims about intellectual functioning of children of alcoholics: "We find in our groups that children of alcoholics, like most alcoholics themselves, according to research, are bright and of above average intelligence" (p. 106). However, the author does not indicate how she obtained her "findings," nor does she cite the research about the intellectual levels of alcoholics.

Finally, Bennett, Wolin, and Reiss (1988), using WISC-R full scale I.Q.s of 64 children from alcoholic families and 80 children from non-alcoholics families in the Washington, D.C., area, determined that the COAs scored "significantly lower" (113.1) than the controls (117.7). However, since both of these scores fall within the same I.Q. range of "bright normal," an obvious question arises concerning the practical "significance" of this difference, especially when attempting to provide services to school-aged children of alcoholics.

Intelligence test findings should be used to assist children of alcoholic/addictive families on an individual, case-by-case basis in areas of learning, adjustment, and remediation of difficulties. Rather than generalizing from an I.Q. score or I.Q. range (such as "bright" or "superior"), we concern ourselves with how a child's scores in the various cognitive functions have fluctuated around his/her *own* individual average level of functioning.

In conducting a retrospective analysis of psychological testing which I had administered to children of alcoholics over a ten year-period (1977–1987), I noticed several trends which emerged on the Wechsler (WISC and WISC-R) tests:

1. The score for Performance (nonverbal) abilities is usually higher than that for Verbal abilities in terms of I.Q.s. The gap between the two I.Q.s is often a significant one for the age level (seven–eleven years).
2. Because of the wide Performance-Verbal gaps, a child's Performance I.Q. score may be in one range (such as bright normal) while the Verbal I.Q. falls in another (such as average).
3. Because of the leveling effect of the lower Verbal score on the composite Verbal-Performance average, the Full Scale I.Q. also tends to be lower than the Performance.
4. However, the Full Scale I.Q.s of children of alcoholics tend to be normally distributed, i.e., the scores follow a bell-shaped curve, with the majority of scores clustering in the average range.
5. Within the Verbal grouping, there is a tendency for the *Information* and *Vocabulary* subtests to be lower, indicating a deficit in language and verbal concepts from previous environmental learning derived from the culture of the home and family.

The lowered *Information* and *Vocabulary* subtest scores may well be measuring the childhood corollary of the deficit in "basic life information" observed in Adult Children of Alcoholics by Woititz (1983) and Kritsberg (1985). Kritsberg, writing on the Adult Child syndrome, concludes:

ACoA's as a rule do not possess concrete information on how to live life. When they were growing up, there was no one to answer their questions. When an ACoA says, "I don't know," or "I don't understand," it is not a lie. The lack of information is both in concrete knowledge and in the ability to deal with emotional states. (p. 42)

The score obtained on the WISC-R measure of verbal common sense judgment (Comprehension subtest) is usually in the average or above-average range for the majority of children of alcoholics during the years of middle childhood. There are a couple of reasons which might explain this: (1) Comprehension appears to measure the child's ability to manipulate strategic information necessary for *inde-*

pendent coping (surviving) in the social milieu. (2) The ability to manipulate strategic information necessary for coping appears different
from the cognitive skills necessary to utilize verbal life information
concepts. These latter abilities require not only adequate inputs
from the environment, but also a child's ability to perceive, accept,
process, store, and retrieve these inputs. The child is affected by the
presence or absence of an enriching family environment, as well as
by the emotional milieu which either facilitates or precludes verbal
interactions.

When the family culture is characterized by tense, bitter interactions, a child's anxiety may be so high that it interferes with her ability
to process and store incoming information. Although she may be able
to perceive sound, and even to accept it, the interference of anxiety will
block short- and long-term memory storage. The child might be exposed to information, but be unable to recall it for later use.

The tendency of young children of alcoholics to be more adept in
nonverbal than verbal functions suggests that — already by the years
of middle childhood — they have developed compensatory coping
strategies. Through vigilant perceptual processes, a child is able to
scan the environment and make sense of the world without access to
verbal cues. Strategies for coping depend on the ability to accurately
size up a social situation. Doors slam, an automobile screeches out of
the drive at odd hours in the night, food is scorched and left on the
stove — all these nonverbal cues are translated into cognitive
meanings.

A child of a practicing alcoholic once told me, "I can always tell
when my parents are mad at each other by the way they *vibrate*.
When they're mad, they don't talk, they just *vibrate*. I can pick up
their bad vibes at the supper table, and before I know it, I've got a
stomachache."

The WISC-R profile in Figure 5 is an example of how a girl such
as the one described might display very high functioning in her
visual-perceptual ability to scan the environment in order to sift out
what is essential from what is non-essential (Picture Completion
score=16). The child also shows a high ability to size up a social
situation without the benefit of any verbal cues (Picture Arrangement score=15). Thus, without the benefit of words, this child has
the capacity to make sense of her world. The equivalent Test Age in
the far right column shows the dramatic fluctuations in this girl's
functioning. In certain areas, she is precocious, while in other areas
she has major limitations.

Limitations in functioning are seen in the low scores on two tests,

Figure 5 Wechsler Intelligence Scale for Children-revised

	Year	Month	Day
Date Tested	87	3	3
Date of Birth	77	5	5
Age	9	9	26

	Raw Score	Scaled Score
VERBAL TESTS		
Information	11	08
Similarities	15	12
Arithmetic	13	13
Vocabulary	23	08
Comprehension	18	12
(Digit Span)	(08)	(07)
Verbal Score		53
PERFORMANCE TESTS		
Picture Completion	23	16
Picture Arrangement	37	15
Block Design	27	11
Object Assembly	25	14
Coding	25	05
(Mazes)	(20)	(10)
Performance Score		61

	Scaled Score	IQ
Verbal Score	53	103
Performance Score	61	115
Full Scale Score	114	109

NOTES: Female child of practicing Alcoholic Mother.

one in the Verbal and the other in the Performance group, both tests indicating the presence of high anxiety. The Digit Span test (08) shows problems in the girl's ability to take in spoken information due to her anxiety. The Coding test (25) reflects the likelihood that anxiety also retards coordinated visual-motor functioning. For example, this girl might have difficulty completing math homework because of the tediousness of writing numbers — even though her high score on the Verbal test of Arithmetic (13) shows numerical ability. Recovery efforts initially would be directed towards anxiety reduction.

In summary, we are cautious about using the Full Scale I.Q. to make definitive statements about the children of alcoholism and addiction. As we see from the example in Figure 5, the Full Scale I.Q. usually conceals as much as it reveals.

Intellectual Development and Academic Achievement

Wechsler defined intelligence as "the aggregate or global capacity of the individual to act purposefully, to think rationally, and to deal effectively with his environment" (Lutey, 1972). Most psychologists would support this definition, although they may disagree on the methods for determining a correct measure of this capacity.

The relationship between intelligence and achievement has to do with how a child makes use of his ability. An "overachiever" is a child whose school achievement is above what would be expected from the scores she attains on an intelligence test. For example, referring to the intelligence test profile in Figure 5, the child obtained a high score on the Verbal subtest, "Arithmetic," which requires attention and concentration but also may be measuring facility with numerical concepts. If this same child were to obtain failing grades in math in school, we might think of the child as "underachieving." (Of course, since the intelligence test simply tells us about the child's verbal and auditory facility with mathematical ideas, we should reserve judgment until we understand more about the child's visual-perceptual abilities. As we have seen, visual-motor functioning is lowered, probably by an anxiety factor. This little girl may suffer a handicap — despite *ability* in math — as she labors under the influence of high anxiety, which interferes with her ability to listen to the teacher and to complete written homework.)

AFFECTIVE DEVELOPMENT

Affective or emotional development begins in earliest infancy. The neonate enjoys the simple pleasures of being fed and cuddled and will express distress when not being responded to adequately by the caretaker. These primitive affective reactions form the basis of later emotional states, which become more fully elaborated through maturity.

During the years of middle childhood, children normally have difficulty expressing their feelings. They begin to employ more elaborate defense mechanisms to protect themselves from emotions which threaten to overwhelm ego integration. The temper tantrums of the two-year-old child are no longer socially acceptable outlets for a school-age child. Yet, a child who is being scolded harshly, or beaten, or humiliated, or sexually violated *will* experience rage. What happens to these emotions in children who are not allowed to express them?

Dissociation is one reaction. This defense mechanism allows the child to split off strong feelings and memories of these feelings from consciousness. Although the defensive operation of dissociation ranges on a continuum from healthy functioning (fantasies, dreams, selective amnesia) to dissociative disorders such as multiple personality disorder (MPD), a traumatized child is particularly prone to dissociate whole segments of the self experience. (The signs and symptoms of these dissociative reactions in childhood are summarized on page 141.)

School and family socialization experiences encourage a child to use emotional control and socially desirable behavior. Children who wall off troubled emotions behind the defense of disavowal will have no access to feelings at times when it would be appropriate to show strong emotions. School personnel sometimes describe these youngsters from practicing alcoholic/addictive families as "dulled" emotionally, lacking in enthusiasm or spontaneity.

When a child enters recovery, these problems in emotional development are apparent. A child may vary from being boisterous and overreactive in one session to being bland and apathetic the next week. The numbed feeling states which have been described in these younger COAs appear to be related to their primary emotional defense of *disavowal*. Disavowal protects the child's maturing psyche by establishing a barrier against painful emotions. Thus, children will have all the cognitive *recall* of the horrors of alcoholic family life; however, they will *disavow* the emotional significance of their trauma (Jesse, 1987). When such a child is seen in session, he will usually respond with a shrug to the question, "How did you *feel* about . . . ?" These youngsters truly don't know how to articulate feelings in the language of adult emotions. Disavowal protects the fragile self from being flooded by overwhelming feelings.

Emotional Integration

If we refer again to Figure 4 (page 113), we see that the self is depicted in a state of cohesion as the various ego functions are integrated and organized. When a particular aspect of self functioning is split off, such as when emotions are dissociated, it is likely that compensatory functioning will occur in another sphere. For example, a lack of emotional integration may result in an overcompensation by another modality, such as the cognitive or perceptual sphere.

As represented in the schematic, Figure 6, affect has been walled-off from the conscious segment (see "X") of the self experience. The result is an overcompensation by any one or more of the other

Figure 6 Walled-off Affect

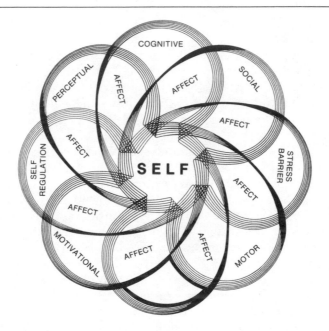

modalities, experienced as increased tension and somatic distress, social anxiety, perceptual distortions, intellectualization (cognitive sphere), stress, problems in self-regulation (overeating, acting-out, etc.) and decreased motivation, to name just a few examples.

The child's ability to modulate and contain strong, discrepant feelings within the self is developed by the parents' calm acceptance of the child's emotional life. Despite constitutional differences of temperament from child to child, an important selfobject function of the parent is to assist the child in comprehending and integrating sometimes bewildering and rapidly fluctuating emotions. The parent does this by empathic attunement to the child's inner state, reflecting these states back to the child in the language of emotions. This activity develops the child's tolerance and acceptance for his own emotional reactions. Feelings then can be integrated into the self experience.

However, when a parent is unavailable or shows an intolerance for the child's emotions, the child will experience his feelings as bad, shameful, wrong. (This is the same as saying that *he* is bad, shameful, wrong.) When feelings are split off from the conscious self experience through repression, disavowal, or dissociation, any reappearance of the dreaded emotions becomes disruptive to the self. The child's emotional life comes to be linked with being unacceptable.

Children of alcoholics appear to suffer an arrest in their emotional development. The Adult Child of Alcoholics (ACA) syndrome attests to the potential for the adult personality to fragment or breakdown into its childhood components under stress. Kritsberg (1985) describes the ACA's tendency towards emotional outbursts of rage or deep grief. These extreme emotional states are typically walled-off or unintegrated into the total personality. In Figure 7, a disruption of the walled-off affects has occurred. Strong emotions (such as rage, grief, etc.) break through and are experienced as fragmenting to the sense of self.

Research in Emotional Development

Nylander's 1960 report is still one of the most comprehensive studies of children of alcoholics. When 229 children of alcoholic fathers in Stockholm were compared with 163 children of non-alcoholic parentage, the subjects could be distinguished from the controls on the basis of seven symptoms, which occurred only in the COAs: tics, tiredness, nausea and vomiting, confabulation, encopresis, aggression, and unsociability. A highly significant difference was found to exist between the two groups in four other symptoms as well: emotional lability, anxiety, headache, and other sleep disorders. These occurred with greater frequency among children of alcoholics.

Another large-scale study was conducted by Haberman (1966) in a representative community in the U.S. Children of alcoholics were rated by their mothers for childhood symptoms of emotional problems, and these ratings were compared to those by mothers of children from two different non-alcoholic control groups. The children of alcoholics had a higher frequency of eight specific symptoms: stuttering or stammering, unreasonable fears, staying alone and rarely playing with other children, frequent temper tantrums, constant fighting with other children, bed wetting after age six, frequent trouble in school because of bad conduct or truancy, and often in trouble in neighborhood. The overall pattern of symptoms in the Haberman study is consistent with that found by Nylander (1960).

Children of alcoholic fathers have been reported to show more

Figure 7 Affective Imbalance

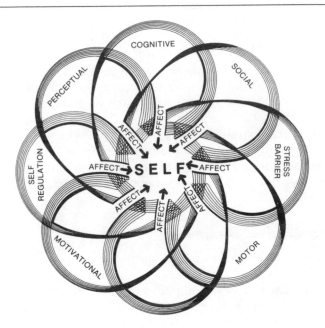

positive emotional functioning when they have enjoyed a positive relationship with their mothers (Obuchowska, 1974). Without this positive maternal contact, the children are negative, resigned, or aggressive.

In a study conducted by Fine et al. (1976) latency aged children of alcoholics showed emotional disturbance on one psychological instrument, the Devereux Behavior Rating scales. Among children in the eight-to-twelve-year-old age group, the COAs were significantly more impaired than children of other psychologically disturbed parents on the following scales: *emotional detachment, social aggression, pathologic use of senses* (behavior seen in schizophrenic children), and *inadequate need for independence*. When compared with normal control children, the COAs were significantly different on these scales as well as on *social unresponsiveness* and *isolation* behavior rating scales.

Another psychological instrument, the Personality Inventory for Children, was administered to children whose parents were in treatment for alcoholism (Anderson and Quast, 1983). The COAs scored higher than test norms on *anxiety* and *adjustment* scales.

These studies suggest that, by the years of middle childhood, children of alcoholics demonstrate interferences in emotional development through a variety of mental and physical symptoms. Ongoing stress and the excessive emotional stimulation of chaotic family life take a toll on a child. When there is a compensatory relationship with the nonalcoholic parent (as suggested by Obuchowska, 1974), the child's emotional development may be less severely affected.

MOTOR DEVELOPMENT

A child's motor development can be observed through the often random and otherwise deliberate movements so typical of the years of middle childhood. A child may be seen spinning, jumping, twisting, kicking, fidgeting, wiggling, turning, leaping, hopping, and even break-dancing. These are all examples of the kind of muscular activity that is governed by motor development. During the years of middle childhood, motor coordination becomes increasingly important as the child is required to use the fine motor skills for academic tasks and gross motor skills for success on the playground. Sports, games, musical activities, hobbies, and various other activities of childhood require coordination and agility of the child's muscular movements.

Impairments in motor functioning may be related to other aspects of development. Problems with fine motor control which lead to difficulties in the classroom may be related to a developmental problem in cerebral functioning. Autistic-like movements where a child self-stimulates through rocking, head-banging, or spinning may be indicative of serious emotional disturbances. However, certain of these behaviors may occur in even so-called "normal" children at various times.

Hyperactivity is one disturbance which is commonly linked to children from alcoholic and addictive families (El-Guebaly and Offord, 1977). Whether these hyperactive disturbances result from some neuropsychological disturbance or chemical imbalance or emotional disturbance is unknown. As we have already learned in our earlier case illustrations with several children, nutritional problems also can lead to a form of increased motor activity. In other cases, when children are overwhelmed emotionally, they may express their arousal through increased motor symptoms.

On the other hand, children from alcoholic/addictive families who are suffering a depression may be listless or inactive. Stereotyped movements and gestures also may be used as a part of the compulsive defense system of middle childhood.

Research in Motor Development

The first studies linking hyperactivity to alcoholism were conducted by Morrison and Stewart (1971), who interviewed the parents of 59 hyperactive and 41 control children. Among the hyperactive children, 20% of the fathers and 5% of the mothers were alcoholic, compared with only 10% of the fathers and none of the mothers in the control group. Among the alcoholic parents, twelve had been hyperactive during childhood; six of these later became alcoholic. In another study of hyperactive children, Cantwell (1975) found a higher incidence of alcoholism, sociopathy and hysteria in the parents. Although these studies suggest a genetic link between the childhood disorder known as "hyperactivity" and parental alcoholism, future research will need to elaborate the exact relationship.

More recently, Kyllerman et al. (1985) studied 21 children of middle childhood who were born to alcoholic mothers. Compared to a matched control group, the COAs had significantly lower fine and gross motor age test scores and inferior coordination. There were no significant differences between study group children in foster homes or those raised in the homes of their biologic mothers.

SOCIAL DEVELOPMENT

To assess a child's development we look at the external façade or observable social behaviors. Is the child gregarious and constantly seeking the company of others, or does he prefer to be alone? Does she mix easily with peers or resort to aggressive tactics? With children of alcoholics we are particularly alert to the outward manifestation of seemingly normal social interactions accompanied by isolation, or the tendency to pull into oneself, away from social interactions. This is a prominent defensive posture observed in both adult children of alcoholics and alcoholics themselves. Problems in peer interactions, sibling relationships, and social conformity have been observed in the latency aged children of alcoholics.

Research Findings in Social Development

Nylander (1982) following up with COAs studied in earlier research (1960), found maladjustment and addictions in adulthood. Children from the highest social class in the study were just as likely as those from the lowest social class to show problems in social maladjustment, including the use of alcohol and drugs.

In one of the earliest studies on school-aged children of alcoholics, European researchers Aronson and Gilbert (1963) attempted to infer a personality predisposition to the adult onset of alcoholism. They abstracted six personality dimensions from their studies of adult alcoholics, believing that these might be characteristic of pre-adolescent sons of male alcoholics who were between the ages of seven and thirteen. These investigators then examined 41 sons of alcoholic fathers on these dimensions. Each of the children was compared to three other control children by classroom teachers, who rated them on the following characteristics:

- *Acquisitive* — a desire to receive both emotionally and materially from those about him. This reflects a need for overt proof of love. For the adult alcoholics, this dimension might be stated in the language of Alcoholics Anonymous (1976): "We never got enough of what we thought we wanted."
- *Inappropriate emotional expression* — emotionally immature, impulsive, excessive, inappropriate response to emotional stress; unable to cope with frustration and anxiety; unable to express direct hostility.
- *Dependent*.
- *Manipulative* — friendly and agreeable; uses charm to influence or control those about him; shallow emotional relationships.
- *Evades unpleasantness* — unable to cope with demands of society; denial.
- *Self-dissatisfaction* — low self-esteem.

All five characteristics were seen significantly more often in the children of alcoholics than in controls. Since the teacher ratings for these categories actually appear to describe social development as seen in the classroom, rather than personality, let us review how these boys were viewed by their teachers.

- *Acquisitive* — "Requires extra attention, needs proof that he is liked, does not wait his turn."
- *Inappropriate emotional expression* — "Sensitive to criticism, impulsive, emotionally immature."
- *Dependent* — "Wants frequent reassurance, is not self-reliant, is not dependable, gives up easily when alone, cannot make or stick to decisions."
- *Evades unpleasantness* — "Daydreams over long lessons, does not face up to unpleasant situations, exaggerates for good effect, blames others."
- *Self-dissatisfaction* — "Compares self unfavorably, often moody and depressed, is not happy or content."

The social development of these sons of alcoholic fathers was viewed by their teachers as different from that of their peers of non-alcoholic parents.

In another European study (Bell and Cohen, 1981), a German translation of the Bristol Social Adjustment Guide was completed by teachers of children whose mothers had a history of alcoholism. The teachers judged the children of alcoholics as being more overreactive in their behavior in school than a control group of children whose mothers had no prior history of alcohol abuse. Additionally, the alcoholic mothers rated their own children as more overreactive.

An important study by Werner (1986) examined child characteristics distinguishing those children who are "invulnerable," that is, who remain resilient and unaffected by parental alcoholism. Forty-nine COA subjects (22 male) of a multiracial cohort of 698 children on the island of Kauai, Hawaii, were followed at ages one, two, ten, and 18. Although within this group males and the offspring of alcoholic mothers showed more serious psychosocial problems in childhood and adolescence than did females or children of alcoholic fathers, those children who developed *no* serious coping problems differed from those who did in characteristics of *temperament, communication skills, self-concept*, and *locus of control*. Additionally, these children had experienced fewer stressful life events disrupting their family unit in the first two years of life. Werner emphasizes the importance of the early childhood caregiving environment, as well as an interactional model of human development. To those of us working with COAs the findings suggest that early intervention in the areas of emotional development, improving verbal communication skills and self-concept, and the fostering of personal accountability is crucial.

MOTIVATIONAL DEVELOPMENT

The development of motivation revolves around how a child has been able to have basic needs met in the past by the caretaker. However, in addition to the basic needs for food, shelter, and safety, a child has a variety of other psychological and social needs. When children have a history of being deprived or frustrated in their parental interactions, they will show interferences in the capacity for delaying gratification. Children who have experienced inconsistent parenting or who have had to rely on parent surrogates usually develop anxiety about their own ability to provide for themselves. Other children develop precociously, insisting on self-reliance and never trusting anyone else to meet their needs.

Problems in motivation can be seen in high-achieving children of alcoholic and addictive families who push themselves beyond their developmental capabilities. These compulsively driven youngsters usually experience imbalanced functioning in some other sphere of the self experience, for example, the social sphere. When children are driven to succeed, they will usually do so without regard for the rights and feelings of others. These "bossy" or "show off" children may have difficulty in their peer relationships.

An opposite motivational problem occurs in children who are listless and apathetic. Since they have enjoyed few social reinforcements in the family, their motivation is lacking. Many youngest children of alcoholics tend to exhibit motivational problems. Having always relied on older peers or parents, these children may not achieve commensurate with their abilities. Such children may be clownish in behavior, overemphasizing the social sphere.

Research in Motivational Development

Motivation can be inferred from how persistent a child is in completing tasks or how he applies himself to situations such as academics, given that he has the ability to perform. Children of alcoholics often have been described in the research literature as impulsive with a low frustration tolerance. On the other hand, they have also been described as compulsively driven to succeed. What accounts for the difference?

Child-rearing practices appear to have some bearing on a child's motivation. Marcus (1983), in a comparison of alcoholic and nonalcoholic mothers of elementary school children, found that the low achievement of COAs was associated with certain maternal behaviors. In particular, the mothers' control through guilt together with laxity in discipline accounted for low achievement in the children.

Children of alcoholics from lower socioeconomic families were followed by Miller and Jang (1977) in a 20-year longitudinal study. Although these children were no different from their peers in cognitive and intellectual abilities, according to the authors, they were less likely to complete high school. The fact that these children were from stressful, multiproblem, divorced families must be considered alongside parental alcoholism as contributing to their problems in motivation.

Substance abuse and delinquency are common outcomes of motivational problems in the children of alcoholism and addiction. When a child's spirit has been broken by harsh, punitive family conditions, that child will tend to experience a sense of hopelessness and despair. These symptoms are often masked by early substance use behaviors.

DEVELOPMENT OF SELF-REGULATION

From earliest infancy the developing child relies on the primary caretaker to attend to the function of self-regulation. When he is hungry, he signals to the mother. When he needs safety and protection, his cries will be interpreted by the sensitive caretaker. These caretaker interactions come to form a part of the child's inner self experience. He later will be able to signal through the use of words, "I am hungry," or, "I am afraid." However, when the caretaking milieu is complicated by ongoing stressful interactions, or when the caretaker repeatedly fails to accurately interpret the child's signals, the child will become insensitive to his own self-regulating requirements. When he is afraid, he will eat. When he is hungry, he will express anger. When he is lonely, he will look for some way of gaining attention, even through negative behavior.

The capacity for self-regulation is usually grossly disturbed in children from alcoholic and addictive families. Through their lack of attunement to their own inner signals, these children follow the patterns laid down by their addictive parents. They turn to some external substance or activity as a way of bolstering the missing part of the self. Addictive practices may not be as obvious in children; however, through ongoing observations one can find subtle indications of the child's struggle to achieve a sense of inner regulation. Most of the case illustrations in the previous chapters provide examples of these problems; some of the more dramatic examples are provided in the cases of Buff, Claudine, Franky, Louise, Nedra, and Oscar.

The ego function which has been identified here as the "stress barrier" derives in part from Freud's (1920, 1926) notion of a hypothetical protective shield or "stimulus barrier" which screens out the perception of acute traumatic events. A "traumatic" situation is one so overwhelming that the protective shield is acutely weakened and the ego flooded with painful stimulation.

More recent discussions of cumulative trauma (Khan, 1963) describe how this protective shield comes to be weakened over time. When a child is exposed to ongoing stress throughout his childhood years, there is a slow, gradual weakening of the ability to screen out excessive stimulation. Thus, the stress barrier can be rendered ineffective either by sudden, acute trauma or by ongoing stress.

The parents' role in serving as an auxiliary protective shield for a child has been discussed by Freud and later psychoanalytic writers. Kohut introduces the expanded concept of the parental selfobject unit which provides calm, soothing caretaking interactions that come to be internalized by the child. The absence of these interactions, particularly during times of acute stress, has a direct bearing on the child's resilience to stress. Traumatic parental interactions, such as incest and physical abuse, flood the child's ego with excessive stimulation and affect the child's subsequent ability to withstand other life stresses.

I have observed the symptoms of stress sensitivity in children of alcoholics. Their bewilderment and fear increase their sensitivity, which increases the physiological reactions that produce more stress hormones. These children then become hyperaroused and hyperalert, tending to overreact to the slightest stress. When there is no calming adult to assist the child in integrating strong emotional reactions into the self experience, the child tends to remain vulnerable to stress.

Children of alcoholics during their elementary school years appear to have difficulty with a weakened ability to screen out even normal levels of stresses. They often are described as "distractible", or "hypersensitive" to stress, or as "becoming disorganized in the face of stress."

The fact that they are often limited in their ability to self-soothe, leads to an intensification of their stress reactions. This is not to say that these children lack the ability to learn more effective ways of self-soothing. Indeed, the earliest phase of child recovery work should concentrate on strengthening this capacity in a child, thereby improving the child's ability to withstand the normal levels of stress which will be encountered in day-to-day living situations at home and at school.

Post-Traumatic Stress Disorder

Cermak (1988) suggests that the diagnosis of post-traumatic stress disorder is applicable to the children of alcoholism and addiction. Previously thought to apply only to adult victims of catastrophic events (natural disasters, military combat, etc.), this diagnosis has come to be used increasingly with victims of other severely stressful traumas. In addition to experiencing the obvious stressors of child physical and sexual abuse, children who grow up in addictive families also witness violence, sexually provocative interactions, and many other types of destructive family scenes outside the range of normal childhood experience.

In discussing the diagnosis of post-traumatic stress disorder, the *DSM-III-R* (APA, 1987) indicates:

> The traumatic event is persistently reexperienced in at least one of the
> following ways: (1) recurrent and intrusive distressing recollections of
> the event; (2) recurrent distressing dreams of the event; (3) sudden
> acting or feeling as if the traumatic event were recurring (includes a
> sense of reliving the experience, illusions, hallucinations, and disso-
> ciative (flashback) episodes, even those that occur upon awakening or
> when intoxicated; (4) intense psychological distress at exposure to
> events that symbolize or represent an aspect of the traumatic event,
> including anniversaries of the trauma. (p. 250)

The symptoms which the *DSM-III-R* delineates for the diagnosis of PTSD include:

> Persistent symptoms of increased arousal (not present before the trau-
> ma), as indicated by at least two of the following: (1) difficulty falling
> or staying asleep; (2) irritability or outbursts of anger; (3) difficulty
> concentrating; (4) hyper-vigilance; (5) exaggerated startle response;
> (6) physiologic reactivity upon exposure to events that symbolize or
> resemble an aspect of the traumatic event. (pp. 250–251)

When we attempt to make a determination of whether or not a school-aged child is suffering from post-traumatic stress disorder symptoms, we must be concerned about the course of that child's development prior to the onset of the observed symptoms. Was the child's developmental progression essentially normal up until the time of a significant stressor? Or had the child's development been compromised in gradual, insidious ways by ongoing stress and family instability, resulting in major interferences in development?

When chronic parental alcoholism and addiction take place from the time of early childhood, it is likely that interferences in development have occurred along the way. A child whose ego functioning has been compromised repeatedly will show less resilience in the face of stress, but this should not be confused with a post-traumatic stress disorder. On the other hand, when a child's functioning has been supported by a relatively stable caretaking environment, an abrupt trauma, for example, from a parent's act of violence, may result in post-traumatic stress disorder.

During the course of my practice in forensic psychology, I have examined a subgroup of children from non-alcoholic families who have suffered psychological injury as a result of sudden trauma, such as a serious automobile accident or being mauled by a large, vicious dog. In these cases, a diagnosis of PTSD was justified. Certain differences exist between these child trauma cases and PTSD in children from alcoholic/addictive families. These differences include:

1. Psychological testing, specifically the WISC-R, for the children from non-alcoholic families does not usually show the sawtooth pattern of uneven development typical of children from alcoholic/addictive families (see Figure 4).
2. In most instances, traumatized children from non-alcoholic families have better verbal facility, enabling them to give a more articulate description of the major stressor than COAs.
3. Traumatized children from non-alcoholic families usually do show *some* emotions, even if only a few tears, when describing their trauma. COAs have a blunted, resigned affect.
4. The schoolwork of non-alcoholic child trauma victims, if affected adversely by the impact of the trauma, usually improves within a relatively short period of time. With COAs there is a more gradual decline in school performance, and the recovery time is longer.

Childhood Symptoms of Post-Traumatic Stress Disorder

From intensive, ongoing observations of a group of previously normal, psychically injured children, Lenore Terr (1984) has distinguished those features of PTSD idiosyncratic to the childhood manifestation of the disorder:

1. Children over three or four years of age do not become partly or fully amnesic regarding their perceptions of external events. Children do not employ repression or denial of external reality, as do adults. (As I have indicated throughout this discussion, children from alcoholic/addictive families recall the horrors of alcoholic family life. They do *not* use the defense of denial.)
2. Children, unlike adults, do not demonstrate psychic numbing. (Terr notes that adults probably experience psychic numbing because of their denial and repression — defenses which children do not employ after psychic injury.)
3. Children, unlike adults, do not experience intrusive visual flashbacks.
4. Children experience a shorter decline in school performance after psychic trauma, as opposed to the long-term performance

decline seen in adults. (This observation tends to hold for previously normal children who have experienced acute psychic trauma; however, I have not found it applicable to children from alcoholic/addictive families who experience cumulative trauma.)

There are three remaining post-traumatic symptoms which, according to Terr, occur in children more frequently than in adults, although they may occur in adults.

5. Post-traumatic play and reenactment of the trauma occur frequently in children.
6. Time skew occurs more frequently and dramatically in children.
7. A foreshortened view of the future is particularly apparent in childhood PTSD. Here the child often has a very pessimistic outlook.

DEFENSIVE OPERATIONS IN MIDDLE CHILDHOOD

Before discussing the defense mechanisms commonly seen in school-aged children from alcoholic/addictive families, let us briefly review the traditional understanding of defenses.

As originally proposed by Sigmund Freud and later extended by Anna Freud in her work with children, defensive operations are viewed as a way that the conscious segment of the personality (the ego) prevents the experience of anxiety. In the face of threat, protective measures (known as defense mechanisms) operate to protect the individual from overwhelming anxiety. Threat may be from the internal forces of the sexual and aggressive instincts or from the external world. All defense mechanisms have two commonalities: (1) They operate at an unconscious level; and (2) they alter reality in some way by distorting, ignoring, or falsifying what is actually occurring.

During Anna Freud's extensive clinical work with children, she concluded that children required defenses to protect them from the excessive stimulation of their instinctual drives. The various drives associated with a particular psychosexual stage of development resulted in characteristic defenses of that stage. Anna Freud (1927) influenced the work of later psychoanalysts, such as Erik Erikson (1950), who studied the relationship between instinctual zones and ego defenses.

Defense mechanisms were believed to be arranged hierarchically, beginning with the least mature psychosexual stage of development. However, the primary defense underlying many of the others is *repression*, which consists of blocking an idea or feeling from conscious awareness. An overview of the hierarchy of defense mechanisms begins with those believed to be the least mature according to the psychosexual stage:

- *Denial*—Negating the perception of internal or external reality by refusing to acknowledge what is seen or heard or felt, thereby avoiding painful conflicts.
- *Projection*—Unacceptable impulses, attitudes, or feelings are attributed to others rather than to the self.
- *Distortion*—Grossly altering external reality to suit inner needs.
- *Regression*—A return to an earlier developmental stage or mode of functioning to avoid the anxiety associated with more mature functioning.

Increasingly mature defenses are associated with the progression in psychosexual stages of development:

- *Displacement*—Shifting feelings toward one person to another.
- *Intellectualization*—A split in consciousness where one segment of the personality functions apart from the other.
- *Isolation*—A separation of feelings from thought, with the emotion repressed or expressed in disguised form.
- *Rationalization*—Justifying one's attitudes or beliefs.
- *Reaction formation*—Controlling unacceptable impulses by expressing their opposite.

The defenses of maturity—*altruism, humor, sublimation*, and *suppression*—are not often seen in the years of childhood. The more mature defense of suppression, which is a conscious or semiconscious decision to postpone attention to a feeling or conflict, is often confused with repression; in fact, the two defenses are very different.

Self psychology makes a distinction between a defense used to ward off intrapsychic conflict and one resulting from an arrest in ego development. This notion views *defense* as a function of the *ego*, and so requires a certain level of developmental maturity. When ego development has been compromised by traumatic environmental conditions or failures in parental empathy early in a child's life, an arrest in development leads to failures to perceive and acknowledge reality accurately.

. . . it is of the utmost importance clinically to distinguish between mental activity that functions principally as a defense, warding off aspects of intrapsychic conflict . . . and superficially similar mental activity that is more accurately understood as a remnant of an arrest at a prestage of development. . . . (Stolorow and Lachmann, 1980, p. 45)

This distinction is especially relevant when we talk about a child's *denial*, for example, of the loss of the parent to alcoholism or drug use. We would not expect a child to be capable of mourning the loss of a parent to alcohol or drugs when the child was not able to perceive and assimilate reality, as in the case of infancy or early childhood.

Figure 8 illustrates a developmental continuum for the defense of "denial." As the child becomes increasingly able to ward off intrapsychic conflict, he also is able to use denial as a defense. A prestage of the defense occurs when reality is not synthesized, as in the earliest period of childhood. Stolorow and Lachmann (1980) propose that every defense has this type of developmental line, ranging from the most primitive functioning to mature defensive functioning.

In our clinical work with children of alcoholism and addiction it is important that we pay attention to their developmental level when interpreting defenses. In many instances, a child may be erroneously believed to be using denial defensively to avoid painful emotions, when the child simply does not have the foggiest notion of feelings.

Figure 8 Denial Continuum

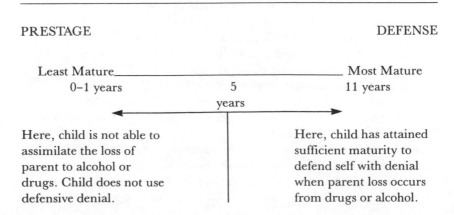

PRESTAGE   DEFENSE

Least Mature_____ Most Mature
     0–1 years   5   11 years
                                      years

Here, child is not able to   Here, child has attained
assimilate the loss of   sufficient maturity to
parent to alcohol or   defend self with denial
drugs. Child does not use   when parent loss occurs
defensive denial.   from drugs or alcohol.

When, for example, the loss of a parental relationship to alcoholism or addiction occurs early in the child's life, the loss will not be experienced by the child as sadness; rather, the child will simply experience a void or emptiness.

Dissociation as a Major Childhood Defense

Children from alcoholic/addictive families who are the victims of child sexual abuse or physical abuse or psychological cruelty commonly use dissociation as a primary defense. Dissociative tendencies occur spontaneously in childhood, as imaginary companions and other aspects of a child's make-believe world are generally kept psychologically separate from other aspects of reality. Thus, what may be a normally occurring phenomenon of childhood cognitive development comes to be used in the interest of self-preservation.

When the ego is flooded with painful stimulation, the stress barrier is so weakened that the remaining ego structures are not able to integrate the psychological trauma. One compromise solution is to dissociate, or wall off, entire segments of the self experience. As conscious memories are blocked from recall, an amnesic reaction occurs.

Kluft (1985) defines dissociation:

> . . . as a complex psychophysiological process, with psychodynamic triggers, that produces an alteration in the person's consciousness. During this process, thoughts, feelings, and experiences are not integrated into the individual's awareness or memory in the normal way. Two characteristic features are found in most major dissociative reactions. The first is a disturbance in the individual's sense of self-identity. . . . The second feature is a disturbance in the individual's memory that is usually manifested by amnesia for past events or complex acts. (p. 67)

The concept of dissociation has been used largely to discuss the condition known as multiple personality disorder, where different aspects of identity are dissociated or kept mentally separated. While I am not suggesting that MPD is common among the children of alcoholics and addicts, I do find regularly occurring instances of dissociative processes. A little girl may show an identity disturbance, for example, by showing a hysterical reaction when looking into the mirror, telling her parents that she is "turning into" her friend. Or the same child may show regressive play on one occasion, preferring baby toys, and then choose age-appropriate toys the next time. A dazed, trance-like state may lead the child to wander off from home without telling her parents. When we understand these dissociative symptoms, we can provide the child with therapy that aims to strengthen self-cohesion.

Table 2 lists childhood signs and symptoms of some commonly occurring dissociative reactions. Although a child may evidence one or several of these symptoms, this does not necessarily warrant a diagnosis of a dissociative disorder. Problems in self-cohesion which result in dissociative symptoms are more common than not in younger children of alcoholics, particularly when these children have suffered sexual or physical abuse or have been witnesses to family violence.

Characteristic Defenses of Children from Alcoholic/Addictive Families Used for Self-Preservation

Many children from alcoholic/addictive families are believed to be suffering arrests in development. By obtaining a thorough developmental history of the child, as well as of the parents, we can ascertain when the general and specific traumas associated with addictive family life began. In most instances, the child will be employing defense mechanisms in the interest of self-preservation rather than to ward off intrapsychic conflict. Mechanisms of defense used to protect the fragile, tentative self include:

- *Acting-out* — Giving in to impulses as a way of relieving inner tensions.
- *Depersonalization* — A sense of estrangement from one's body or mind. (The origin of this defense arises from early trauma in which the child's actual accomplishments were met with undermining, discounting, or criticism from the parent, increasing the bond to the parent and decreasing the child's autonomy. In later life, each new activity or success carries a quality of unreality — as though it were being performed by someone else.)
- *Dissociation* — A severing of aspects of consciousness as a way of regulating overwhelming tensions and stimulation which threaten the self organization.
- *Disavowal* — A blocking of the affective component of a painful experience. The painful reality is perceived, but the affective implication is repressed.
- *Hypochondriasis* — The expression through physical symptoms of

Table 2 Childhood Signs and Symptoms of Dissociative Reactions

1. Children who do not remember the actual abuse.
2. Children who seem to go into a "daze" or trance-like state at times.
3. Children who show marked changes in personality, e.g., going from shy and timid to hostile and belligerent, from passive and dependent to autonomous and aggressive, from feminine mannerisms to masculine behavior. One may also note changes in voice.
4. Children who seem unusually forgetful or who seem confused about very basic things, such as the names of teachers and friends, important events, possessions, etc.
5. Children who show marked day-to-day or hour-to-hour variations in skills, knowledge, food preferences, athletic abilities, etc., which would be expected to be stable, e.g., handwriting, knowledge of arithmetic or spelling, use of tools, or artistic abilities.
6. Children who demonstrate rapid regressions in behavior or show marked variations in age-appropriate behavior, e.g., a ten-year-old playing like a four-year-old at times.
7. Children who appear to lie or deny their behavior when the evidence is obvious and immediate.
8. Children who have many rapidly fluctuating physical complaints, especially headaches, and/or hysterical symptoms, such as epileptic-like seizures, paralysis, loss of sensation, blindness, etc., where no medical cause can be found.
9. Children who refer to themselves in the third person or insist on being called by a different name at times.
10. Children who self-mutilate, who engage in dangerous or self-destructive behaviors, or who are suicidal.
11. Children who are abnormally sexually precocious and who initiate sexual behavior with other children or adults.
12. Children who report auditory hallucinations.
13. Children who report conversations with an imaginary playmate beyond age six or seven.

Reprinted with permission, Justice for Children, P.O. Box 42266, Washington, D.C. 20015

difficult feeling states when the self has suffered losses in self-esteem (through criticism, ridicule, etc.).

- *Projection* — Painful ideas or feelings which originate within the self are experienced as though they originate in the other.
- *Somatization* — Difficulties in self-regulation are expressed as somatic disturbances (headaches, nausea, stomachache, etc.).

- *Splitting* — Contradictory feelings about the same person or situation are held separate to alleviate intense ambivalence.

Ego Compromises in False Self-Development

Distinctions between the true and false self were described by Winnicott (1960), who, as a pediatrician, made early childhood observations of mother-child interactions, and later, as a psychoanalyst, observed the childhood components of what he called the true-false dichotomy in the same adults he had treated as children.

The relevance of the true-false self adaptation to the children of alcoholism/addiction will become clear. Winnicott believed that one of the functions of this false self was to preserve the real self despite "abnormal environmental conditions." Here we are not talking about the dissociation of aspects of identity from conscious awareness. The false self was a defensive function in response to parental failures to acknowledge or affirm the real self.

The real self, that core of one's being which is experienced as the real *me*, is sealed off from the world. A child who hides his or her needs to be capricious, whimsical, magical, omnipotent, creative, admired, applauded, *and* loved will express an outward display of false self defenses by being self-effacing, polite, well-mannered. These are the responses which are rewarded by parents and siblings. The false self is built upon identifications with parents, siblings, peers, and others, but it conceals a lonely, unmirrored real self from the world.

The false self becomes organized around compliant, people-pleasing gestures. Children who use these mannerisms and attitudes seek to please and to win the approval of the adult onlooker. They become overadapted, good little boys and girls who seek to overachieve or carry out role functions to win the praise of their self-absorbed parents.

The false self facade appears to be strengthened during the years of middle childhood because of the typical defenses associated with this developmental phase. Compulsive defenses of the school-age period lead a child who is academically inclined to compensate with high achievement. Indeed, Winnicott describes the false self as being associated with a "rigidity of defenses." These rigid defenses protect the inner true self from the feelings of worthlessness which are being driven home in the blame-and-shame game of the alcoholic/addictive family culture. However, there is a more basic determinant of shame which stems from the lack of parental acknowledgment of the child's very selfhood. Since the child is not valued as an independent center of initiative, a separate self, the real self goes into hiding. The false self façade may come to form the adaptation commonly seen in what is known as co-dependence, where the person continues to adjust the external self to meet the whims or needs of another. A false self adaptation is also commonly seen among adult children of alcoholics.

The child's drawings in Figure 9 illustrate the false self compromise. The little girl, an only child, had been expected to "be seen but not heard" by her warring parents, who were preoccupied with each other. Psychologically, they had abandoned the child, giving her negative attention when she misbehaved and providing positive responses contingent on her quiet, subdued behavior. After several months of recovery, the parents were beginning to acknowledge their daughter and to interact as a family unit. Although the child was not consciously aware of her dilemma, her drawings provided the clue to the problems which she experienced in self development.

The first drawing was made by this seven-year-old girl at the beginning of recovery, when her parents were in recovery but separated from each other. Asked to draw herself, she replied, "I'd rather draw a butterfly than me. I *like* butterflies." The lines which encase the self (butterfly) were said to be a "rainbow." However, the encasement (false self façade) makes it impossible for the butterfly to move about freely.

Figure 9 The False Self Compromise

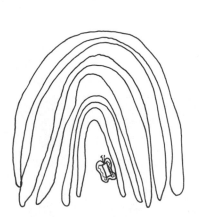

The second drawing was done several months later, after the separated father had rejoined the family. The reunited family is shown under the symbiotic arch of a rainbow on a Sunday outing, flying kites while "butterflies" float overhead freely.

CHILDREN IN RECOVERY

During the normally quiescent period of middle childhood a youngster is often able to hide behind the false self facade of an effective social role. "The squeaky wheel gets the oil," is the traditional way that treatment for these youngsters has proceeded. Problem children are seen and heard, but rarely does *the* problem ever get corrected.

In this chapter I have tried to depict the realities of childhood development. Deficits in self development in school-aged children *cannot* be cured or remedied in a week, a month, or even a year. Because development is an ongoing process, which will continue to stress the maturing child as he or she strives towards challenge and mastery, a slow, gradual process of recovery from the effects of alcoholic/addictive family life will need to take place.

Although there are now a number of alcoholism treatment facilities which provide help to younger children, it is important to remember that this is *only* a beginning. Neither will a child's problems in self development be corrected by the most effective alcoholism education program. These types of programs can identify children and parents who are in need of assistance, but the actual delivery of assistance will need to be long-term and ongoing. In short, the child's recovery process will be parallel to the slow, gradual rate of change that occurs in the recovering parent. For, as the reader will come to realize, this individual work strengthens the child's ability to function as a viable self during subsequent family and sibling meetings.

PART IV

The Family in Recovery

In this part we proceed through the corridors of recovery, beginning with the parents' treatment in Chapter 8. The parents' treatment has an impact, not always positive, on their school-aged children. We explore the problems a child is likely to encounter during the parents' detoxification phase, acute withdrawal, and post-acute withdrawal periods and come to recognize the relapse symptoms of parents in recovery. Known as the post acute withdrawal syndrome, these parental symptoms can have deleterious effects upon the child.

How does a child appear to the outside observer when the parent begins treatment? What are the important features of childhood functioning which will alert us to the child's condition?

We must not be content to view children through our own defensive denial, which blinds us to the extent of the child's trauma. Viewing the child through the opaque lens of a family role is the very way that our vision becomes obscured. Unfortunately, labels have been applied to children of alcoholics in much the same way that they were applied to wives of alcoholics in the early period of alcoholism treatment. Steinglass (1987) comments on the tradition begun by Whalen (1953) in labeling wives of alcoholics seen at a family services agency. Terms such as "Suffering Susan," "Controlling Catherine," "Wavering Winifred," and "Punitive Polly" merely

underscore the labeler's negative professional attitude (albeit unconscious) towards members of an alcoholic/addictive family. Children
too, have been labeled with some binding expectations. Terms such
as "Superkid" or "Alkykid" (Byrne, 1980) or even Black's (1979)
"Placater, Adjuster and Responsible One" may become onerous for
a little child to bear. Although these designations may represent a
more benign intent — the labeler's way of trying to simplify very
complex phenomena — we must extend ourselves to come up with a
more complete understanding of child development issues.

   In Chapter 8 we consider how the coordinated functions of the
developing child become distorted through living in an alcoholic/ad-
dictive family environment. Chapter 9 focuses on the family systems
processes during the early, middle, and later stages of a parents'
abstinence. The imbalances and attempts to reorganize family life
around the fulcrum of sobriety are represented by the "inclusion-
control-affection" trichotomy (p. 168).

CHAPTER 8

Parents in Recovery

In fact, the main thing to point out to people about infants and children is that life for infants and children is not easy even if it has all sorts of good things in it. . . .

—D. W. Winnicott, 1986,
p. 125

When does recovery for the child begin?

As we have learned, the life of the child does not improve automatically when the parent stops drinking. Some untreated children of alcoholics even appear to worsen when the parent begins abstinence. Is there something about a parent's abstinence that contributes to difficulties in a child? Is not abstinence in and of itself a *good thing*?

The child, like the parent, cannot be expected to recover from the destructive effects of alcoholism in a few short weeks. There is no easy, rapid method for correcting the impact of cumulative family stress on the young child's still developing psyche. The parent's recovery alone does not imply that the child is in recovery.

As we are about to learn, cessation of drinking in a parent does not mean that the parent is in *recovery*. Recovery implies changes beyond abstinence which improve the quality of life. Whether or not a child enters into the recovery process will depend on whether or not the parent puts forth the effort to ensure that child a better way of life. Likewise, whether or not the parent succeeds in recovery depends on the positive contributions of the entire family.

In order to better understand the implications of parental recovery for the child, we begin by reviewing the phases of a parent's recovery. After discussing the still drinking parent, we consider intervention, detoxification, and post-acute withdrawal. Child and family systems process issues corresponding to each aspect of recovery are also described.

THE PRACTICING ALCOHOLIC/ADDICTED PARENT (PAAP) SYNDROME

Children from addictive families often find us through agencies such as juvenile courts and the welfare system. At such times, remember this caveat: Anytime a child is referred for neglect, physical and/or sexual abuse, *suspect substance abuse in one or both parents*. If this seems to be an overprediction of substance abuse, bear in mind the recent findings of one metropolitan juvenile services program (Willingham, 1988), which reported that 70–80% of such cases involved chemical dependency. (Also note that in this same community there was no mandated training for mental health care professionals in the identification, treatment, and prevention of addictive disorders.)

Symptomatic children of alcoholics frequently appear in social service agencies long before a diagnosis of familial alcoholism has been made. For example, school-aged children typically show stress-related symptoms that may lead to a referral to the school nurse or to their own family physician. Vague somatic complaints such as stomachache, headache, lethargy, lassitude and general malaise should be taken seriously as signs of a practicing alcoholic/addicted parent (PAAP) disturbance.

Attention deficit disorder or hyperactivity in a child should be another clue of the likelihood of parental addiction. Verbal and physical aggression on the school playground may reflect the effect of parental modeling which has occurred in the wake of the PAAP's destructive drinking.

The child's physical makeup, such as the unusually skinny or chubby child, may suggest nutritional inadequacies associated with an addictive family lifestyle. Elsewhere (see Chapter 1) I discuss the "junk food syndrome" as it pertains to these children. An unkempt, sloppy appearance is often indicative of parental neglect commonly associated with an uninvolved, addicted parent.

Problems in coordination which appear not to have a physical basis are seen in certain children from PAAP homes. Occasionally, one may even observe a type of "staggering" gait (which may be due in part to a parent's modeling of poor physical coordination during intoxication). These children will seem unaware of their surroundings, as though they are dissociated from the environment. In the play therapy room they may walk around distractedly, stepping on toys, seemingly oblivious. Elementary school teachers often describe them as "spacey."

Children of alcoholics in the still drinking household have developed a complex set of survival defenses. Certain of these defenses have to do with perceptual and cognitive functioning. Children can become so adept at tuning out troubling incoming information that they use these defenses indiscriminately. Problems in attention and concentration lead children from addicted families to show an apparent memory deficit. Unable to retain information because what has been heard is not stored in memory, these youngsters are a source of frustration to teachers and parents. Often seen as deliberately disobedient, the child who fails to carry out a set of instructions because he "forgets" will be punished. Thus, the very defenses which have been used for survival may become maladaptive.

Problems with emotions in the PAAP syndrome child manifest in one of two extremes: Either the child is prone to temper outbursts or he is bland and flat emotionally. The emotionally labile child may use behavior, such as engaging in destructive, chaotic play, to express hostile rage. By contrast, the emotionally numb child will show a low energy level with little spontaneity or enthusiasm.

Unusual fears and phobias may be present in PAAP children, who tend to displace their terror of alcoholic family life onto a concrete object or situation. Vague fears of monsters or the dark or of being left alone often lead to nightmares, sleep walking, or other forms of sleep disturbance.

The problems of the PAAP child are summarized in Table 3. Do we overreact by suspecting parental addiction when a child presents with several of these symptoms? In this culture, at this time, the answer is "no." We live in an addicted society, according to Schaef (1987), who tells us:

> To say that society is an addictive system is not to condemn the society, just as an intervention with an alcoholic does not condemn the alcoholic. In fact, those of us who work with addicts know that the most caring thing to do is not to embrace the denial but to confront the disease. (p. 4)

Table 3 The Practicing Alcoholic/Addicted Parent (PAAP) Syndrome in Children

Areas of Ego Functioning	Symptoms	Examples of Disturbance
1. Perceptual	"Tunes out" incoming information; doesn't see or hear accurately.	Doesn't recall instructions; vision appears "clouded."
2. Cognitive	Memory problems; unable to think clearly; distracted.	Child seems "spacey," confused; tangential.
3. Affective	Emotional overreaction or bland, flat affect.	Shows temper outbursts or labile affect.
4. Motor	Physical coordination problems. Hyperactive.	Awkward, clumsy, sometimes "staggering" gait.
5. Social	Disturbances in peer and sibling relationships.	Aggressive with peers and siblings or withdraws, isolates.
6. Motivational	Listless, apathetic, or driven, compulsive, striving.	Either underachieves or compulsively overachieves.
7. Self Development/Regulation	Lacks cohesive self; tends to fragment under stress. Poor self-esteem. Poor self-care.	Preoccupied with eating junk food or may be anorexic. Anxiety. Identity problems.
8. Stress barrier	Somatic complaints. Sleep disturbances. Nutritional imbalances. Enuresis/encopresis. Anxiety; tension. Easily distracted.	Vague complaints such as headaches, stomachaches, nightmares; listless; falls asleep during school; hyperaroused.

It is *not* an overreaction to suspect familial addiction when a symptomatic child seeks assistance. With the epidemic of drug and alcohol problems currently affecting all levels of society, we must screen for these influences upon children.

A consultation with one or both parents is usually the first step in confirming that the child is experiencing a PAAP syndrome. With the parent we begin with unobtrusive yet highly predictive questions. A format suggested by Steinglass et al. (1987) facilitates the rapid assessment of the significance of alcohol in the life of the family: Three family behaviors — short-term problem-solving strategies, daily routines, and family rituals — all appear to be disrupted by the invasion of alcoholism into family life. After we inquire about these three areas, we may progress to more direct questions about actual addictive practices in the home. If there is strong reason to suspect familial alcoholism, this impression is openly shared with the parent(s).

Help for the child is explained as requiring the participation of the parent(s). At times parents will persist in their denial, urgently demanding that the child's problems be ameliorated at once. There is always the risk that the parents will be uncooperative not only about their own treatment but also about help for the child.

What can be done when the parents resist becoming involved in the child's recovery? First, we recognize that an oppositional parent may be exercising the rights of an adult in choosing to disengage from his or her own need for treatment. However, that parent is *not* behaving as an adult when refusing treatment to the child. Our first therapeutic task is to confront the parent's refusal with our honest conviction. When accountable behavior is required of parents, this actually becomes a front-line intervention. Disruption of the addictive game rules of denial and deception is the goal. At such times, the following suggested intervention has been adapted from Boszormenyi-Nagy and Ulrich (1981), who advise: "Parental refusal to bring children into treatment is seen in terms of disengagement from ethical considerations." At such times, "The therapist is persistent" (p. 183).

The following is a suggested response to the parent who resists bringing a child into treatment:

> I have reason to suspect that your own (or your spouse's) addiction is contributing to the problems in your child. I'm here to help you deal with these problems. Right now your child seems to be crying out for help through troubled behavior. I want to see you do right by this

child, because every day counts in her development. She urgently needs help now — my help and *yours*. You won't be able to help your child until you face your own addiction. You do have a parental duty to provide help.

Sometimes a co-dependent parent readily admits that there is a problem within the home, but indicates that the addicted parent will strongly resist receiving help. The therapist then works with the co-dependent and the children to implement an intervention.

PARENT RECOVERY—EARLY PHASE

Intervention

The period of acute recovery for the parent is established from the time of *intervention* or of the parent's acceptance of the need for treatment. Intervention refers to a specific method of confrontation by a trained intervention specialist working with any combination of the alcoholic's family members, friends, or employer. Most intervention models are based on the early intervention plan developed by Vernon E. Johnson at the Johnson Institute in Minneapolis. Previously, alcoholism treatment had been considered premature until the alcoholic "hit bottom," becoming so devastated by alcohol-related crises that the need for treatment was accepted. However, working with alcoholics at St. Mary's Hospital in Minneapolis, Johnson became convinced that these life crises could be induced much earlier than final stage alcoholism.

> Earlier intervention means less destruction to the chemically dependent person's life and body. More important, it produces a greater likelihood of recovery. (p. 43)

The rationale behind the Johnson intervention model is that the alcoholic suffers from impaired judgment as a direct consequence of alcohol use, since alcohol affects the higher brain centers having to do with reasoning and judgment. Such poor judgment results in ongoing alcohol use, which maintains pathological denial and leads to continued drinking, which leads to denial, which leads to drinking which leads to. . . . This vicious cycle impairs the alcoholic parent's ability to see the reality of his mental, physical, social, and spiritual deterioration. Objective evidence must be presented by other people.

A group of persons who are meaningful to the alcoholic — family members, friends, employer, or physician—is coached by a trained intervention specialist for a confrontation with the alcoholic. These individuals take turns reviewing for the alcoholic the destructive impact of his/her alcoholism on their lives. An ultimatum is then imposed: Either the alcoholic agrees to treatment or some serious loss will occur. A spouse might threaten the end of the marriage unless the alcoholic gets help; an employer may threaten job loss; a physician may be frank about the alcoholic's physical decline. Young children may be included during a part of the intervention; however, caution should be exercised. Only adult children should be allowed to participate in a full intervention session, since young children can become extremely frightened by the threats spoken to the chemically dependent parent during a complete confrontation session.

Children can derive therapeutic benefit from being able to openly air their feelings and concerns to the affected parent without threat of retribution. When this is done in a controlled setting and facilitated by a therapist, the results can be very positive for the family.

Even without a formal intervention process, the alcoholic parent may face serious threats from significant others or society that motivate him to seek help for his addiction. An ultimatum from a legal authority such as when there has been an alcohol-related traffic arrest, a spouse's threat of divorce, a physician's order, an economic threat—all such types of crises may lead the alcoholic parent to stop drinking.

A parent's recovery can also begin when a therapist intervenes. If ongoing care is to be provided by the therapist during the acute phase of recovery, it is crucial to facilitate the parent's involvement in Alcoholics Anonymous or one of the other twelve-step programs (Narcotics Anonymous, Cocaine Anonymous, Overeaters Anonymous, Al-Anon, Nar-Anon, etc.). The program must be started as soon as possible to support the parent's recovery efforts.

Therapists overcome their own resistance to the twelve-step approach by a more thorough understanding of the purposes and functions of these self-help groups. An excellent discussion by Brown (1985) describes the growth process achieved through AA for the individual alcoholic as a "developmental model of recovery." Our understanding of the dynamic interplay between self psychological and systems influences during recovery leads us to explore this perspective in the discussion of the twelve steps in Chapter 11.

Finally, to those therapists who would debate the superiority of family therapy or group therapy or some other psychotherapy modality over the twelve-step programs, a remonstration. When we are talking about abstinence or sobriety, or when we are examining some aspect of ritualized family functioning, perhaps we may enter into debate by comparing and contrasting models of psychotherapy to the Anonymous programs. However, when we are talking about *recovery*, there is *no* long-term, cost-effective, holistic psychotherapy that provides strong community support among its members. In other words, when we are talking about *recovery* — and what is needed to sustain *recovery over time* — we must remain open to the benefits of the twelve-step programs.

How frequently should the parent be attending self-help meetings during the acute phase of early recovery? The answer is: *at least daily*. If detoxification is to be accomplished while the parent remains at home, this parent will require a great deal of support. If daily twelve-step program attendance seems to require the alcoholic parent to spend an inordinate amount of time away from home in a smoke-filled meeting room, there are several points to bear in mind. First, there are today many "smokeless" A.A. meetings where the parent who is not nicotine addicted will be comfortable. Second, the alcoholic parent who is attempting outpatient recovery will be spending only one to two hours daily at a meeting in pursuit of recovery. Contrast this to the 24 hours a day spent in recovery by those parents fortunate enough to receive inpatient care. Third, the alcoholic parent will require — and will *deserve* — maximum support from recovering peers during the acute withdrawal phase. Finally, and perhaps importantly for scientific minded professionals, the patient receives a *physiological* benefit from attending A.A. meetings. Research (Morrison, 1985) has shown that recovering alcoholics derive a measureable increase in their body's natural tranquilizing substances — the brain chemistry which has to do with calming and soothing — just from *attending* Alcoholics Anonymous meetings. Although we do not know as yet just why this is so, any longtime A.A. member will tell you of this secondary gain to be derived: "Why, I always *feel* calmer after I go to a meeting!"

Regardless of whether the parent agrees to inpatient care, outpatient care, a combination of outpatient and A.A., or simply A.A., the next phase of acute recovery begins with the period of physiological withdrawal from the substance.

Detoxification

The time from the cessation of alcohol and drug use to the complete elimination of these substances from the body, usually about a week, is considered the detoxification phase. Although modern treatment approaches encourage inpatient hospitalization or some type of medically supervised or closely monitored detoxification process, the addicted parent often remains in the home during this time.

In the history of Alcoholics Anonymous, a parent who remained in the home received intensive, sometimes round-the-clock support from A.A. peers during the period of detoxification. Today, a parent who recovers strictly through A.A. may still receive assistance from the fellowship. Folk remedies, such as orange juice laced with honey to offset physiological withdrawal, are recommended to the newly sobering parent as a way of curbing the urge to drink. This makes sense when we realize that alcohol, in addition to being a powerful drug, is also a foodstuff. During the final stages of alcoholism, the parent may have been consuming vast numbers of calories in ethyl alcohol. Metabolic imbalances, including severe hypoglycemia with the attendant psychological symptoms, may be very pronounced during withdrawal. Neuropsychological symptoms, such as tremulousness, agitation, and insomnia, are lessened by prescribing physical activities, although this may sound bizarre at face value. For example, one alcoholic mother who became agitated called her A.A. sponsor for help and received the unusual command, "Go wax your kitchen floor." Without question, the sponsoree did as she was told. Her agitation improved following the mindless physical activity.

Early on, the alcoholic is cautioned by A.A. peers, "Don't listen to your mind. Your mind will only get you into trouble." This sage advice recognizes the extreme mental confusion, obsessive thinking, and often frank paranoia that accompany the early detoxification period.

A parent undergoing home detoxification may be told by an A.A. sponsor to attend even more frequent A.A. meetings — sometimes as many as two or three a day — in order to get through the period of acute withdrawal. Although the children may experience a relief in tension when the parent is away from home, they tend to disavow the emotional significance of the parent's absence from the home. That is, life for the child appears unchanged from the time the parent was away or unavailable when drinking.

If the period of active alcoholism was marked by parental self-absorption, the detoxification phase is likely to be characterized by continuing interference in the parent's capacity for empathy. As one recovering father observed during his home detoxification period:

It was hell having this two year-old kid grabbing onto my leg when all I really wanted was to be left alone. OK, so he was my son. But sometimes I just felt so irritable that I wanted to kick him across the room.

When the parent detoxifies in the home, this period can be as frightening to the family as when the alcoholic was still drinking—if not more so. At least when the parent was still drinking, alcohol could be used as *the* excuse for crazy behavior. However, the bizarre actions of the detoxification period often frighten the children, who now see the alcoholic parent as *really* insane.

From the mind's-eye view of one little girl, aged ten, we can see the impact of home detoxification:

The last night my Daddy got drunk and ran us out of the house with a gun, we ran to our neighbor's house and stayed there all night and for the rest of the next day. But then they told us that it was OK for us to go home because my Daddy wasn't drinking anymore. But when we got home, it was *worse* than before. My Mom was taking care of him just like he was a baby. He was sick and shaking and yelling at her that she couldn't do anything right. He kept us awake half the night with his yelling. That's when I got really mad at him and started hating him, and I wouldn't be nice to him for a long, long time after that.

Another parent who found it necessary to detoxify at home spoke about the problems which she experienced when her six-year-old son began to act out viciously.

I think he knew I was trying to stay off booze and drugs, and I think he was trying to get back at me for everything I did to him when I was drinking—like yelling and screaming and cursing. Because here I was only three days sober, and my nerve endings exploding all through my body, and he decides to go wild. He started roaring through the house yelling and cursing at me and knocking things over and kicking, and all because I wouldn't cater to him. It was taking all I had just to stay off the booze. I wanted to scream. I felt like we both had gone crazy.

The effects of the parent's home detoxification should be evaluated carefully during the assessment of the child. Often this acute phase has contributed to significant trauma in the child. This possibility will need to be explored during psychotherapy. Parents usually provide the therapist with information about the home detoxification phase, being able to vividly recall their own struggles. However, they are frequently unaware that this period has taken its toll on their children.

The likelihood that children have experienced trauma during a parent's home detoxification is especially strong in lower socioeconomic families. Unfortunately, the more recent phenomenon of the inpatient treatment center—which has made recovery a class act—has not been extended to all levels of society. A welfare mother, for example, will face an economic barrier to receiving treatment center care for her substance abuse problems. Even if welfare were to underwrite the cost of her inpatient care, this mother would face the problem of how to provide care for her children during her absence. In a society that has neither extended families nor free childcare, these single-parent families will continue to face difficult, turbulent recovery periods. Ironically, it is among lower socioeconomic families that chemical dependency problems abound.

At a family level, the recovery phases of intervention and detoxification precipitate a crisis. The previous accommodation of the family to the still drinking alcoholic was marked by a high tolerance for a lifestyle based on crisis; nevertheless, this pattern of unpredictability had become predictable. These ongoing mini-crises of family life resulted in an equilibrium marked by an unconscious, as well as conscious, allegiance to alcoholism. The structure for *belonging, leadership,* and *intimacy* had incorporated alcohol as the catalyst for systems maintenance. Removal of alcohol (and by inference the alcoholic) from the family throws the system off balance and exposes the instability of the underlying structure.

Residential Care

Perhaps one of the most important contributions of the treatment center to the family is the removal of the chemically dependent parent from the home during the acute withdrawal phase. At a time when this parent is physically and psychologically disabled, his or her removal from family burdens and accountability tremendously bolsters sobriety.

When the alcoholic parent is able to enter a treatment center for detoxification and recovery, the children are spared many of the negative associations and interactions of the acute withdrawal phase. Brief contact with the parent is important to reassure the children of the parent's whereabouts and safety; however, certain residential treatment programs discourage a parent from contact with the family during early withdrawal. Sensitivity to the effect of this upon the child — to the child's experience of loss and uncertainty — will lead us to intervene on the child's behalf.

The symptoms of the acute withdrawal phase range from severe neurological symptoms, such as delirium tremens and seizure, to mild tremulousness and agitation. Symptomatic treatment also varies from bedrest with administration of intravenous medications to closely monitored ambulatory care and some type of oral sedative to facilitate sleep.

A parent who receives residential treatment enjoys the benefit of a thorough medical workup, as well as family and social assessment, all of which provide the focus for ongoing treatment. The treatment center usually offers a combination of group and individual therapies and requires patients' participation in Alcoholics Anonymous.

Many programs now include some type of family involvement during the recovering parent's stay. The spouse alone or the spouse and the children may be asked to participate in a "family week" or to attend a series of evening meetings. These events usually include some type of family counseling specific to alcoholism, as well as alcohol and substance abuse education. Rarely do issues of child development govern the work done with children at this stage in the parent's recovery. Unfortunately, the treatment center continues to focus attention on the chemically dependent family member and/or the co-dependent. Outside referrals for children are not made. Or, if they are made, they usually have not been informed by a thorough assessment of the child's difficulties. Children will continue to need a structured process of recovery and support after the parent has completed inpatient treatment.

Whether acute treatment is provided in a residential setting, an outpatient clinic, or a therapist's office, the parent claims the recovery spotlight. The tradition of individual, rather than systems, case management often complicates recovery for the alcoholic as well as for the family. If the alcoholic is being treated by one therapist and the co-dependent and children by other therapists, family instability is perpetuated. Unless the various therapists are alcoholism specialists who embrace a common philosophy about treatment and recovery, such fragmented treatment is a disservice to the family.

As soon as possible after the parent has been stabilized in acute recovery — that is, within one to two weeks — the therapist should require that the children and spouse become involved in treatment. An alternative to the typical "alcoholism education" model, which asks children to process their reactions to the parent's problem (alcoholism), is recommended. This child-centered approach asks the parent to become aware of the child's dilemma. The children's PACT (parents as co-therapists) model is described in detail in Chapters 11 and 12.

For a more comprehensive description of inpatient and outpatient treatment programs, the interested reader is referred to the excellent discussions provided by Gallant (1987) and Nace (1987).

Post Acute Withdrawal

Over the years recovery work with alcoholism therapy groups led me to conceptualize a discrete set of behaviors and affective states as "the 90-day cycle." (Was it merely coincidence, I wondered, that Alcoholics Anonymous awarded 90-day chits or tokens to its members? I continued to pose this question as I observed the struggles of the newly recovering alcoholic who, without Alcoholics Anonymous, would often return to alcohol shortly after the first 90 days of sobriety.)

Typically, during the first week of recovery, the alcoholic is preoccupied with physical withdrawal to the exclusion of all other interests or people. This extreme self-absorption comes as no surprise given the physiological demands of acute withdrawal. During the second week of recovery, the post acute withdrawal picture improves, but there are still definite symptoms of hyperarousal, including restlessness, sleep disturbance, irritability, and so on. By this time in recovery, substitute addictions have begun to replace the void left by the alcohol or other drug of choice. Symptoms of hyperphagia—increased food cravings—lead to gorging on chocolate and other sweets. Increased caffeine and nicotine use seem to provide substitute "highs."

After the first month or six weeks of recovery, the affective state of the recovering person seems marked by a depression resembling a grief reaction. The loss of the primary relationship with the bottle and the need to grieve this loss appear to be cardinal features of group work at this point in recovery. Part of the grief work includes having the alcoholic admit that his best friend—the bottle—has been an object of betrayal. Often this admission leads to the expression of grief about earlier object losses and betrayals as far back as childhood.

By the end of the first 60 days, the alcoholic begins to experience the first benefits of ongoing physical recovery. Although psychological dependence on the addicting substance might still be strong, there is some evidence of nutritional and metabolic recovery, for example, weight gain or weight loss, improved skin color, and clear eyes. This period often marks the onset of a type of euphoria known in A.A. circles as the "pink cloud." The danger for the novice therapist with these pink cloud patients is to accept the euphoria as a bona fide mark of progress. It is essential to recognize that this brief interlude of improvement from 60 to 90 days is equivalent to the "flight into health" often seen in other types of psychotherapy patients. However, this "flight" seems to be physiologically based and is soon followed by a physiological "low." Shortly after the 90-day mark, the recovering alcoholic begins to demonstrate severe symptoms of anxiety and depression. These sobriety-based symptoms were not completely understood until Gorski and Miller (1982c) articulated the post acute withdrawal syndrome.

> After the symptoms of the acute abstinence syndrome have subsided, the symptoms of post acute withdrawal (PAW) begin to emerge. Post acute withdrawal syndrome is a group of symptoms resulting from neuropsychological (brain and central nervous system) impairments that persist into recovery. PAW surfaces seven to fourteen days into abstinence and grows to a peak intensity over the next three to six months. (p. 99)

This post acute withdrawal syndrome is a stress-induced set of symptoms which the parent experiences during recovery. Since change produces stress, any type of change in the alcoholic's life becomes a precipitant of the PAW syndrome. Changes which are internal to the person, such as changes in awareness or cognition, are just as liable as external changes to initiate stress. For example, an alcoholic parent who becomes flooded with a return of loving feelings toward his mate after years of being emotionally numb may suddenly slip into the PAW syndrome.

The PAW syndrome described by Gorski and Miller (1986) consists of six major types of symptoms having to do with cognition, memory, affect, sleep patterns, physical coordination, and sensitivity to stress. When these symptoms are not managed effectively, the recovering parent is likely to return to the addictive substance as a way of coping; hence, the relapse syndrome is an untreated post acute withdrawal syndrome. It is important to remember that the symptoms which are shown in Table 4 are neuropsychological in origin and stress-induced.

In my work with recovering parents, it became necessary to expand the above list of symptoms to account for the *experiential* compo-

Table 4 Types of PAW Symptoms
in the Recovering Parent

1. Inability to think clearly

2. Memory problems

3. Emotional overreaction or numbness

4. Sleep disturbances

5. Physical coordination problems

6. Stress sensitivity

From Gorski and Miller (1986, p. 59)

nent of post acute withdrawal. Self cohesion problems were prominent. A patient who suddenly began to have problems thinking clearly while in post acute withdrawal would begin to fear that he was going insane; an immediate drop in self-esteem accompanied this fear. Although the stress might persist, when the patient was reassured that he was *not* going insane, he would begin to feel improvement—not only in self-esteem but also in his thought processes. Similarly, a mother who was emotionally overreactive during a sudden verbal outburst might fracture a tenuous parent–child relationship. This *social* complication might affect the sense of self or identity of the parent, leading to the conclusion that she was an "unfit mother." Her *motivation* then might be affected, and she would decide to quit trying, and perhaps even to separate from her child. *Self-regulating* functions in this parent might be ineffective during highly stressful events. Thus, poor self-care, such as irregular eating patterns, nicotine abuse, overwork, and destructive relationships might be the parent's way of compensating for her *sensitivity to stress*.

Symptoms which have to do with the *self* experience of the individual emanate from disturbances in one or more of the various functions of the ego. Here the *ego* is used as a hypothetical construct to imply the coordinator or executor of the various psychic functions. The *self* is that independent center of initiative experienced as the "I" or "me" which experiences fragmentation when ego control begins to weaken. Ego strength refers to the resiliency or recovery rate of coordinated functions when the *self* has experienced a lack of cohesion.

It is important to remember that the symptoms of ego disturbance during post acute withdrawal tend to be neuropsychological in origin; however, they may also be purely psychological or functional in origin.

The ego functions and examples of the types of disturbances in post acute withdrawal are presented in Table 5. If the categories in Table 5 seem familiar, the reader is referred to Table 3 in this chapter. The same areas of ego functioning disturbed in PAAP children are also disturbed in the recovering parent. These ego disturbances,

Table 5 Types of PAW Symptoms Affecting the Parent in Recovery

Areas of Ego Functioning	Symptoms	Examples of Disturbance
1. Perceptual	Distorts incoming information; feels perceptually overloaded.	Doesn't hear and/or see accurately.
2. Cognitive	Inability to think clearly; memory problems; problems in abstract reasoning.	Confused; common sense judgment impaired; loses or misplaces items; sober "blackouts."
3. Affective	Emotional overreaction or dissociated from feelings.	Apprehension; fear; anxiety; irritability; depression; flat affect; emotionally numb.
4. Motor	Dizziness; clumsiness; awkwardness; jerkiness.	Tends to drop items, break things; makes mistakes.
5. Social	Relationship problems; may withdraw socially or seek addictive clinging relationships.	Argumentative, fault finding; becomes resentful and isolates or refuses to be alone, clingy.
6. Motivational	Low drive or engages in driven, incessant activity.	Listless, can't get started; apathetic; or involved in workaholic activity.

(continued)

Table 5 *(continued)*

Areas of Ego Functioning	Symptoms	Examples of Disturbance
7. Self development/regulation	Loss of sense of self; poor self care; uses addictive methods to self-regulate.	Becomes overinvolved in the lives of others to try to define self; overeats; overworks; overspends, etc.
8. Stress sensitive	Difficulty tolerating both internal and external changes; seeks order, control; emotionally reactive.	Tries to control and manipulate others; fault finding, irritable; insomia or sleeps excessively; nightmares; drinking dreams.

together with symptoms of the acute stress reaction, continue to be apparent in children whose parents have begun recovery. Here it is important to clarify that the elaboration of these ego disturbances is in no way an attempt to suggest a genetic component which *transmits* these disturbances. Rather, we are proposing a common sense explanation which may have already occurred to the reader.

When we speak about the development of ego functions in a child, we are talking about a forward progression of coordinated psychological functions. Yet at times these coordinated functions in children may be subject to a regression or a shift to earlier modes of functioning. In the face of difficulties and environmental stresses, a child may briefly show behavior of a backward nature, indicating the regression (or "relapse") into modes of functioning which occurred at an earlier age.

And, so it is with the recovering alcoholic parent, who shows a gradual improvement functioning in coordinated ego functions until the advances are temporarily derailed by stress. The similarity between children and recovering parents has an obvious explanation: Their functioning is governed by complex neuropsychological mechanisms. *Rates* and *quality* of development in children and *rates* and *quality* of recovery in alcoholic parents are influenced by the interaction of these mechanisms with other factors, such as *time* (length of time in recovery; age of child), exercise, proper rest, sleep, nutrition, environmental stimulation, and stress.

According to Gorski and Miller (1986),

> Recovery causes a great deal of stress. Many chemically dependent people never learn to manage stress without alcohol and drug use. The stress aggravates the brain dysfunction and makes the symptoms worse. The severity of the PAW depends upon two things: the severity of the brain dysfunction caused by the addiction *and* the amount of *psycho-social stress* experienced in recovery. Recovery from the nervous system damage usually requires from *six* to *twenty-four* months with the assistance of a healthy recovery program. (p. 58, italics mine)

Heretofore, *recovery* as a variable which influenced the stress level of the alcoholic had not been discussed in the alcoholism literature. When the influence of stress on the adjustment problems of children of alcoholics had been discussed in the literature (Nylander, 1960; Jesse, 1977), the emphasis was on the chronic alcoholism of the parent as a stressful situation in the lives of children or on stressful family relationships during recovery. If we come to understand *recovery* as stressful not only for the recovering parent but also for the family, then we have broadened our treatment perspective. The child who is living in a home with a still practicing alcoholic/addicted parent and the child living in a home with a parent in recovery are *both* encountering stressful family dynamics.

Difficult family relationships as a source of stress to the recovering alcoholic parent must be considered in the light of the post acute withdrawal syndrome. If the recovering parent becomes highly stressed, this is a threat not only to sobriety, but also to family systems maintenance.

A majority of alcoholic/addictive parents are themselves the victims of abusive, addictive families of origin. It is estimated that 80–85% of recovering alcoholic women are also adult incest survivors. What may be expected during the recovery of these women who also happen to be mothers? Courtois (1988) has indicated that the recovery from chemical dependency for these women is affected by a resurgence of symptoms of post-traumatic stress disorder:

> Survivors in such treatment programs can be forewarned that as they progress in their detoxification they may begin to experience more intense symptoms of PTSD, since alcohol/drugs have been found to suppress these symptoms. (p. 313)

CHAPTER 9

The Process of Family Recovery

> *. . . our needs from and toward*
> *other people are three:* inclusion,
> control, *and* affection. *We*
> *achieve interpersonal joy when we*
> *find a satisfying flexible balance*
> *in each of these areas between*
> *ourselves and other people.*
>
> *— William C. Schutz, 1967,*
> *p. 18*

Within the body of family theoretical approaches, there are many different ways to view the overall workings of a system. However, what I have found exceptional about the inclusion-control-affection trichotomy is its *simplicity*. We do not need to engage in excessive theorizing to apply this model to the family in recovery. Equally important, now that the model has withstood the test of time as I have applied it over the years to many groups and families in recovery, is its continuing *relevance*. The model has been further strengthened by incorporating a family relapse dynamic (derived from Gorski and Miller, 1983).

The contributions of Gorski and Miller (1982a,b,c, 1983, 1986) have greatly furthered my understanding of the impact of parental abstinence on the life of the child. However, work with children in recovery has required an extension of the post acute withdrawal syndrome (PAWS) to incorporate the family relapse dynamic of systems functioning. In Figure 10, the family in recovery is seen as cycling through a series of process phases which have to do with

Figure 10 The Inclusion-Control-Affection Trichotomy

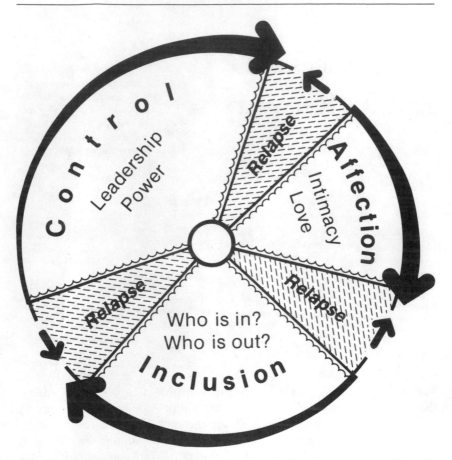

The different sizes of the wedges for the inclusion, control, affection phases indicate the relative period of time that the family spends in a particular process phase. Relapse phases are evenly distributed between the three process phases. The backward movement of the relapse arrows indicates a regressive movement to the preceding phase. The family group continues to cycle through these process phases throughout the course of recovery.

central themes of *belonging, leadership,* and *intimacy.* The greatest stability occurs near the end of each phase, just before the brief period of systems imbalance known as "family relapse." As noted in Figure 10, there is both forward movement, or systems striving to approach the next phase, and resistance, or a regressive backwards swing towards the previous phase. This momentum sets up the un-

THE PROCESS OF FAMILY RECOVERY

stable period known as family relapse, which is a process phenomenon that attempts to hold the family in the previous phase at the same time that it enters a new phase.

Experientially, the recovering alcoholic parent might experience various disturbances in ego functions as a result of the increased psychosocial stress. Apprehension, worry, and argumentative, fault-finding behavior might occur in relationships with the spouse and children. Similarly, the spouse might experience a threat to the integrity of the self, leading her to become overinvolved in the lives of her children. To cope with the excessive stress, she might begin addictive behaviors, such as compulsive overeating. The children would experience the anxiety and tension in the parental relationship; accordingly, their attempts at self-regulation would be disrupted. Behavioral or psychological problems might be expressed through indirect strategems, such as sleep disturbance, enuresis, academic problems, stealing, or lying. Interventions to relieve the family disturbance would be directed towards facilitating the family's progression into the next process phase.

The inclusion-control-affection trichotomy of family process phases during recovery has been derived from the work of Schutz (1958, 1967), who found that these three fundamental issues were present in all human interactions. Family work with recovering alcoholics has demonstrated the pre-eminence of the inclusion-control-affection dynamic during the phases of recovery. When this model has been extended to assimilate the dynamics of relapse, the process of recovery has been strengthened for the alcoholic, as well as for the spouse and children. Although there is a tendency for families to cycle in and out of these various phases throughout their life history, the predominant theme of a particular phase will be apparent at any one point in time. Also, while there may be thematic issues associated with other phases present during one of the ascendant phases, it is the theme of the ascendant phase which will govern the family's processes. (For example, one might observe interactions which were based on control or affectional motives during the inclusion phase; however, these would be transacted at a superficial level. During their respective phases control or affectional issues would be far more obvious and transacted more intensely.)

EARLY RECOVERY: THE INCLUSION PHASE

In the early phase of recovery, issues of belonging predominate. From the time of intervention, the family's organizational processes are concentrated on who is *in* the family and who is *out*. Those *in* the family are preoccupied with finding their place among the different family members who represent the "in crowd."

Since the recovering alcoholic parent has usually been temporarily excluded from the family as a result of intervention and treatment, this parent is perceived as being of "low status" and hence has no legitimate power. This parent's early recovery will be marked by low intimacy and low influence exchanges with the other family members. Children typically maintain an alliance with the "high status" or non-alcoholic parent, even to the detriment of family recovery. In cases where both parents are alcoholic, or where there is a single-parent household, or where the non-alcoholic parent is viewed as deviant, the "high status" family leader may be found among the sibling subsystem.

Recovery may be ushered in by an actual shift in family membership, for example, when there is a divorce or separation. This happens in the majority of families where the mother is alcoholic. These women, unlike their male alcoholic peers, are often abandoned by their mates just at the point of entering treatment. One explanation is offered by a co-dependent spouse who talked about his decision to separate from his wife during her second week of recovery.

> Before she got sober, I felt like I had to stay home and take care of her and the kids. I used to hate being tied down like that when she got drunk. She'd start to scream and yell, or belittle me in front of the kids, and it was all I could do to keep from belittling her, but I couldn't leave then. I was afraid that she would hurt herself or the kids if I left. Now I think she is really serious about her recovery, so I'm free to go.

Although this man reconciled with his wife during her second year of recovery, the inclusion phase centered around his decision to opt out of the family.

A mini-regrouping of the family occurs when the alcoholic parent leaves the home to begin treatment. Even if the alcoholic parent remains in the home, his frequent attendance at A.A. meetings or an outpatient treatment program represents a new intermingling of the family with the outside world.

When the parent begins a relationship with an A.A. sponsor, this individual begins to assume an increasingly important role in family functioning. Although A.A. sponsors are external to the immediate family, their sphere of influence on the newly recovering person extends to family functioning. A sponsor may, for example, provide directives about the marital relationship and parenting issues. Because a sponsor's authority with the alcoholic affects the balance of power within the family, the sponsor may be resented by the spouse and children as an unwelcome intruder. A similar attitude may be directed towards the co-dependent's Al-Anon peers or the alcoholic's therapist.

Independent of the parents' comings and goings (in treatment, out of treatment, A.A., separation, divorce, etc.), children function during the inclusion phase to maintain the family homeostatic balance. Elsewhere (Jesse, 1988) I have described in detail how the sibling subsystem functions during early recovery to maintain the status quo. Children will continue to perceive the alcoholic parent as deviant despite the parent's sincere efforts to rehabilitate. Without a perceptual shift among the child members, the sibling subsystem behaves exactly as it did during the parent's time of active drinking.

Inclusion behavior has to do with seeking belonging and togetherness. The desire to be included, to feel a part of the group, is experienced as a need for attention, interest, or approval. Children reveal this most basic need within the family through either positive or negative attention-gaining behaviors. One child may be driven to achieve in order to gain attention and approval. Another child may seek approval by being quiet and dutiful. Still a third child may have learned that the only way that he will be recognized is through outlandish behavior. A child who suddenly begins to act out after the parent begins recovery is attempting in this manner to have his attentional needs met, to ask, "What about *me*? Don't *I* count?" Even if the attention is negative, it is better than no attention at all. Lack of attention is the same as being excluded, as not belonging.

At the beginning of the inclusion phase interactions are characteristically superficial. Fear, mistrust, loneliness, and bitterness are the predominant affective states. Deeply buried resentments dictate an avoidance of intimacy at all costs. These attributes of an unstable family constellation lead to the members' being segregated as social isolates and accounts for a lack of family cohesion (Jesse, 1977).

If inclusion is not facilitated, the alcoholic parent's recovery may be impeded. The desire to belong may be seen in the newly sobering parent who, in his remorse, is oversolicitous and indulgent with family members; when they do not respond in kind, the alcoholic becomes bitter and resentful. These resentments usually portend a return to drinking. An alcoholic parent who concentrates his energies on being included in the family rather than on his own recovery (which will ultimately raise his status) risks becoming stuck in early relapse. Whether the relapse process involves the state of a perpetual "dry drunk" or an actual return to drinking, the family will not move beyond the inclusion phase of recovery.

Inclusion motives are usually behind the co-dependent's attempts to control the alcoholic's recovery. Obsessive preoccupation with whether or not the alcoholic will return to drinking expresses the issue of trust-mistrust, which will not be resolved fully until the affection phase of recovery. Similarly, the co-dependent's feelings of being excluded from the alcoholic's involvement in A.A. or an after-care program is based on the need for more contact and together-ness.

As the family stabilizes, there is usually some consensus about family membership. Although the alcoholic and spouse may not have fully articulated a commitment to stay together, there is an awareness, albeit superficial, that they will move in that direction. The children's sense of belonging also stabilizes near the end of the inclusion phase. A child who may have left the family has made the transition to the extra-family setting (such as foster care, a divorced parent, etc.), while a child who has returned from an extra-family setting has been fully integrated into the immediate family group. By the end of the inclusion phase, a separated spouse has reconciled and returned or a new spouse has come to be accepted as a part of the family. In short, the family will *not* move into the next phase of recovery until the current family membership has been consolidated and stabilized.

Transition/Relapse to the Middle Phase

The regressive period marking the end of the inclusion phase usually begins shortly after the parent has been abstinent about six months. This time is often a depressive period, not only for the recovering alcoholic parent but also for the entire family. For the alcoholic, there is an existential crisis. A review of the difficult one-half year just passed leads to the recognition that recovery — if it is to be successful — consists of nothing more than day after day of a lifestyle based on moderation. For the recovering parent who has been used to years of tempestuous addictive living, there is a sense of emptiness. How can one live with such predictability? Another grief reaction occurs as the parent further releases the past. Grief, depression, disillusionment, and fear are the predominant affective states.

Family relating during this brief regressive interval continues to be superficial, low key, and marked by uncertainty. There is a continuing sense of alienation from other people within the family, as well as from the outside world. Negative emotional states (fear, anger, shame, mistrust) are still largely unexpressed. This time marks the transition between the inclusion and control phases of recovery. If the recovering parent and family have not been involved in some type of therapy program, this is an excellent time to begin, for within a few months into the second-half of the first year of recovery, the family will begin to face the essential question: *Who is going to provide the leadership for this family in recovery?*

At some time in the organizational history of every group, the question of leadership must be addressed. This issue will expose invisible coalitions, allegiances, and hence, hostilities. No one wants to be on the losing side in a power struggle. Accordingly, individuals typically resist moving into the control phase of family interactions by keeping their contacts and interactions superficial. Or there may be premature moves toward intimacy, often with disastrous results. Intimacy — true intimacy — simply cannot be achieved until control phase issues have been resolved.

Heretofore, the recovering alcoholic parent has felt no legitimate power to influence anyone within the family. Now, passing through the transition phase, the parent's confidence increases, leading to tentative bids for power and control. The family will staunchly resist these bids. However, it is the recovering parent's renewed involvement in the family which advances the family forward into the next process phase, that centered around *control*.

THE CONTROL PHASE

In the development of all groups, the determination of power relationships among people occurs after the group has been formed and group membership has been secured. According to Schutz (1967):

> Control behavior refers to the decision-making process between people, and the areas of power, influence, and authority. The need for control varies along a continuum from the desire for power, authority, and control over others (and therefore over one's future), to the need to be controlled, and have responsibility lifted from oneself. (p. 118)

Control is a word which has come to be synonymous with addictive family dynamics. Schaef (1987) explains how and why control governs these interactions so intensely:

In an addictive system everyone tries to control everyone else. The family tries to control the addict, the addict tries to control the family, the spouse tries to control against being controlled; everyone is involved in some sort of manipulative behavior. The worse the addiction becomes, the more desperate the need for control. The belief that anyone can get a handle on it is an illusion. Addictive relationships are founded on the illusion of control. (p. 41)

How, then, can a process issue which is said to be normal in the development of *all* family groups be transacted successfully in a system where it has become so distorted that it is a part of the family pathology?

In so-called normal families, the leadership function usually rests with the parents. Although one parent may, at times, exert more influence and hence more control than the other, usually the leadership is fairly equally distributed between these two adults. However, in the alcoholic/addictive family system, family leadership has usually been abdicated by the alcoholic to the co-dependent or by both parents to the children. As we have learned, power and control that may have been resting covertly within the sibling subsystem are not easily returned to the parents.

The beginning of the control phase is a very risky time for the family. Having just consolidated family membership, all feel the question of who is to be in charge of the family as an organizational threat. The parents in recovery usually have a poor history of conflict resolution. They may not even be aware that consensus — where no one person comes out on top but everyone wins something — is possible when there is a dispute.

When we examine the issue of control as it tends to become exaggerated in the alcoholic/addictive family, we note that the emphasis is always on controlling someone or something *outside of oneself*. Whether the spouse is attempting to control the alcoholic, or one sibling is attempting to control another, or the children are attempting to control their parents, or the alcoholic is attempting to control substance intake, the effort is always to bring about some kind of external control. Thus, the need for control becomes exaggerated and distorted as a way of achieving inner comfort, for behind the exaggerated need for control is *fear*. *Addictive families are fear-ridden systems*. Often fluctuating from rigidly controlled to chaotic, these families shield themselves from the outside world by an impenetrable wall of fear/anger/control. Attempts to remove the control usually result in the second line defense of anger, which is the more superficial emotion masking fear.

Commonly, the fear has to do with the impending loss of *internal* control. Individuals within the addictive system try to maintain the integrity of the self through controlling other people. The need to control another person (or selfobject), who is experienced as a part of the self, occurs when there is a perceived threat to the sense of self. Independent expression is not easily understood or tolerated in addictive families. A parent will perceive a child's messy room as a statement about poor parenting. A wife will perceive her husband's excessive drinking as a statement about her as a woman. The recovering father will perceive his son's poor report card as a reflection on his lack of fathering. Many times these efforts to control are based on family myths and values which, although no longer relevant, go back to the parents' families of origin — and even generations beyond.

When both spouses are involved in Alcoholics Anonymous and the Al-Anon family program for spouses, they may have begun to work the twelve steps of these programs. The first step, which has to do with an admission of powerlessness (over alcohol or over the alcoholic), applies to the notion of generally relinquishing control. Parents who have an intellectual understanding of this premise have made considerable progress. However, it is quite another task to have parents make the leap from an intellectual understanding to internalizing an emotional comprehension of powerlessness, i.e., lack of control. Commonly, this phase of therapy involves a grief reaction. The following excerpt from a co-dependent therapy session involves a wife's expression of grief over the awareness that she lacks control over her husband.

> I just feel sad every time I'm forced to admit that I don't *really* have any control over my husband. How will I get him to do things for me? Like the bills? Or taking care of the vehicle when it needs repairs? If I have to keep my mouth shut until the mood strikes him, *nothing* will ever get done.

When this woman was able to acknowledge that her efforts to control by nagging had not produced results, she began to consider that there might be another way.

The task of therapy during the control phase is to bring family members to a place where they can consider negotiation and consensus as a way of conflict resolution. Clarifying the differences among articulated rules, implicit rules, and "requests" becomes important to the parent-child work done during this phase of therapy. Parents in recovery are often very unrealistic in their notions of what they can and cannot control with their children. A parent will attempt to control some superficial aspect of a child's appearance, such as hairstyle, but will perceive absolutely no control over rules for the child's verbal behavior. For example, a parent who was beginning sobriety had a tremendous struggle the entire first year with his teenage daughter's verbal profanity. He believed that he had no right to send her to her room or use other disciplinary measures when she cursed him or his wife. However, this same man believed he had every right to tell his daughter that she could not cut her hair.

Without professional assistance, families are likely to become mired in power struggles. Or they will move back and forth between the phases of inclusion and control. When some members are rigid and unyielding in their efforts to exert power and influence, others will opt out of the family. Children may leave the home. A spouse may separate from the family. Anytime family membership shifts there is a new organizational crisis; hence, the family is thrown back into the phase of inclusion. This may lead to family disorganization and disruption.

A successful resolution of the control phase establishes the parents as bona fide leaders who are acknowledged by the children. Ideally, the control phase is resolved near the end of the parent's first year of abstinence; however, control phase issues may sometimes persist for years.

Transition/Relapse to Long-Term Recovery

At the end of the control phase, there is another transition period marked by regressive interactions. Old leadership styles and power coalitions may reappear briefly. For the recovering alcoholic parent, the physiological manifestations of post acute withdrawal may be exacerbated. The co-dependent and children also experience the negative affective states of the relapse syndrome. This transition period signals family resistance to moving forward into the next phase of *affection*, which revolves around issues of emotional closeness and intimate relating.

THE AFFECTION PHASE

The family members have been successful in forming a viable structure where everyone is included, they have become differentiated as to responsibilities and leadership, and now they must become integrated emotionally (Schutz, 1958). While the inclusion phase is concerned with whether or not a relationship even exists between any two members of the family, the control and affection phases have to do with transactions in relationships which have already been formed. Efforts to protect the self in each of these phases lead to a characteristic interpersonal defenses against anxiety. During the inclusion phase, the interpersonal anxiety involves a self which is felt to be worthless and empty; during the control phase it involves a self which is felt to be stupid and ineffectual. However, the deepest anxiety occurs during the affection phase — this involves a self which is believed to be unlovable or unworthy, or a self which will cease to *be* through the intimate merging with another.

The major concern of the affection phase is how to give and receive love. For members of an alcoholic family who have rarely experienced interpersonal closeness, the fear of love is as great as the need to receive it. Similarly, expressions of love to other individuals do not come easily in a family where interpersonal antagonisms have been characteristic. To receive love means that one becomes vulnerable and runs the risk of being controlled by the other person; to express love means that one risks the shame which is anticipated from rejection.

It is important that the therapist understand that members of an alcoholic family may not have known or experienced the ordinary emotion called "love." The need for love has to do with behavior which is aimed at becoming emotionally close. One of the most important tasks of therapy during this phase is to teach the family members how to develop a congruence between *feelings* and *behavior*. For example, a husband may claim to love his wife but have a great deal of difficulty showing affection, consideration, or respect. He may attempt to relieve his interpersonal anxiety by using humor or sarcasm, so that his wife feels his clumsy attempts at "love" as hostile jabs. Similarly, a mother may purport to care deeply for her teenage daughter; however, her interactions with the girl are colored by attempts to control and manipulate through guilt-laden messages, such as, "After all I've done for you, you should be more grateful than to disobey me." The goal of therapy will be to have this mother separate control phase issues, which have to do with exercising leadership functions, from affection phase issues.

Problems encountered during the affection phase have to do with family members' attempts to avoid closeness. The alcoholic typically has related to others at a superficial level, preferring interpersonal distance. During his drinking days he may have been overly indulgent and clinging while under the influence of alcohol, but distant when sober. Locked in interpersonal ambivalence, the alcoholic expresses a wish for emotional attachment while using behavior which repels it.

Conversely, a family member may profess a desire to remain distant while really longing for contact. The alcoholic and the co-dependent may reject others and avoid the anxiety of close interpersonal ties through workaholic behavior or by spending an inordinate amount of time away from the family at A.A. meetings (which gives the illusion of an intimate association with others). Here the subtle technique is to appear emotionally involved with everyone, which is really a safeguard against getting too close to any one person.

According to Schutz (1958), "To become emotionally close to someone involves, in addition to an emotional attachment, an element of confiding innermost anxieties, wishes, and feelings" (p. 24). Being close and personal means risking one's ego through surrendering one's most private concerns and feelings to another. The dyadic relationship is threatening, for it is perceived that the other person now has the ability to control, manipulate, or evaluate the fragile, unprotected self.

Sometimes an opposite problem is found in the overly social style of the alcoholic and co-dependent. These overly social individuals are very caught up in a people-pleasing style; their goal is to be liked by everyone. The illusion of being liked provides a safeguard against feelings of being unlovable and rejected. Two styles of overpersonal involvement are seen: A direct style is outwardly people-pleasing, personal and confiding; an indirect style is more subtle and manipulative. Indirect individuals use guilt as a way of controlling others and punish anyone who strays from their expectations or sphere of influence. For example, a mother whose child expresses a desire to have a relationship with a divorced father might use subtle methods of controlling the child through guilt, or the child might be told outright that he is selfish, ungrateful, bad. The indirect, subtle message is, "How dare you want to stray from me."

Both undersocial (distant) and oversocial (people-pleasing) styles reflect a strong, underlying anxiety about being unlovable, as well as a strong need for closeness and affection. The goal of therapy in each case is to have these parents begin to verbalize their underlying emotions, rather than using destructive behavior to safeguard against them.

While inclusion and control issues might involve any two people in the family or a triangular relationship or one person and the rest of the family, the affection phase involves only two people interacting at any one time. During this phase, the emotions which are expressed may range from direct personal hostility to love.

As noted in Figure 10, the period of affection is the briefest period in the family recovery cycle. The family will continue to cycle back through the other phases, from control to inclusion, or from inclusion to control, before again arriving at the predominant phase of affection. It is important to realize that any time a family member leaves or enters the family, the process issues are automatically shifted back to those of inclusion, and hence the process commences again.

PART V

Children in Recovery

In this part we concentrate on reparative work with the child. As we begin in Chapter 10 with the comprehensive approach to child assessment, the reader may suspect that our focus has become too narrow, that what is being proposed is how to locate the source of *the* problem, once again, within the child's troubled psyche. If this were so, it would constitute a move backwards some three or four decades in time. However, this is not the case at all.

What I am emphasizing is respect for the child-self as system. Making up this organic whole called "child" are combined genetic, constitutional, and environmental influences which produce some unique *effect* on a child's developmental status. I am encouraging therapists, for the sake of children in recovery, to determine this effect to the extent that it is possible to do so. Before involving the child in family therapy meetings which may only frustrate and complicate a child's weakened self, begin to assess the child's ability to withstand these meetings, as well as to explore the child's specific needs for recovery.

Even in Chapter 11, when I recommend that early phase recovery work with a child consist largely of individual sessions, I am not proposing a return to an individual model of child treatment. For, as the reader will come to realize, this individual work strengthens

the child's ability to function as a viable self during subsequent
family and sibling meetings.

During my earliest work with children of alcoholics (Jesse, 1975),
I proposed a group treatment model for children in recovery.
Because of the salience of the peer group during middle childhood,
I expected the group to act as a "psychotherapist." By providing peer
support, alliance, and more positive identification, the group was
expected to facilitate a child's improved functioning in the family.
However, the group failed to have the desired effect. I have reported
on the problems of group treatment of younger children of alcoholics in another publication (Jesse, 1988). Essentially these children
have difficulty forming a cohesive, selfobject milieu. Their problems
in verbal skills and difficulties in self-regulation interfere with a
"therapeutic" effect. Coleman (1978) observed a similar difficulty in
the group treatment of siblings of drug addicted teenagers, noting:

> It is felt that the behavior of the group represents a microcosm of the
> youngster's internal environment, the roots of which lie within the
> families' historical milieu. These developmentally produced defenses
> are still too rigid to penetrate. . . . It is still questionable if any
> internal pathology has been altered. (p. 125)

While group methods for the treatment of school-aged children of
alcoholism/addiction may be used adjunctively, it should be kept in
mind that the group will not significantly alter a child's developmental deficits. The primary purpose of group treatment with this age
group should be:

1. to decrease feelings of alienation associated with parental
   addiction;
2. to provide substance abuse awareness and education in a peer
   milieu;
3. to improve peer functioning through planned activities and
   recreation.

The child's most *therapeutic* agent will be the parent(s), and the
milieu which is most conducive to supporting lasting change is the
family. As I have maintained throughout, work with a child which is
separated from the family context, especially the parental selfobject
unit, ignores the very systemic forces which comprise a child's
emotional environment. Unfortunately, family therapy which does
not emphasize the realities of child development also obscures our
ability to apprehend this child-self embedded within the system.

Chapter 12 presents the middle and ongoing child recovery issues, particularly the key concepts of control and intimacy. Control is recognized not only as a family systems process but also as a factor in the external social system, including the therapist. During the final phase of therapy the ultimate control for children in recovery is returned to the now empathic milieu of parental caretakers. In many ways, this model of child recovery is an ideal, for it stretches the imagination about what can be accomplished when "recovery" becomes a process towards an improved way of life for a group of individuals called a "family."

In this day of mental health cost containment, there doubtless will be many critics of this model who champion brief intervention, questioning, "Who in the world is ever going to foot the bill for long-term child recovery work?" To those critics, I would raise another question: Who is *already* footing the bill for the enormous public costs to courts and agency helpers who must intervene in the lives of families and children who are being destroyed by addictive processes? Who is already footing the bill for the multitude of secondary physical complications which result from alcoholism and addictions?

Who already is footing the bill for the enormous amount of family dollars which are being paid daily for consciousness-altering substances? Alcohol, tobacco, caffeine, sugar, illicit and over-the-counter drugs are also *brief* solutions to those isolated individuals who call themselves "a family," enmeshed by their addictions.

Who will foot the bill, indeed!

I have known families — simple folks, really — who came to understand that exchanging money paid on addictions for the cost of recovery was at least an even trade.

CHAPTER 10

Assessment of the Child

The principle to which we are referring consists then in regarding the child, not as a being of pure imitation, but as an organism which assimilates things to itself, selects them and digests them according to its own structure. In this way even what is influenced by the adult may still be original.

—Jean Piaget, 1964, p. 31

Perhaps more than any other client population, children require an assessment — or inventory — of their developmental strengths and limitations prior to intervention, especially since there are natural variations in the rate and level of maturation from child to child even within a specific age group. These individual differences are often more profound than the commonalities among children from addictive families.

Recovery begins when we start to know each child as a uniquely developing self. Our efforts to know must include respect for the coordinated ego functions through which the self experience is being filtered. Otherwise, we will be making the same mistake that has been made by caretakers in the family — denying the realities of a child's uniqueness. When we respond to a child with only partial knowing, that child will feel misunderstood by us. Following Piaget, we must recognize that children often possess knowledge that they cannot communicate to others, although their need to be understood is as strong as their need to understand (Anthony, 1976).

How do we come to *know* the child in recovery? Then, how do we translate that knowing into words that the child will understand? Then, how do we facilitate this understanding for parents?

An assessment of the different layers of the self experience of the children of alcoholism and addiction is an important first step. The combined assessment procedures provide a photograph of the relative contributions from various sectors of the outer world on a child's inner functioning. As the different aspects of coordinated ego functions are assessed, we can better understand the nature of a child's participation in the alcoholic/addictive family system.

THE PROCESS OF ASSESSMENT

How can we purport to *know* the impact of years of complicated addictive family life on the child? Interviews and verbal interactions alone will not provide the complete picture. At such times, it is tempting to borrow from our professional armamentarium any one of a number of labels or types to attach to a child's observable behavior. But what purpose do these labels *really* serve? The process of child recovery is neither enhanced nor strengthened by seeing the child as a role — such as the dutiful child or the noncompliant child. These labels merely obscure the lost child-self, which is screaming for full expression.

Recovering alcoholic and addicted parents as a group are amazingly perceptive people. They can see through phoniness and sense uncertainty. To admit to them that we cannot begin to know how to proceed with their child until an evaluation has been completed *establishes* rather than diminishes our credibility. Professional grandiosity has no place in alcoholism and addiction recovery work.

Most recovering parents are very grateful to have their child receive a thorough assessment. At some level they are aware that the cumulative stress of addictive family life has affected their child adversely. Parents have a right to view their child through the informed position of psychological assessment or even if indicated, neuropsychological assessment.

Usually, the assessment process has an immediate stabilizing effect on family functioning. This appears to be true for at least a couple reasons. First, the assessment *is* an intervention. Because of important family process shifts when the parents turn to the therapist to provide leadership, a therapeutic effect commences. Second, the assessment is an intervention at the level of the family system.

From the time of the first contact onward, the therapist begins to perform leadership functions.

Those who are new to child and family work often mistakenly fear that assessment will serve to alienate a family seeking help. Such a family often presents in distress, with an urgent request that change be provided, NOW! To investigate rather than to intervene seems a cold, sterile way of proceeding in the face of crisis. This viewpoint holds assessment within the tradition of scientific psychology, where evaluation and treatment are separate, disparate approaches. In that tradition the evaluation consists of measurable behaviors or traits being counted and classified by a neutral objective observer. The observer always maintains an external frame of reference to the child. We need to be reminded, however, that the earliest approaches to the treatment of childhood disorders, notably those of Anna Freud, Erikson, and Melanie Klein, made no distinction between assessment and treatment. This seems to have been true because the *process*, or interpersonal influences of the assessment, had a therapeutic effect upon the child. This process, which is believed to be essential in work with children in recovery, is described as the *empathic mode of observation*.

The self as a psychological entity had not been the topic of concentrated study until the work of Kohut (1971, 1977). Kohut introduced a method of observation called *empathy*, which is that process where the observer occupies an imaginary point *inside* the individual with whom he empathically identifies. Although Kohut contrasted this empathic mode with the empirical method which is used in psychometric examinations, the challenge of assessment is how to *empathically* integrate all sources of information about the child, that is, how to make our assessment *both* empirical and empathic. Because a child cannot speak to us about many of the limitations of his/ her inner functioning, the sensitive translation of psychometric information can serve as an empathic bridge.

The following discussion is intended to acquaint both novice and experienced family clinicians with those child assessment procedures most relevant to work with school-aged children in recovery.

THE ASSESSMENT INTERVIEW

Usually a first consultation has been scheduled by the parent, who has provided some information about the child's problems. In other instances, the appointment may have been scheduled by treatment center personnel, case workers, or other helping professionals associated with the family in recovery.

The initial assessment consists of an interview with parent and child together, and then time spent alone with the child. Our observations begin immediately upon meeting with the child and the parent. In fact, the first indication of a child's reaction to the consultation may be observed through waiting room behavior ranging from hesitancy and withdrawal to noisy, frenetic play. The therapist's attunement to the child's inner state, which is seeking behavioral expression, is reflected back as a way of building rapport to support the therapeutic work that will follow. For example, a child who stubbornly refuses to leave the waiting room even with parental coaxing is respected in her reluctance. Most children will respond to the therapist's verbal echoing of their conflict:

> You're not too sure that you want to be here today. You don't know me, and you don't know if you're going to like me. All right, I'll show your mother into my office while I leave the door open for you so that when you *are* ready, you and I can meet in the playroom.

Providing the child with the awareness that you comprehend her fear is *empathic reflection*. At the same time, the therapist has made a family intervention of establishing herself in the leadership role, intimating that part of the interview will occur apart from the parent through the child's medium of play.

We are reminded here that there is an inner child-self of the parent which is being stimulated during our interaction with the child. Through identification with the child, the parent will experience our empathic reflection as belonging to *both* of them.

The Parent-Child Interview

After the child is given a brief introduction to the playroom (or, if no playroom is available, to a corner of the therapist's office which is designated for play), the child, the parent, and the therapist meet for the initial interview. An office or room which is furnished informally — and which does *not* include the therapist sitting at, behind, or near a desk — is favored. Recovering children and parents have built up years of resistance to authority. Even though one of the COA defensive styles may be outward compliance to authority, rest assured that an inner rebellion is often stirred by a therapist who holds herself aloof behind a desk. The child, as well as the parent, needs to experience the therapist as a friendly ally. Any room setting which introduces intimidation or control is to be avoided.

After brief conversation to put the child and parent at ease, the therapist always begins by directing the first question to the child:

> What did your mother (or father, or parents) tell you about coming here today?

It is important to uncover the child's expectations, as well as to determine how much preparation will be required to educate the child. Often children have been told *nothing* by their parent. Fearful of the child's negative reaction, the parent will simply tell the youngster that "we" have an appointment. Or the child may have been told vaguely that she is going to the "doctor." Children who arrive completely uninformed need to be prepared with simple, straightforward explanations. When the therapist models honest communication with the child, the parent's education is advanced. The therapist, turning to the parent, counsels the parent to explain to the child why the appointment has been scheduled for the two of them:

> Let's pause for a moment, Mrs. Johnson, so that you have the opportunity to explain to Mary why you have brought her here today.

The parent's explanation is then facilitated by the therapist's drawing attention to the problems at a family level rather than leaving the child singled out as "the problem." If, for example, the parent's explanation highlights the child's problem behavior only, the therapist can reframe the statement:

> Your mother knows that you are not very happy sometimes, Mary, and she doesn't understand what she can do to help you. That is why she has brought you here today so that we all can help each other by talking about the problems in your family. What are some of the problems that you see happening in your family?

"Why" questions are to be avoided, since they will lead the child to respond defensively. Dutiful children will try to provide the therapist with the best rationalization possible. Passive or aggressive children will retreat completely from these "why" questions. The process of empathic attunement does not require the children to *produce* for us by understanding their own motivations, such as, "*Why* don't you like to clean your room?"

Children of alcoholic and addictive families are often relieved when we invite them to talk about the problems in the family from their perspective. Since the child's perception may be entirely different from the presenting problem just articulated by the parent, the therapist explains that each member in a family views problems through his or her own eyes, and there may be as many different perceptions as there are members of a family. None of these is wrong; they are simply *different*.

If the parent does not mention alcoholism or addiction as a problem for the child and the family, the therapist introduces the topic of addictive family dynamics.

> Mary, your mother has shared with me that she used to drink a lot of alcohol. She believes that her drinking has something to do with the unhappiness you have been feeling. What can you remember about your mother's drinking?

If the child shrugs, or otherwise seems reluctant to broach the subject, the therapist respects this silence and then moves into the area of recovery.

> What are some of the ways your family has changed since your Mom stopped drinking?

Open-ended questions elicit the child's views of the family. To be avoided are questions that lead the child to the interviewer's predetermined conclusions. Questions that can be answered "yes" or "no" will also fail to facilitate the flow of the child's ideas. In addition, we discourage questions that may arouse fear in the child. For instance, asking "Do you think your Mom will return to drinking?" may set off *obsessive* worry in a child about the threat of relapse. Recall that children during the years of middle childhood are naturally obsessive in their thinking. Children in recovery need to know that they have no (magical) power or responsibility for their parent's addiction.

Sometimes a child will adamantly refuse to discuss family alcoholism. The shame motive is a powerful one which preempts the need to talk about hurt feelings. Shame feelings are kept secret. A child's right to privacy in the interview is honored.

Attempts to elicit feelings in the language of adult emotions are avoided. An interviewer's exhortation, "How did you *feel* about this or that?" is often met with an honest shrug from a little child who truly doesn't experience or know how to articulate complex emotional states (Jesse, 1987). Words such as "depressed," for example, may be translated by the child as simply "bad," as in, "I felt *bad*." Through the interviewer's empathic attunement to the child's inner state these elaborated emotions can be inferred. We do not need to ask.

At the first sign of tension or discomfort from the child, such as restlessness, irrelevance or agitation, the parent-child interview is concluded and the child is excused to the playroom.

The Child at Play

During the initial interview play activities are used not so much to promote change as to further the process goals of maintaining contact and cooperation with the child. The play situation also is used to soothe the child if excess tension has built up during the course of the parent-child interview. Tension reduction for the child in recovery is a major consideration with each scheduled session. For these youngsters who lack internal self-regulating capacities, the therapeutic milieu must leave them feeling better than when they came and eager to return.

The rules of the playroom are stated simply but directly to the child.

> You may play with any of the toys that you like, and we may talk about anything that you like. But you may not leave the playroom (or play area) until I let you know that our time is up for today. Anything that you talk to me about here is not discussed with your parent(s) unless you give me permission. If there is something that I believe we should discuss with your parents, I will let you know and we can come to an agreement about when you want to tell them.

The need for a confidential relationship with the child has already been discussed with the parent. Most recovering parents are quite respectful of this confidential contract between the child and the therapist. (An exception is presented in Chapter 12 in the case illustration of Ulric, whose mother demanded to know the complete details of my therapy sessions with her son.)

After the initial rules have been presented the play therapy observation is nonstructured. The child is allowed to make play choices from a variety of toys, such as dollhouse, puppets, sandbox with small animal and human figures for sand pictures, a large bin of building blocks of various shapes and sizes, modeling clay, paints and colors for artwork. Games, which may be utilized later, are for the time being kept out of reach on a high shelf.

The child's reactions to the play therapy situation are observed.

As Ornstein (1985) has indicated, the child's play provides us with insight into both emotional and cognitive realms of the mind. We observe the content of a child's cognitions, as well as his attitudes, associations and feelings while he interacts with the play therapy media. We note whether his play is constricted or chaotic. We note the kinds of toys chosen, as well as the manner in which they are chosen — whether constructively, apathetically, or destructively. We do not interact with the child unless he invites us to do so.

Finally, we note the child's reactions when separating from the playroom. When he is told that it is time to leave, does he linger, attempting to engage the therapist? Or does he rapidly dash past the examiner to join his parent in the waiting room? Each interaction will provide some information about the child's problems in attachments. Children will often bond to the play therapy room (or area, or toys) before forming a strong attachment to the therapist.

The Parent Interview

An interview is later scheduled to discuss with the parent(s) the child's history, as well as their own individual, marital, and substance-abusing history. Recovering parents are usually intellectually prepared for the interviewer's questions; however, they may be unprepared for the emotions which are elicited as they review their addictive past in relation to their maltreatment of their child. Supportive interventions are required to reduce parental guilt associated with this aspect of the assessment process. At one level, the parent in recovery is aware that his addiction has had deleterious consequences for the child. Although he may not even recall many of the destructive events which have been harmful to the child, the parent does have a general sense that his child's difficulties are in response to his addiction. However, at another level, the parent has difficulty accepting that the child is anything other than a thorn in the side. Why, the parent will ask, in the face of his own sobriety, has the child deliberately chosen problem behavior or psychological symptoms? The recovering parent, like many health care professionals, tends to view abstinence as a panacea. In truth, it is only a beginning.

Empathizing with the recovering parent is not difficult *if* we accept the disease concept of alcoholism and addiction. Such an empathic response is mindful of the parent's helplessness and lack of choice under the influence of the drug when harm was inflicted on the child. If, on the other hand, we view the addictive conduct as a moral issue, we will find it difficult to be congruent in our counseling efforts with the parent.

Overidentification with the child in recovery leads to subtle breakdowns in our attempts to be effective change agents with the parent. When we recognize that the key to successful treatment of the addictive family unit is reeducation and training of the parent, so that he/she can become the child's chief advocate, we recognize our need to maintain a collaborative relationship with this parent.

When the recovering parent appears to be blocking the recall of pertinent history from the period of active alcoholism, it is precipitous to judge this as defensive forgetting. Often the parent's *ability* to recall such material has been impaired by the effects of chronic alcohol use. This type of neuropsychological deficit tends to improve as the parent progresses in sobriety. Most alcoholic parents, even with substantial recovery, continue to play the "shame and blame game" with their children. Shame about their own inadequacies leads to defensive blaming of the child — or spouse — or other children in the family who now absorb the shame. Continual refocusing of the child's problems as "a family problem" alleviates much of this blaming and shaming.

Crucial information about the parent's recovery, including history of their involvement in treatment programs, Alcoholics Anonymous, Al-Anon, or other psychotherapy programs is deemed important. An assessment of the parent's phase of sobriety, as discussed in Chapters 8 and 9, should include an evaluation of physical, emotional, and interpersonal functioning at the time of the assessment. The context and content of parent-child interactions when a parent is six months sober will differ from those when a parent is two years sober.

During the parent interview, we begin by focusing on the parent's beliefs about the child's problems and how these have been dealt with in the period of drinking and recovery. Information about the parents' current marital relationship and family histories also are obtained. A complete developmental history of the child is obtained by providing the parent with a written format for completion and return at the next visit.

PSYCHOLOGICAL ASSESSMENT

The purpose of psychological assessment with a child in recovery is to gather information about that child's unique functioning so as to intervene more effectively. The underlying assumption is that parental alcoholism and other forms of addiction leave some kind of mark on the delicate psychological structures of a child. At the same time, the child's psychological functioning is disrupted by the envi-

ronmental influences of familial alcoholism. A comprehensive understanding of the child as a psychological self within the interactional context of the family serves the best interests of the child and
the family.

The following discussion is intended for psychologists, as well as
for those helping professionals who may be referring children in
recovery for assessment purposes. Understanding the rationale for
psychological evaluation and the types of tests most commonly used
facilitates an informed referral and interpretation of the psychologist's report and recommendations.

As a general rule, children in recovery should be evaluated by a
clinical psychologist, within either a private or an agency setting,
who has some experience in the field of alcoholism and addictions.
Although such specialists are not always immediately available, community treatment centers or hospitals can usually locate them
through their referral network.

When making the referral, the child therapist should provide the
psychologist with a "referral question", which is often a statement of
the child's presenting problems and symptomatic behavior. The following example suggests how a referral question might be posed to a
psychologist.

> Mary's mother and teacher claim that she is unable to settle down
> in the classroom, and, as a result, she is failing in many of her
> subjects. Mary appears to have average ability, but she seems distract-
> ed, fidgety, and unmotivated. When she is confronted by her mother
> about these failing grades, she flares up with temper outbursts.
>
> Mary's father is a recovering alcoholic who has just begun treat-
> ment. How have these family problems contributed to Mary's present
> school difficulties? How can Mary best be helped in counseling? In
> school? What kind of feedback should be provided to the family about
> Mary's problems so that she can be helped at home?

The child therapist may request that this information be provided by
the psychologist in the form of a report written in language easily
understood by the therapist and parents.

Perceptual Assessment

Psychological tests used to measure perceptual assessment include
the Bender-Gestalt Visual Motor test, where a child is asked to
reproduce drawings of a series of geometric forms. Another test, the
Marianne Frostig Developmental Test of Visual Perception, some-

times referred to simply as the Frostig, tests a number of different visual and visual-motor functions. Tests in auditory perception may be inferred from certain of the tasks on the standard intelligence tests or by administration of other tests of auditory discrimination.

Cognitive Assessment

Cognitive development may be assessed by using standard psychological tests of intellectual abilities, such as the Stanford-Binet and Wechsler Intelligence Scale for Children-Revised (WISC-R). While these tests provide quantitative data which yield an intelligence score, or I.Q., they also provide more than measures of "intelligence." Valuable information may be obtained about the content of a child's cognitions or the processes of her thinking, as well as perceptual abilities. Neuropsychological functioning is indicated by the evenness or variability in measured scores. In addition, important indicators of emotional conflict can be derived from the WISC R.

Other evaluation procedures which psychologists use to measure a child's cognitive processes include such tasks as the Peabody Picture Vocabulary Test, the Incomplete Sentences Test, Story Telling Techniques, Rorschach, Children's Apperception Test, and Tasks of Emotional Development. With the exception of the Peabody, which is a test of general word knowledge, the other tests are considered to be projective personality tests. The child's verbalizations provide an indication of his cognitive processes as well.

Clinical Illustration — Rudolph

Rudolph was the seven-year-old son of a recovering alcoholic divorced mother, who also had a two-year-old daughter. When Rudy's mother was six months into her recovery, she began to voice considerable frustration about Rudy's noncompliant behavior.

Rudy was a dawdler. He sat in front of the television set morning after morning, or dawdled with toys and games, ignoring his mother's repeated nagging to get himself ready for school. Rudy's Mom resented what she believed was the boy's deliberate stubbornness. On these frustrating mornings, Rudy reminded her of his father, a stoic man who had divorced his alcoholic wife during the final months of her heavy drinking. Rudy also reminded his mother of her own father—a cold, stubborn alcoholic man who had abandoned her during her childhood.

Although Rudy's mother was attempting to practice the principles of her twelve-step recovery program, which emphasized love and tolerance, she found this almost impossible with her son. She resented Rudy's dependence, particularly since her toddler-aged child required her constant vigilance. She was unwilling to cater to Rudy's apparent dependency needs. His seeming helplessness reminded her of her own mother, with whom she had experienced a role reversal during her childhood.

Rudy's mother believed that the boy was using negative attention-gaining behavior deliberately to spite her. During his morning and evening rituals, when Rudy seemed to be using his dawdling to frustrate her, she would experience herself as a failure as a mother. Filled with self-hate and agitation, she would feel hatred towards Rudy. These difficult feeling states often were accompanied by an urge to consume alcohol. She became increasingly fearful of relapse. She admitted that she would now seek emotional release by yelling at Rudy and accusing him of trying to drive her back to drink. The more she yelled, the more the small, cowering boy seemed to dawdle. To the mother, Rudy was not a frightened, disorganized child; he was the hated, unacceptable tormenter who reminded her of her inadequacy as a parent.

When mother and son presented for the initial interview, Rudy, a child with apparent average verbal intelligence, seemed to converse easily. The initial impression was that the boy had many unmet dependency needs for caretaking functions to be provided by the mother. Also, it appeared that the parent-child interactions were based on faulty, but deeply ingrained, habit patterns. Attempting to communicate either of these impressions to the mother raised a great deal of defensiveness around the issue of "bad mothering," her worst inner fear.

A comment about habitual patterns met with the mother's, "So what? There's no *need* for him to keep repeating these bad habits. Since I've been sober, I tell him over and over the right things to do, but he just *won't* do them." Empathizing with the mother's frustration and supporting her in her genuine concern for Rudy established the necessary bond to enlist her support in the assessment process.

When the comprehensive assessment procedures were completed and discussed with the mother, she began to develop a very different picture of her son. She learned that Rudy's intellectual functioning was impaired significantly in certain key areas. Although his verbal fluency and verbal common sense reasoning were average, he had almost no social judgment when verbal cues were not provided in a calm ambience. Without his mother's calm words to describe the correct social behavior for him, Rudy simply could not grasp the right course of action for himself. Moreover, he was limited in his ability to anticipate or plan the correct sequence of behaviors to arrive at a desired goal without verbal assistance. Also, Rudy's ability to attend and concentrate on the verbal cues that were provided was greatly reduced in the face of disruptive anxiety. When he felt anxious and afraid, Rudy's ability to remember verbal cues was blocked by these temporary anxieties.

The cyclical nature of the parent-child conflict soon became apparent. When the mother's expectations of Rudy were not commensurate with his cognitive abilities, she became impatient and demanding. Her angry demands increased Rudy's anxiety to the point that he was even less capable of functioning adaptively. The less Rudy complied, the more the mother felt inadequate. The more she felt inadequate, the angrier she became with Rudy.

When Rudy's mother learned about his cognitive impairment, she became far more accepting of his limitations. She saw that in certain areas his test-age was really not that much different from the chronological-age of her younger child. At this point she became more receptive to the education that she needed to parent Rudy effectively. She saw herself as collaborating in both therapy and academic situations to help Rudy overcome his specific limitations. Freed from recriminating guilt, the mother was able to demonstrate patience and sensitivity with Rudy for the first time.

Rudy soon began to experience himself as worthy of attention from his mother and other helpers. His increasing self-esteem was evident as he reported more initiative in his home behavior. With consistent training at home and remediation in school, Rudy soon began to show maturation in his cognitive functioning.

In Rudy's case, child assessment served both educative and strategic functions. It was educative in the sense that it provided the therapist, the school personnel, and the parent with important information about Rudy's capabilities and limitations. It was strategic to the extent that the intervention provided an immediate shift in the family context. Rudy's mother moved from an adversarial role with her son to one of parent and guide. The rigidified adversarial role that had been maintained by Rudy's limitations and his mother's projections was no longer relevant.

We might speculate that the interferences in Rudy's development were somehow related to the neglect he suffered during the years of his mother's active alcoholism. However, this becomes a moot point when we need to plan interventions for the child in recovery.

Emotional Assessment

Through the psychologist's use of *projective tests* an understanding of a child's inner states may be inferred. For example, the child may be asked to draw a picture of a person, or a house, or a tree, or even the family. Other tests used with school-aged children involve having them make up stories to a series of pictures. One such test is the Children's Apperception Test (CAT), which shows pictures of animals involved in human-like activity. A child may tell a story with an aggressive or violent theme or present some other emotionally laden conflict. A theme with a happy ending provides some indication of a child's optimism and hopefulness.

The Tasks of Emotional Development (TED) test includes photographs of boys and girls of latency age involved in various scenes believed to be representative of developmental tasks. A child is assumed to identify with the child in the picture and to project onto the picture his/her own typical emotional reaction in a similar situation. Themes of trust, socialization, aggression, learning, conscience development, identification, separation, sibling and parent relationships, the acceptance of limits, and self-concept are elicited on the TED.

Another technique is the Rorschach (or "inkblots") test, which is concerned with visual-perceptual, motivational, and emotional responses. A child is presented with each of the ten cards of the Rorschach and asked to tell what he sees. Children in recovery who have been emotionally damaged through physical, sexual, or psychological abuse respond to these cards very differently from children whose development has not been so affected. Red areas on the card may be seen as blood or fire. Often emotionally labile children become so affected by their inner reactions to an inkblot card that they quickly withdraw from the card, asking that it be placed out of sight.

Assessment of Academic Achievement

Achievement has to do with what a child has accomplished in the school curriculum, while intelligence has to do with a child's *ability* to accomplish. Although there may be a relationship between intelligence and achievement, the two are not synonymous. Psychologists are concerned with the discrepancy between *ability* and *achievement*. If a child is not living up to his ability in certain areas, what does this mean? Often the discrepancy is due to perceptual problems and cognitive deficits or a combination of cognitive-perceptual deficits. More often, children from an addictive household show problems in *motivation* stemming from low self-esteem and stress-filled lives. A child who has begun to experience himself as a failure has little interest in working at his optimal level.

A child who is an overachiever—that is, one who excels in academics beyond what would be expected for his or her intellectual capabilities—would not necessarily be evaluated as problem free. Such a child from an alcoholic family may be using compensatory striving as a defense against self-esteem and family problems. A psychologist would consider all psychological test information and try to determine what was at the basis of the high-drive performance.

Achievement tests may be administered to the child with his classroom peers in the school environment. School personnel are interested in seeing how a particular child is doing compared to other children in the classroom at that grade level. These achievement test scores often can be obtained from the parents or the school.

When a psychologist administers an achievement test, it is given to the child during an individual administration. The advantage here is that the child's behavior can be observed and any signs of stress noted. Examples of these individually administered achievement tests include the Peabody Individual Achievement Test (PIAT), which measures mathematics, reading recognition, reading comprehension, spelling, and general information, and the Wide Range Achievement Test (WRAT), which measures spelling, reading recognition, and arithmetic.

Assessment of Social Development

One procedure for assessing a child's social development involves looking at his/her perceptions of the basic biosocial grouping, the family. A child may be asked to draw a picture of his family, including or excluding any member of the family he chooses. These drawings become particularly relevant when children enter recovery.

Case Illustration—Sammy

Sammy, age seven, was the only child of poly-addicted parents who had just separated prior to the mother's beginning inpatient recovery when she was six months pregnant. Sammy, left in the care of a grandparent, was beginning recovery work during his mother's treatment.

During the assessment phase, when Sammy was asked to provide a drawing of his family, he sat with a puzzled look on his face, staring at the paper. After several minutes, he claimed that he could not draw the picture. Suspecting problems in visual, visual-motor, or motivational spheres, I asked the child to talk about the problems that kept him from drawing. "Coz, I ain't got no *family*," Sammy said woefully.

After several months of recovery work, the parents had reconciled and Sammy's baby sister had been born. At that time, he eagerly provided a family drawing, showing a family gathered together opening Christmas presents.

A child's peer group membership or other group relationships (school, church, clubs, foster care) can be assessed from parent reports, teacher reports, sibling reports, etc.; however, none of these provides the child's unique perceptions of his interpersonal world.

Within the context of each social grouping, a child receives as well as generates social interactions. Parents often assign a role to a child within the family, but the child has to accept that role in order to carry it out effectively. As children learn to discriminate the roles that others play, they begin to make judgments about the meanings of these part-whole relationships. They then choose their own roles from an array of possibilities. This sorting out of roles is commensurate with the cognitive functioning of children in this age group and is an ongoing process as children continue to develop and refine their place within their social networks. As the desired outcome of role behavior, children look for social rewards in terms of power, support, nurturance, and attention.

Children in middle childhood have not acquired sufficient self development to stabilize their social role behavior or personality development. Most of these children do *not* display one characteristic role. Often, a child's role will vary from family to school to peer group, and may vary within these social groupings over time. I have rarely found it useful to label a child in terms of a social role.

As the family's context shifts during recovery, a child may display a number of roles as he seeks to find his place among changing familial roles. As a child perceives the social roles which govern group interactions, he will vary his role so as to maximize his gains and minimize his losses. Role behavior may have very little, if anything, to do with the inner self of the child, which is protected from outward observation by the false-self façade of the social role.

FAMILY ASSESSMENT

The family assessment is usually scheduled as soon as possible after the initial interview. When the parent indicates that a certain member of the family will refuse to come for the appointment, the therapist simply and gently repeats that the meeting is for the *entire* family, leaving it up to the parent to arrange for the member's presence. If the family does appear without a certain member, this becomes part of the material for discussion in the assessment meeting.

Despite the emphasis on information-gathering, the family assessment appears to have a therapeutic effect on the family. Consequently, it is recommended that the therapist who will be working with the family be the one to do the assessment. Sensitive material often emerges at the family interview, and the therapist who facilitates this process makes an initial therapeutic bond with the family. It is countertherapeutic to change therapists at this point.

By the time the assessment begins, the therapist has many other sources of information about the child in recovery. She knows, for example, how capable the child is of tolerating the strong affect which may surface in the family assessment.

When all family members have gathered in the session and initial rapport is established, a child-centered method of information-gathering commences. The therapist announces that the family is going to play a game. This immediately reduces anxiety for the child. As the therapist distributes blank cards and pencils to the family members, they are asked to anonymously provide a one-sentence (or shorter) description of what they consider to be *the one most important problem in the family*. If there is a young child present who is unable to write, the therapist may allow the child to whisper a response to her; she then writes it on the card.

After all cards are gathered, the therapist plants two cards having to do with control dynamics. The cards are then read, one at a time, allowing time after each for discussion. One of the planted cards will be read with the words, "'Too strong.' The person who wrote this doesn't explain, but that person apparently believes that someone in the family is too strong." Family members usually look at each other with puzzled expressions and sometimes make open accusations about who might have written the card. Meanwhile, information is provided through their discussion about the power relationships in the family. Finally, before all the rest of the cards are read through, the therapist reads from a second planted card. "'Too weak.' Again, someone in the family believes that someone is too weak." Discussion proceeds as the family discusses who is too weak.

After all the cards have been read, the therapist explains that each family member appears to have a different perception of the "main" problem in the family, but that this does not mean that one person is more right than another. It simply means that people in the family *see* things differently, each through his or her own eyes. Whether or not the family notices that there were two cards too many, the therapist admits that she, too, played the game anonymously.

Family members are then told that they will be given a chance to play the game together as a group, but that they must reach consensus on the main problem in the family. They will be allowed 15 minutes for their discussion. The therapist then leaves the room, but remains behind a screen or within hearing distance, or views the family from behind a one-way mirror. This part of the exercise will disclose important information about communication styles, coalitions, power relationships, and cooperation. Often a family will not have reached consensus at the end of the 15-minute period; however, important information will have been gathered about the family's problem-solving capabilities.

During the family assessment information provided on questionnaires previously completed by one of the parents may be discussed. Of particular importance is the family's development in recovery, the support system being utilized, such as the twelve-step programs, and the other intimate relationships, such as sponsors, who have a direct bearing on family functioning.

PARENT FEEDBACK SESSION

As soon as possible following the family assessment, the therapist provides feedback to the parents. Children in recovery are not present at this time. From material in the initial interview, child play observation, psychological assessment, and family assessment, the therapist conceptualizes the key points of intervention with the child in recovery and presents these recommendations to the family. In the following chapter, we will consider the parents' involvement in the PACT (parents as co-therapist) child recovery model.

CHAPTER 11

Children's PACT Model of Family Treatment, Early Phase

[Empathic] responses have to be available in the child's everyday life-experiences, and preferably in relation to the primary caretakers; the proud glance or an encouraging word by a parent cannot be replaced by the most comprehensive and well-timed interpretations [by a therapist].

—Anna Ornstein, 1985, p. 361

In child recovery work it is important to think of the child's treatment and the parents' treatment as simultaneous. While developing the empathic potential of the parent, we are continually facilitating the development of a more adequate and responsive caretaking environment for the child.

As we discussed in Chapter 3, the concept of the child-self in relation to its selfobjects (caretakers), which is derived from Kohut's psychology of the self, is the bridge between individual and systems functioning. Reality considerations remind us that we are likely to spend only one or two hours a week with a child; the child will need to function many more hours within the selfobject (caretaking) milieu of the family. During beginning recovery work the parents are told that, of all available relationships, theirs will be the most valued and therapeutic for their child. Parents also are told their development as the child's most essential therapeutic allies is a goal of therapy.

However, just because they are no longer using chemicals, these parents are not immediately capable of providing their children with empathic responsiveness. In the early phase of recovery work, a parent may be so preoccupied with his own physical recovery that he continues to turn inward. This self-centering is essential for the parent to become more effective in performing his own self-monitoring functions. Krystal (1978) describes this most basic of problems in the chemically dependent individual:

> He is unable to claim, own up to, and exercise various parts of himself. . . . Without being consciously aware of it, he experiences himself unable to carry out these functions. (p. 215)

In other words, the alcoholic/addicted parent whose family of origin did not acknowledge him as a separate, autonomous self will require a period of growth in order to experience himself as whole. Much of the success of Alcoholics Anonymous and the other twelve-step programs derives from the fact that they provide a selfobject milieu. Here, the newly recovering parent is able to function within a supportive "holding environment" until he can internalize healthier self-care activities to replace the old, addictive behaviors. Until he has begun to experience himself as whole, it is unlikely that the newly recovering parent will be able to see his child as a separate, unique individual. Until the parent's self is strengthened in sobriety, he may not be able to exercise enough self-forgetting to cross the empathic bridge to understand his child's inner state.

In this chapter, we will consider how work with the family in recovery proceeds through the early phase of recovery. Specifically, we will formulate the PACT (parents as co-therapists) model of family treatment.

TREATMENT PLANNING

When a chemically dependent parent accepts treatment, the child may become involved in some aspect of the parent's inpatient or outpatient care. Ideally, the parent's acute treatment phase should provide the parents with a wealth of basic information about the recovery needs of their children. Parents simply do not know about many of the problems affecting their school-aged children. If they are led to believe that their own recovery is the cure-all, the child will suffer. Parents also should not be led to believe that a "family week" is going to resolve problems for their children once and for all. The message, communicated in an informative, educative manner, needs to be simply, but directly, stated:

> Children from chemically dependent families are known to suffer from numerous problems during their elementary school years. This is a rule, not the exception.
>
> Certain problems in development may not even be detectable without a complete evaluation, but may affect a child's ability to learn. Often these learning problems contribute to conduct problems in the classroom. Other problems include emotional conflict, stress-related symptoms, eating problems such as obesity or anorexia, and many confused attitudes about the self and the family.
>
> Your child will need to have a sustained period of recovery. In the same way that you are going to need special assistance during your recovery, your child also needs ongoing attention.
>
> You will be improving your child's chances of realizing good mental health if you begin now. Make a commitment to the children in your family to see that they are given the resources they need for care during their childhood years.

Parents must be educated early in their recovery about their children's need for assessment to clearly document *how* they have been affected by addictive family life — not *if* they have been affected, but *how* they have been affected.

As we learned in the previous chapter, an assessment of the child's psychological and academic picture will point out the key areas for intervention. Because of the complexities and vicissitudes of development, we cannot make assumptions about a particular child's functioning simply from appearances. Through viewing the still photograph of a child's unique position in perceptual, cognitive, affective, motoric, social and motivational spheres, as well as examining stress resilience and self-regulation, we soon visualize where child services must begin. I am often amazed when parents tell me that their child was in a previous therapy experience for as long as a year or more, but no assessment was ever completed.

We are doing the child a disservice if we do not build the therapeutic relationship with a regard for his or her unique development. Empathic relating means receiving the child's signals and responding to the messages that the child is sending. Unless we have a developmental map to guide our interaction, we are likely to ignore or misinterpret the child's signals.

Societal agencies, such as children's services, adoption agencies, probation, etc., are usually cooperative in providing psychological reports that have already been completed on a child. Ideally, treatment centers would provide this same service to families — *if* psychological services for children were valued as a priority in the treatment package for the recovering parent. Although alcoholism is espoused to be a family disease, in practical application evaluation and treatment are reserved for the affected parent. More reasoned feedback to alcoholic parents regarding their children, followed by appropriate referrals, increases the likelihood that children will receive ongoing recovery. I am convinced that the prevention of serious alcohol and drug problems affecting our nation must concentrate on providing recovery to these high-risk youngsters.

In planning services for the child, we must determine where the first points of intervention should be concentrated. If a child is having serious problems in the classroom of either an academic or behavioral type, we need to collaborate with the teacher, the parents, and the child. Work with children in recovery means that the child therapist must often take a strong advocacy position for the child's academic and social well-being (see the case Illustration of Martin, Chapter 4). For example, arranging a classroom observation, where one is able to view a sample of the child's actual behavior in the academic setting, is helpful. These observations can be made without the child's awareness and are usually arranged by the teacher or other school personnel. Teachers are usually eager for information on how to work with a troubled child, especially when they understand the background of the child's struggles. In most instances, parents are cooperative about allowing this exchange of information to take place between the school and the therapist. Tutorial assistance, visual and neurological examinations, and/or remedial classes might result from a school observation.

CHILDREN'S PACT MODEL OF FAMILY THERAPY

When children in recovery and their parent(s) are seen for the initial session, the major intervention with the parents is to elicit the cooperation in allowing the child to participate in recovery work. Newly sobering or drug-free parents are extremely guilt-ridden and fearful about their children. The following are some of their common fears:

- That the child may reveal to the therapist events which may have happened while a parent was in a blackout and which are unknown even to the parent.

- That the therapist will form an alliance with the child against the parent.
- That the therapist will form an alliance with the spouse against the parent.
- That the therapist will form an alliance with other societal agencies, such as juvenile services, against the parent.
- That the therapist will be punitive and blaming.
- That the therapist will be ineffective with the child.
- That the therapist will be effective with the child and family change *will* occur.

No doubt there are many other fears which are idiosyncratic to a particular parent. The bottom line is that the early phase of recovery work with the child is extremely tenuous — *unless* there are other individuals, such as a spouse or agency personnel, persuading the parent to seek treatment for the child. For this reason, a parental agreement, or PACT, is obtained. This allows the child to remain in treatment for a period of approximately one year and is subject to renegotiation at the end of that time.

The major interventions with the parent during this time are based on a supportive/observational model. Supporting the parents through early phase recovery work, the therapist models empathic interactions with the child. These interactions comprise the first 10–15 minutes of the child's session. Later, in a session with the parents, the therapist processes observations and corrects misperceptions. However, any "correcting" must be done with tact and sensitivity. Anna Ornstein describes this basic difficulty in child-centered family work:

> Not to take sides appears to be the greatest challenge to child therapists, who, more often than not, are deeply identified with the child and are tempted to "educate" the parents in their parental responsibilities. Giving advice and educating the parents, however, appear to increase parental guilt and defensiveness and may have serious consequences for treatment: the parents, unable to follow the advice because of their own imperative emotional needs and because they do not feel heard by the therapist become increasingly resentful toward the child for making them feel inadequate as parents. (p. 361)

The empathic-supportive relationship with the parents during their entire first year of recovery may offset guilt and defensiveness about parenting issues. As trust increases, a parent may admit to the therapist that he actually doesn't know the first thing about how to parent his children, that his own role models were faulty, and that he even fears he may have already damaged his offspring. A therapist who is seen as being able to provide valuable information on child-rearing practices is not viewed as withholding or depriving by a parent who truly doesn't know and has a genuine need to know.

Stage I — Disavowal

Children *are* aware of the horrors of alcoholic and drug-abusing family life. They *are* aware when, in these families, they have been sexually or physically violated, or emotionally bruised, or ignored and neglected. They do recall witnessing violent or sexually provocative parental interactions.

A child beginning recovery will be able to recount many of the vivid details of traumatic family scenes. These details are typically told in the form of an emotionless soliloquy. The absence of affect leads the adult observer to the mistaken notion that the child, like the other adults in the family, is denying feelings — as though the child had access to emotions which are deliberately being avoided.

However, denial, as a defense against the *awareness* of a painful aspect of reality, assumes the ability to cognitively and emotionally assimilate the problem. A drunken alcoholic mother has the *ability*, when she sobers, to see and comprehend that her intoxicated behavior may have harmed her children. She may even experience guilt and remorse. But children in the middle years of childhood have not developed the capacity in logical thinking to assimilate many of their bewildering experiences in the addictive family system. A child such as seven-year-old Kyle in Chapter 3 could not reason that this father was breaking all the upstairs windows as a way of shocking the drunken mother into compliance. Moreover, Kyle was not capable of extending his perceptions into the logical explanation: "Both my parents are under the influence of the drug, alcohol, and while this has nothing to do with them as people, they're sick and they need help, and, further, their self-centeredness is making them ineffective as parents to me." Limited by his developmental position, Kyle was able only to huddle inside the closet, listening to the shattering glass, experiencing abandonment anxiety, but disavowing the meaning of parental neglect and psychological maltreatment.

Without the assistance of a calming, soothing selfobject to provide him with adult logic and verbal explanations, Kyle could not be expected to assimilate and integrate the full meaning of his parents' conduct. The disavowal of meaning was walled off behind a false self who had to face the external world—the very next day—in the second grade classroom. There, among 26 other children, Kyle was expected to function adaptively. Listening and comprehending his teacher's instructions and behaving cooperatively with his peers, he behaved as though the previous night of family destruction had not even happened. When Kyle's ability to self-regulate broke down, he became fidgety and agitated in the classroom and began to displace his aggression by punching a classmate. He was then sent to the principal's office and labeled "conduct problem."

Youngsters from nonaddictive homes whom I have treated for the post-traumatic effects of accidents and injuries differ from the children of alcoholic/addictive families in one important respect. When the young accident/injury victims are seen initially, they will usually show some sign of emotion associated with the painful recall of the traumatic events. A child may become weepy, for example, when describing a particularly upsetting scene, such as crossing the street with a peer who was struck down by a drunken driver and fatally injured. Children from alcoholic/addictive families are protected from their emotional injuries by the wall of disavowal.

Case Illustration—Tamara

Seven-year-old Tamara had lived with her heroin- and alcohol-addicted parents, traveling from one motel room to the next, sleeping in the same bed with her mother and father, suffering neglect, and often being without food. But she had been most frightened, according to the social worker, by seeing her parents self-administer heroin by injection.

When Tamara was taken into foster placement and began recovery, she did not want to talk about her life with her parents. She remembered, but she did not want to experience the unsettling agitation which accompanied the memories. During her exploration of the playroom, she came upon a play doctor's kit with a plastic syringe. During her explanation of the purpose of the syringe, she began to talk about when her parents used to shoot heroin. Then, quickly, she asked me to take the syringe away, and within the course of the next ten minutes she asked several times to make trips to the water fountain.

Disavowal shields the child from emotions that may be directed towards the source of the trauma—in this case, the mother and father. A child can ill-afford to become rageful towards the parent(s) whom he loves. Even youngsters who have been removed from their families because of harsh physical or sexual abuse by a parent will be bland and emotionless when talking about the abuse. Their feelings of rage, despair, and fear are effectively contained within the cloisters of the real self, sealed off behind the wall of disavowal.

Basch (1983), in his comprehensive discussion of the differences between disavowal and denial, provides an example regarding the child's experience of parent loss. Although the reality of the loss is accepted, the disavowal of the meaning of the loss results in an arrest in development. This arrest can only be resolved later, when the affect appropriate to the loss is stimulated and worked through in the therapy. This rings familiar to the condition we describe as "the adult child syndrome," where the apparent developmental arrest accounts for the preservation of aspects of the self in its original childhood form.

Terr (1988) has determined that very young children who have experienced trauma do not use repression or denial to defend against these memories. Rather, these children can recall these events with "impressive accuracy and detail" many years later. Terr conducted a study on 20 young people who had suffered severe trauma (such as sexual abuse, witnessing a death, etc.) at a very early age. As long as the child had been at least 28 months old at the time of the trauma, the child had direct access to verbal memories of the trauma. A child's ability to construct grammatically ordered verbal phrases appeared to account for his/her ability to recall these traumatic happenings.

Children from alcoholic/addictive families typically do not talk about many of the conflicting aspects of their family life, even though they retain accurate recall. These children simply have not been socialized to realize that the transfer of ideas through words is a preferred mode of dealing with conflict. They observe the adults in the home "acting" rather than talking. They see physical aggression and escape into addictive practice as common modes of communication. Verbal communication is not used by either parent or child to address grievances. It is not so much that there is a "rule" at the level of the family system that no one *should* talk; rather, most of these children do not talk because they lack the verbal prowess to do so. No one talks to them. It does not occur to them that talking can resolve one's innermost turmoil. Accordingly, "talking" therapy will be very awkward for these children in the early phase of recovery.

There are three major goals in this early disavowal stage of child-centered recovery work:

(1). *Recognize the child's legitimate, phase-appropriate need to ward off painful emotional stimulation.* Accompanying any stressor is a response that produces in the child a set of biochemical reactions. When the child is in the relaxed state, the two branches of the central nervous system — the parasympathetic and sympathetic — are balanced in a state of homeostasis. Under stress, the sympathetic nervous system becomes aroused to secrete the chemical, adrenaline. In a hyperaroused state, the child is bewildered and fearful. A child who is continually sensitized by stress develops a predisposition to overreact to the next stress. The cycle goes something like this:

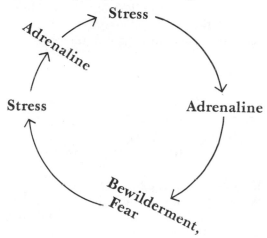

. . . and on and on. In children from the poly-addicted family these hyperaroused states are usually expressed behaviorally. A child will *not* tell us: "I feel panicky, out of control, subject to the whims of my parents' craziness, and I cannot bring about my inner self-regulation to recover homeostasis." The child expresses this message through fidgeting, eating candy, busyness, or driven, compulsive striving. Busyness is simply another way of dealing with agitation. Agitated children are the ones about which a parent complains: "This kid is driving *me* crazy."

Children need to experience calm internal states, particularly during the period of latency development. They need to have a way of deescalating their anxieties. Assisting children in recovery begins with helping them reduce arousal to more normal levels of frequency and intensity. I do not believe that children receive this tension reduction when we continue to focus on the source of their trauma, the abusive family interactions, *unless* they initiate the discussion.

(2) *Recognize the likelihood that the child lacks internal psychological processes for self-soothing*. Children from addictive families have not internalized calm, soothing caretaker experiences. They suffer a deficit in their ability to perform self-soothing functions. A therapeutic forum for soothing is provided through the child's medium of play. Activities which promote self-soothing include games, art, music, puppets, sand tray, dollhouses, and the like. The encouragement of fantasy through play is the route towards stabilizing latency development. When we increase the capacity for fantasy through play, we enhance the child's ability to be in a calm, pliable state. A naturally cooperative attitude accompanies normal latency states. With an increased cooperative attitude, the child will be more receptive to verbal interactions in sibling and family group meetings or parent-child meetings.

Fantasy play also provides information for the therapist about the child's developmental position and conflicts. An eight-year-old boy who fills the sand tray with immature, oversized toys placed in a random, chaotic manner may be functioning in a regressed state. Over time, as we begin to see the child order his sand play in a more refined and age-appropriate manner, we observe his developmental progression.

With the therapist sitting quietly by, allowing the child to take the lead, the mirroring function is the key therapeutic strategy. A therapist used to being more active in a session will likely feel anxious and begin to question what possible good this play does for the child. Recall, however, that these children have rarely, if ever, enjoyed the luxury of having an adult mirror their creative productions, or engage in dialogue as they directed, or join in the play alongside them (*if* they request it).

(3) *Recognize the child's desperate need for self articulation and affirmation and the need to develop a bond with a trusted adult who can facilitate the expression of that self*. When we talk about the child's need for "self" articulation, we are not talking about "identity" or "identification." We already assume that the child's process of identification with parental role models has been faulty (see Chapter 5). We assume that she has suffered humiliation and ridicule, that her self-esteem is virtually lacking. We can also assume that a child's identity—her sense of who she is—has been blurred by the addictive family system. Self articulation, however, refers to the freeing of the real, spontaneous child-

self which has been imprisoned behind a false-self façade of protective defenses seen in the playing of a social role.

Anna Ornstein (1985) explains that the therapeutic potential for liberating this child-self is *created* in the very act of therapist and child playing together. Psychotherapy with play is indeed the method for facilitating the expression of the child's innermost self.

Too much verbal interaction between therapist and child often limits this process. The therapist's words may be experienced as invading the child's sense of self. Words, which can be used to build an empathic bridge to the child's inner world, can also be used to intrude, and thereby separate and alienate. Respectful silence during fantasy play can join, and thereby accomplish a sense of union or bonding.

Because of the likelihood that the parent cannot function as a soothing selfobject during early recovery, it is important to recognize the child's need to feel a sense of attachment to a calming adult. During this early phase, the child needs to have a feeling of connectedness with the therapist as a source of calm.

Sibling Interventions

When a child referral does not include all children within the family, the therapist requests that all siblings be brought in for the family assessment. Later, a meeting of the sibling subsystem, where the children function apart from their parents, is observed.

Joining is best served by seeing each sibling individually. A child needs to be known and respected for his/her uniqueness. As each child's special place in the family is acknowledged, the therapeutic leverage for changing the dynamics of the sibling subsystem is developed.

Bonding between therapist and the various siblings is best accomplished not through talking therapy but through the childhood media of play. (If one or more of the siblings are of pubertal age or adolescence, they are usually seen in a regular talking therapy session.)

Referral of a sibling to an outside therapist may be required because of a child's age, sex, or special therapeutic needs. The family should be told that the sibling will need to return from time to time for family group therapy or sibling group therapy as these become necessary.

Exploring sibling legacies with parents during the early phase of recovery uncovers unconscious parenting attitudes that may exist towards a particular child in the family. For example, a parent who was a middle child may hold an attitude of favoritism towards her own middle child without ever realizing it. These relationships, which are based on ghosts of the past, can be discussed more fully in the parent sessions during the middle phase of therapy.

Parent Therapy — Early Phase

In working with the child-parent unit of the addictive family system, I have been struck by the need to be empathically responsive to a third dimension of this unit, which in Kohut's terms might be called the "self-selfobject-self" or, in my own conceptualization, the child/parent(child). It is this (child)self of the parent which becomes stimulated very early during the inclusion phase of my therapeutic work with children — sometimes even as early as the first interview. Very early I encounter this wounded (child) in the recovering parent or spouse, which has been reached vicariously through my interactions with his/her children.

During this early observational period, the parent and I meet together with the child for a brief 10–15-minute period at the beginning of the child's session. As the parent becomes emotionally responsive to my interaction with their child, I often notice the parent's softening, sometimes becoming misty-eyed. Later, in private, the parent will confide to me a particular hurt that has been revived from behind her own wall of disavowal. For the first time since her youth, the meaning of a particular childhood trauma has been joined with emotion. This is the beginning of the parent's therapeutic "training" in empathy, which will continue to be developed during the course of the PACT work. Empathy for the child's trauma is rarely achieved by a parent who has not recovered access to her own childhood wounds.

Maintaining the necessary therapeutic balance of empathy between the child in recovery and the parent(child) is sometimes a Herculean task. When we remember that during the inclusion phase of family processes the recovering parent experiences low power and low status within the family, we will realize that, in many ways, this parent feels small and childlike. (Indeed, in certain parts of the country, the newly sobering individual is dubbed a "baby" during his first year in Alcoholics Anonymous.)

When we recall that the major family process goal of the inclusion phase is how to find *belonging* among a "family" of strangers, we will not find it difficult to be sensitive to the bewilderment of both parent and child. Working with the newly recovering family is not unlike working with a group of refugees who have been displaced from their native land and are trying to carve out a place on unfamiliar, foreign soil. Sobriety *is* a foreign experience for the family in early recovery.

The Role of the Twelve-Step Program

Parents in recovery are required to participate in Alcoholics Anonymous and/or any of the other applicable programs modeled after A.A., such as Narcotics Anonymous, Cocaine Anonymous, Overeaters Anonymous, Al-Anon, Nar-Anon, etc. The "twelve steps" of these programs are believed to be the most direct avenue towards approaching the grandiose, false-self organization, which dictated the old, addictive style of nonrelatedness.

The therapeutic task has been described in early psychiatric literature exploring the work of A.A. (Tiebout, 1954). Tiebout, who was a therapist to Bill Wilson, one of the co-founders of A A , described the alcoholic individual as having an "inflated-Ego." Tiebout made a distinction between "ego" (as it has been used in our discussion in Chapter 7) and "Ego," which refers to the extreme narcissism or self-centeredness of the parent before recovery. Tiebout describes this type of Ego inflation:

> Such a person appears thick skinned, insensitive, nearly impervious to the existence of others, a completely self-centered individual who plows unthinkingly through life, intent on gathering unto himself all the comforts and satisfactions available. He is generally considered the epitome of selfishness. . . . (p. 3)

Although Tiebout did not discuss the role of psychoactive drugs in contributing to this "self-centeredness," it is recognized that chemicals bolster the enfeebled self to new heights of narcissism. Drugs such as alcohol, cocaine, crack, amphetamines, and others are all "Ego inflaters." They provide inner states of power, euphoria, grandiosity. Rarely do these now alcoholic/addicted individuals begin to use drugs because they *already* possess strength and well-being. They drink or use to *achieve* a sense of competence and interpersonal effectiveness.

> . . . it is from our twisted relations with family, friends, and society at large that many of us have suffered the most. We have been especially stupid and stubborn about them. The primary fact that we fail to recognize is our total inability to form a true partnership [selfobject

relationship] with another human being. Our egomania digs two disastrous pitfalls. Either we insist upon dominating the people we know,
or we depend upon them far too much. If we lean too heavily on
people, they will sooner or later fail us, for they are human, too, and
cannot possibly meet our incessant demands. (*Alcoholics Anonymous*,
1976, p. 53)

A oneness or "merger" with others is made possible through the
omnipotent selfobject of *the drug*, which the individual believes *he can
control* through self-administration. The patient's disorder of the self
is served by the addiction as the powerful regulator of self-esteem
that always works, never fails, and never disappoints . . . well, almost never.

Self-induced states of merger overcome the basic state of nonrelatedness. Major disappointments and lack of trust experienced in the
childhood family of origin have led the addicted parent to seek adult
love and solace, not from his disappointing spouse or his frustrating
children, but from chemicals.

If abstinence is ever to be accomplished and ongoing, Tiebout
says, we must strive for a complete Ego reduction. He stresses the
difficulties a single therapist will encounter in trying to accomplish
this goal. Outside assistance is needed, he claims, and is needed
"urgently." This outside help needs to consist of a selfobject milieu
which offers round-the-clock support to the abstinent individual undergoing Ego reduction work.

Below we review the twelve steps of A.A. from a self psychological
perspective, following the example of others who have explained the
twelve steps from different psychological perspectives (Ryan, 1984 —
eclectic; Brown, 1985 — Eriksonian; Schrenk, 1985 — ego psychology). The steps are effective transformers of the narcissistic layers of
the personality and thereby increase the parent's capacity for empathy with the child. Steps one through five appear to be most relevant
to the goals of the early inclusion phase of family processes. Those
which facilitate control phase issues are six through nine, while steps
ten, eleven, and twelve increase the capacity for intimate relating.

> Step 1: We admitted that we were powerless over alcohol (cocaine,
> food, drugs, etc.) and that our lives had become unmanage-
> able.

In twelve-step programs this first step is usually extended to embrace the notion that we were powerless over other people, places

and things. The first step is an admission that alcohol (or other addictive substances, people, places or things) has failed as a regulator of self-esteem and is no longer an effective way of "managing" the self.

This step expresses traumatic disappointment in the idealized, omnipotent addictive selfobject. Indeed, the previously esteemed "power" whether a chemical, person, place, or activity is now admitted to be a betrayer, even a persecutor, which threatens the total annihilation of the self.

The secondary notion (" . . . and that our lives had become unmanageable") provides some sense of stability to the inner chaos and confusion by offering the first glimmer of reality.

Previously, the alcoholic/addicted parent had been functioning under the delusion of invulnerability, encapsulated by feelings of calm, soothing, power, escape, provided by the substance or activity. This step usually attests to the person's non relatedness to other people. By interfering with the notion of self-sufficiency (admission of powerlessness) it opens up the possibility of change at the family system level.

> Step 2: Came to believe that a power greater than ourselves could restore us to sanity.

At the time of embracing this step, the parent in his helplessness and vulnerability has begun to satisfy "merger" needs with the more reliable selfobject of the A.A. sponsor and A.A. group. "Came to believe . . . " describes the cognitive realization of the self-stabilizing function of this new "higher power" (idealized selfobject) who serves as the all-powerful, all-knowing source of good for the depleted, empty, powerless self.

Note that this step does not seek to define the "higher power," but simply hints at more intact ego functioning and superior reality-testing ("restore us to sanity") that will be provided as a result of this "merger." This step is the beginning of the new, two-person, non-addictive system.

The therapist must keep uppermost in mind the fact that the "new family system" which is being reconstituted will include the A.A. or other twelve-step sponsor and members of the twelve-step group. The sponsor's importance as a prominent selfobject is often overlooked by therapists, who later wonder why the family system has become so confusing. Indeed, the influence of A.A. appears to be one of the reasons why many "pure" family therapists become disgruntled with the twelve-step approach. However, when the contributions of the twelve-step program's selfobject milieu are thoroughly recognized and understood, they may be seen as compatible with family therapy.

> Step 3: Made a decision to turn our lives and our will over to the care
> of God as we understand Him, relying only on knowledge of
> His will for us and the power to carry it out.

Self-sufficiency and the grandiose self are now being relinquished gradually to the "care" of the idealized selfobject, which has come to be made manifest through the A.A. group. Here, the simple remedies of self-care are relearned. These self-comforting or "mothering" functions are turned over to the care of the all powerful selfobject (God, as we understand Him; A.A.). The narcissistic fear of losing one's autonomy or very self, of being "swallowed up" by the other has been forestalled. Yielding to the new "good object" (God; A.A.) is still another cognitive choice for a life apart from the previous destruction at the hands of the addictive persecutor.

> Step 4: Made a searching and fearless moral inventory of ourselves.

This step begins with an inherent contradiction. A.A. takes as its starting point the notion that life has become "unmanageable," and that increasingly the power for one's life is turned over (control is relinquished). But this step begins the emphasis on personal responsibility for one's life. Another paradoxical aspect of this step is the empahsis on the word "fearless," as a way of circumventing resistance to change.

The notion of change, regardless of how vigorously it may be sought, is still dreaded and resisted. Implied in this step is the notion that the former "self" will have to be replaced by a new psychic organization. (The preamble of A.A. drives this notion home even further: "With all the earnestness at our command, we ask you to be fearless and thorough from the very start. Some of us have tried to hold on to our *old ideas*, and the result was nil until we let go absolutely") (1976, p. 58, italics mine).

The notion of a "moral inventory" stresses a realistic self-appraisal, of being able to distinguish immature segments of the personality (character defects) from mature resources, talents, and abilities. This step is the very portal through which one becomes reunited with the ambitions, goals, values and ideals which spring from the nuclear self. "Moral" also stresses superego dynamics and the increasingly realistic ego functions. Old psychic structures are not simply given up, but evolve into new ones which, under the influence of the A.A. group and sponsor (selfobject milieu), become more differentiated as new indentifications occur.

At this juncture in the therapy issues related to problems in parenting and parenting failures typically begin to surface. For the first time, the recovering parent may be able to express some awareness of the implications of his/her addictive practices on the life of the child. Although empathy remains to be fully developed in the parent, this parent may begin to express some regrets to the children for his past treatment of them. These "amends" are usually facilitated in separate parent-child sessions or a family group session after resolution of control phase issues.

> Step 5: Admitted to God, to ourselves, and to another human being the exact nature of our wrongs.

This step is often experienced with dread, as it recreates a time in childhood when parents urged, "grow up, 'fess up, CHANGE." The pressure to change tends to liberate a whole array of old self-protective defenses. However, as the recovering parent steps out into the clear light of day from behind the walls of his false-self prison, he sees that he is able to be his own, competent self-critic, and that he has the mature ability to face his imperfections. By exposing his worst view of himself, he experiences his own deepest vulnerability — and what's more, he survives! No destabilizing of the self occurs; rather, the self is calmed and strengthened. Self-acceptance leads the parent further down the pathway of empathy towards his own children.

The parent's individual recovery efforts, including work with the first five steps, increase his potential to both want and need more participation in shaping the destiny of the family. The parent will be greatly helped in moving in the direction of the middle phase of child recovery work by the following step, which increases the chances for successful resolution of control phase issues.

> Step 6: Were entirely ready to have God remove all these defects of character.

The sixth step concentrates on superego dynamics running parallel to the recognition of more mature personality functioning of which one is capable. By yielding the notion of control to the omnipotent, omniscient selfobject (God; A.A.), one begins to have the experience of — not the dreaded self annihilation — but self stabilization!

The old psychic structures (character defects), which were made manifest in the earlier fourth step moral inventory, are seen as the *source* of one's difficulties. No longer is one able to blame other people, places or things. Personal responsibility is again fostered.

A "readiness" for change nevertheless implies some active participation in the change process. For the alcoholic who has never admitted — let alone surrendered — these parts of the self to anyone (parents, spouse, employers, etc.), the readiness for removal implies giving up control. There is the implicit notion that underneath these defects of character (protective false-self façade) one will arrive at one's own mirror image of perfection, the real self.

The seventh step, which has a paradoxical ring, not only requests change, but requests it *humbly*! This is the pivotal step which leads towards a changed relationship with the children.

Step 7: Humbly asked Him to remove our shortcomings.

Change had heretofore been equated with loss of control; however, asking is an undoing of the fear of God's removal without permission. As these primitive forms of narcissism are transformed through the step, ambivalence and mistrust decrease. There is an acceptance of one's own vulnerability before the idealized parent image (God; A.A.). This is a reworking of the original childhood trauma, when one was completely usurped of selfhood by parental authority — when one was "created" by the parents in accordance with their needs, whims, and wishes — giving rise to the protective layer of defenses which we call "character defects" or the "false-self façade."

After being controlled in childhood without any say in the matter, one now has the opportunity to "ask" for removal of these character defenses from the idealized parent image, God.

The next two steps are important in facilitating the resolution of selfobject failings on the part of each marital partner. Until now, the recovering parent (and even the spouse) may not have entertained the notion of oneself as a disappointing selfobject for others. One simply looked out past one's own hurt and disappointment to one's collection of grievances against others.

Step 8: Made a list of all persons we had harmed and became willing
         to make amends to them all.

This step continues the journey outside one's own egocentrism and the selfobject grievances one has collected to the notion of *oneself* as a disappointing, imperfect selfobject for others. This "willingness" to make amends is another step down the pathway of improved reality-testing, personal accountability, and empathic attunement to others.

The ninth step may not begin until near the end of the first year of recovery, or even into the second year and beyond. However, it is the time when the parent will begin to make verbal restitution to his or her children according to their needs, not his own. This means that the parent must first have some empathic attunement to the child's needs.

> Step 9: Made direct amends to such people wherever possible, except
> when to do so would injure them or others.

Continuing in the same theme of recognizing oneself as a disappointing selfobject for others, one now accepts personal responsibility for the need to acknowledge these failures by making "amends." This step is crucial in helping to neutralize the narcissistic rage that one has collected along the way from previous selfobject failings of others. By recognizing one's own imperfections, one can be more tolerant and realistic when others do not conform to one's expectations.

The additional steps, ten through twelve, greatly facilitate the recovering parent's self-cohesion, thereby increasing the capacity for moving into the other phases of family process dynamics.

> Step 10: Continued to take personal inventory and when we were
> wrong promptly admitted it.

Self-appraisal has become increasingly realistic. This implies the capacity to evaluate one's own limitations and to consider them in terms of their impact on others. This is the gateway to empathic relating.

Superego development has been further strengthened by the internalization of values which affect social interaction. This represents the achievement of a more integrated and cohesive self organization. No longer is the focus on the failings of other people; it is on the conscious assessment of one's own moral turpitude.

Previous steps focused on living up to the standards of the superego (God, as we understand Him; the "Higher Power"). On a daily basis, one becomes aware of one's imperfections. To offset the arousal of anxiety resulting from the recognition that one is, after all, imperfectly human and to restore psychic equilibrium, we have step eleven.

> Step 11: Sought through prayer and meditation to improve our conscious contact with God as we understood Him praying only for knowledge of His will for us and the power to carry that out.

In step ten there was an emphasis on living up to the standards of perfection, while admitting to one's daily imperfections. Finding the self lacking in maintaining the ideal of perfection, a stabilizing merger is sought with the omnipotent, omniscient selfobject. The notion of internalization of this perfected image is implied through the phrase, "God as we *understood* Him." By extending consciousness to the ultimate ideal, one restores inner harmony to the self. Knowing through one's highest experience of reality leads to strength (power) and calm (serenity).

The final step implies the character shifts that have taken place. No longer are others used narcissistically as mere gratifiers of one's own needs; rather, they are viewed as having needs of their own. Unselfish service provided to others now becomes a way of life.

> Step 12: Having had a spiritual awakening as the result of these steps, we tried to carry this message to alcoholics, and to practice these principles in all our affairs.

A life which has been stripped of immature narcissism now integrates interpersonal responsibility and selfless love. This step has an element of transcendence ("spiritual awakening"), asserting an inner life of harmony, lucidity, and tranquility. Self-preoccupation is no longer practiced; rather, internalized values and ideals guide behavior.

Individuals in twelve-step programs are urged to continue "working" these steps, which consists of continuing to apply them to practical problems in their daily lives. The "Ego-deflating" or transforming ability of the steps is dependent on their ongoing application, not unlike the ongoing process of working-through conflicts in psychotherapy.

Psychotherapists historically have looked unfavorably on A.A., and from recent evidence (Schrenk, 1985) it seems that they continue to lag in using the program, despite professed intention to do so.

Even after therapists took part in an educational presentation of the steps in the language of ego psychology, long-term follow-up revealed that there was a lack of congruence between their stated intent to refer and their actual referral process.

Yet, we know that the existence of a supportive social network is one of the major factors which has been found to interrupt the cycle of abuse in alcoholic/addictive parents who were abused as children. A psychotherapist will not be able to provide the intensive, supportive milieu which these parents in recovery both require and deserve.

Parent Education

Parent education regarding child-rearing practices is generally reserved until the end of the early, inclusion phase. One of the major reasons for delaying is that parents in early recovery suffer cognitive impairment which makes it overwhelming for them to absorb more than the most essential of basic information. A secondary reason is our desire to foster the parent's primary concentration on the working of the A.A. steps and recovery program, which includes a number of reading materials.

Very early in therapy, parents are instructed to remove all sugar from the children's diet. This will need to be reinforced with additional education. Recovering parents seem to have a very difficult time with the feelings of deprivation which *they* appear to suffer when their children are not allowed "treats." When the parent is nearing one year of sobriety, certain educational materials are provided to help the parent understand the relationship to alcoholism and nutrition. One of these, *The Care and Feeding of Children of Alcoholics* (Jesse, in press) is an easily read book which is specific to the nutritional needs and parenting problems of children in the middle years of childhood. Another resource which I suggest at this time is *Breaking the Cycle of Addiction: A Parent's Guide to Raising Healthy Kids* (O'Gorman and Oliver-Diaz, 1987). Depending on the parents' other therapy obligations and willingness, a series of local parenting classes also may be recommended.

Although the early, inclusion phase of family processes is considered to span the parent's first year of recovery, this time period may vary. Less time may be required when the family has experienced less disruption and when parental alcoholism has been arrested in the early stages. The inclusion phase may take longer, however, when there is family instability due to separation, divorce, or children moving in and out of the home as a result of extrafamilial placement. With destructive, disorganizing consequences of incest, physical abuse, familial violence, the period of family stabilization may take as long as two to three years.

The average period of about six to eight months is offered as a reasonable indicator of the amount of time that it takes for the recovering parents to begin to move into the leadership role which initiates the control phase of family processes.

CHAPTER 12

Children's PACT Model of Family Treatment, Middle Phase and Ongoing Recovery

Whoever humbles himself like this child, he is the greatest in the kingdom of heaven.

—Matthew, 18:4

Recovery is about change. Recovery for the child is about changing the relationships among her parents, her siblings, and herself. Recovery work with a child establishes a meeting ground where the changes in these relationships can begin to take place.

At a certain point in the child's recovery, a parent must begin to humble himself or herself in the child's presence. To acknowledge that the destructive family processes of alcoholism and addiction were wrongful acts against the child is the beginning of mental health for both child and parent. It is not enough for the parent to say, "I'm sorry if I hurt you with my alcohol and drug using. . . . " That parent must use new skills of empathy to cross the bridge to the child's inner world of turmoil and confusion, to say to the child, "I know how troubled and how frightened you have been, how very much alone you have felt when I was drinking, and how you have had a right to feel hurt and angry. . . . "

A child wants and desperately needs to hear these admissions from a parent—not from a therapist, not from a teacher, not from another relative or trusted adult, or even a peer or sibling — but from the PARENT!

Developing recovering parents' therapeutic potential to provide a healing experience for their own children has been an area of neglect in the field of addictions. The still bitter sentiments of many adult children of alcoholics towards their parents (despite the parents' continuous abstinence for many years) attests to the residual childhood trauma which has not been worked through successfully.

Certainly the emphasis in the addictions field in the more recent past is that "*we*" must *do* something to help younger children recover from their traumatic family experiences. However, this *we* is implied to be a body of helping *professionals*. In all humility, *we* must admit that we are severely limited in our ability to help children through a process of recovery because of a number of realistic constraints:

1. If *we* work in acute care, we may see the child only for one hour a week at the most, with limited access to the family.
2. If *we* work in aftercare, we may see the child for one to two hours a week, perhaps over the course of a year, with a similar limitation in our contact with the family.
3. If *we* work in outpatient services, we still will see a child for only one, or possibly a few hours more, each week, and we may not see the family at all.
4. If *we* work in an institutional setting, we may have access to a residential child during our eight-hour shift, but we will have limited contact with the family.
5. If *we* work in a school setting, we are limited by constraints of time and our human limitations in trying to give quality time to a number of children all at once.
6. If *we* work in court-mandated programs, we may have considerable leverage to control the life of a child and even the family — within certain parameters — but we cannot exert much influence on how successful these individuals are in going about the business of being a family.

MIDDLE/CONTROL PHASE THERAPY

Control has become a nasty seven-letter word in much of the recent literature on alcoholism and addictions. We have learned, even in this discussion, that in these dysfunctional, addictive systems, everyone wants to control everyone else, and no one wants to admit that *everyone* is really out of control. This is what I have found to be the case in working with children and families in recovery: *Everyone wants control (including therapists), but no one wants to admit wanting it.*

The Therapist and Control

Much of the traditional work in family therapy is built upon the notion of the therapist having supreme control. Theorists such as Jay Haley, for example, view control and influence as belonging in the hands of the therapist — not the family. Other therapists who may use psychodrama, or Gestalt role-playing situations, and, yes, even Virginia Satir, would actually stage *direct* the family as a cast of characters, supervising the unfolding of any particular family drama to make a specific point or achieve the desired effect.

Bank and Kahn (1982, p. 300) suggest that the therapist is able to occupy a position of power and authority because the patient colludes — "by being weak, helpless, confused, desperate, amnesic, or shamefacedly manipulative." The PACT model would agree with Bank and Kahn in their observations, but would add the clarification that, yes, in parents who are recovering from physical addictions, the *early* stage of the treatment process is marked by their weakness, helplessness, confusion, desperation, lack of recall of pertinent past, and even manipulation of the therapist to "take charge" of them as well as of their family. Having begun with this admission, I would add that a therapist who does not accept these features as bona fide existential realities in a recovering parent will be making another kind of demand which the parent cannot meet. Expecting a parent to be strong, competent, clear-headed, hopeful, and ready to be attentive to family needs — simply because he or she is no longer using chemicals — is *expecting* a lot.

One needs to feel a sense of legitimacy as a therapist about exercising leadership functions for the recovering family *until* the parents develop their natural potential to serve as leaders. It is a reality of small group dynamics that whoever functions as a leader for that moment in time *is* the leader — regardless of whether or not one has been designated the leader. This is true for parents, siblings, and therapists. In beginning control phase work with families in recovery, I acknowledge that the parents are the leaders; however, *at the very moment in time that I am making this acknowledgement, I am the one who is functioning as a leader*.

Understanding one's own issues and needs for control is crucial before entering into control phase work with the family; otherwise, these needs tend to be denied and projected onto someone else. Control is inherent in any type of professional helping relationship, but too often is denied or exercised surreptitiously. This denial then serves the interest of the misuse and abuse of power and control. Until we become entirely aware of our own innermost responses to being controlled versus being in control, we will encounter a great deal of difficulty with the middle phase of family recovery work. We will be prone to deny the control which we seek, and we will not take responsibility for the control which is a part of our regular therapeutic conduct. For example, establishing the therapeutic framework by setting the time for family members to meet, how often they will meet, beginning and ending the session, deciding on the fee, and structuring the sessions are *all* control functions.

The misuse and abuse of control in child recovery work occur when one usurps the decisions for what will and will not be the agenda from the hands of the rightful owners — the family. When we do not allow the natural family processes to unfold, when we superimpose our own theory of labels and motivations, we rob the family of its spontaneously occurring growth potential to create a new system. On the other hand, when we are intimidated by the whole notion of control, we are likely to be countertherapeutic by relinquishing decisions which should not be made by one or the other of the parents.

Case Illustration — Ulric

Ulric was a ten-year-old boy with four younger siblings and parents who were addicted to alcohol and amphetamines. After Ulric was taken into foster placement because his mother had flailed him with a horse whip, his mother sought to constantly control the situation by almost daily complaints to the social worker. Shortly thereafter, Ulric's nine-year-old sister disclosed that her father had been sexually abusing her for several years.

Now that the family was identified as an "incest family," the fact that there were also severe problems with drugs and alcohol was overshadowed, as was the physical abuse of Ulric by his mother. Court decisions resulted in a host of various group experiences for perpetrators, partners, and victims of incest for the parents and the daughter. Although there was an order to "abstain from drugs," Ulric's mother translated this literally to mean that all they needed to do was to not drink or use drugs. No formal recovery program for chemical dependence was required. Thus, there was no coordinated effort to shepherd the parents and children through a recovery process which dealt with their bio-psycho-social-spiritual needs. No ongoing support network was available.

During Ulric's therapy, when the parents were required to become involved, they appeared to be in a perpetual state of relapse—anxious, sullen, hypersensitive, grandiose—with Ulric's mother demanding control. Indeed, she was angry with the therapist because Ulric's work must proceed, as stipulated by Children's Services. She did not understand why the *therapist* would not delay Ulric's recovery work, or why the *therapist* wouldn't intervene with the social worker to have the court order changed.

The parents stared at me blankly when I suggested that they might benefit from twelve-step recovery work.

"But we have our *work* cut out for us!" Ulric's mother maintained, referring to the numerous assortment of meetings which they were required to attend because of the incest. "We don't have a drinking or drugging problem *now*. And we probably won't ever again. All this has been too hard on us. We can't even take care of our family anymore with all this 'therapy' to do."

The mother's view of recovery was that she was being worn down by "the system," overloaded with the court's expectations. Deterrence, rather than rehabilitation, was the model of recovery which she would no doubt carry away in her mind.

Ulric's father, a horse trainer, maintained that he could escape into his work when the urge to drink or use drugs came over him. He blamed the incestuous relationship with his daughter on his "alcoholism" and his wife's problem with "crystal." He had no interest, however, in participating in any of that "A.A. or N.A. religious stuff." He claimed that he was learning all he needed to know about "communication" in the group meeting for incest couples that he and his wife were attending. Ulric's father did not understand the notion of recovery as a new way of life.

Without the benefit of a coordinated twelve-step effort to support physical and emotional recovery, Ulric's mother remained at high risk to reabuse her son. A supportive network could not be fostered through incest recovery work alone. This mother's need for omnipotent control was so intense that she became rageful when she was not allowed to establish the frequency of their meetings with Ulric, to pay the fee which she had decided his therapy was "really worth," and to come at the time she decided was most convenient for them (regardless of the therapist's schedule). Without the benefit of twelve-step work to neutralize her need for omnipotent control, without a helpful selfobject milieu, Ulric's mother remained incapable of making empathic contact with her traumatized son.

Ulric's father, on the other hand, remained a passive, withdrawing figure who could not recognize his son's intense need for a supportive male relationship.

Social Control

The issue of social control surfaces when the family comes to the attention of authorities because of incest or sexual abuse of a child. Then, the control dynamics of the larger social system impinge on the "family in recovery." The major control issue of this period continues to be: "*Who* is in charge of this family?"

The strength of a cultural taboo to support intervention, once incest or child sexual abuse has been exposed, may explain treatment selection, rather than the superiority of any incest/child sexual abuse treatment modality. There is no such cultural taboo against alcoholism and addiction and their long-range traumatic effects on the life of a child. Indeed, the current thinking about legalizing illicit drugs suggests that our social system *encourages* addictive practices.

Professional denial contributes to the high incidence of alcoholic/addictive practices remaining untreated in incest and physical abuse survivors. Long-term findings of younger incest victims (Courtois, 1988) indicates that there is an overwhelming proportion who begin to practice some type of addiction (alcoholism, drug use, eating disorders) by their teenage years. (This seems to occur despite incest-specific treatment, when there is a failure to treat the family addictive process.)

The inabilities of the alcoholic and addicted parent to process verbal information due to drug-related cognitive impairment are pronounced, especially during the first six months of abstinence. This notion seems to become irrelevant information when the cultural taboo of "incest" has been violated. Incest work then proceeds as the primary focus of the recovery work with the parents and the victim. The family in an incest-specific setting often is treated with a variety of talking therapy modalities by individuals who have no expertise in chemical dependency treatment. Blind to the fact that the addicted parents are still perceiving the world through a haze, professionals lead the confused parents through a variety of exercises in "communication skills" and family dynamics.

Courtois (1988), in her comprehensive and sensitive treatment of healing the incest wound, notes that "incest often occurs in the context of an alcoholic family or when the abuser has used alcohol or drugs" (p. 312). Courtois also identifies patterns of chemical abuse in adult survivors of incest and cautions regarding their treatment: "The incest therapy is secondary and only becomes primary when the survivor achieves sobriety" (p. 313).

Although my discussion may seem unnecessarily critical of current models of incest/child sexual abuse treatment, when indeed these efforts need to be lauded, what we must criticize is the failure to screen and appropriately refer and treat primary physical addictions *before* incest work is begun. Once again, I must emphasize the need for a supportive recovery network to be sustained by twelve-step involvement.

Family Processes During Middle/Control Phase

A parent who has been sober for approximately six months — when control phase processes begin to weigh heavily — appears to be waking up from a Rip van Winkle type experience. He shakes his head, looks around, and begins to question the therapist: "Why is my child still behaving poorly? What have you been doing with him all this time? He still doesn't mind or do his homework!"

That parent may not say it, but his inner thoughts are still concentrated on himself. ("If *I'm* improving and taking these giant steps forward, why hasn't my child succeeded in changing, too?")

The parent then looks over at his spouse and begins to grumble, "And *you*. What have *you* been doing for the past six months while I've been getting sober?"

The recovering parent's ability to see outside himself, while strengthened by physical and emotional recovery, is still limited by his egocentrism. I do not believe that, in most cases, this kind of egocentrism is equivalent to "Ego inflation." It is, rather, as Anthony (1976) has observed in the egocentrism of childhood, "narcissism without Narcissis." Anthony, writing this after his reunion with Piaget, describes Piaget's notion of the childhood ego which has the centeral developmental task of differentiating itself from the rest of the universe.

The egocentric child does not love himself without being aware that he loves himself. He is simply unable to separate himself from his surroundings. He and the world are one; he is the world, and therefore the world thinks and feels and perceives exactly like him. (p. 268)

This description applies as well to the recovering parent who has maintained six months of sobriety or abstinence and who is now beginning to look around at the rest of the world — aware, but not aware that those closest to him are not his mirror images. Their greater differentiation in recovery both stupefies and annoys him. During the course of the control phase, the recovering parent will repeatedly be faced with sorting through these same-different relationships with members of his family. (This is actually very similar to the cognitive sorting, described in Chapter 5, which takes place among children during middle childhood.)

It is the parents' greater individuation in recovery which leads to the spontaneous power struggles and feelings of competitiveness in the family. Each individual in the family has begun to experience and express more selfhood; therefore, each also wants to have an equal say.

For the parents, the control phase processes begin to revive — albeit unconsciously at first — their conflicts from their respective families of origin. Since in these earlier addictive family systems the childhood experience was one of always being controlled without regard for one's selfhood, the current family situation is dreaded and feared. Meanwhile, the recovering parent continues to realize the benefits of improved physical and emotional sobriety, paving the way for regaining leadership. Yet, his efforts to become a fully legitimate leader in the family again are resisted by both the spouse and the sibling subsystem.

The Marital System in the Control Phase

The original two-person system, the marital dyad, again becomes central in the control phase. Leadership activities, which by default were assumed by the co-dependent, are now criticized and challenged by the alcoholic spouse. The co-dependent spouse displays a reluctance to give up power and authority, citing her spouse's numerous failures during the time of active drinking and/or drug-using. Or the co-dependent begins to demand more of an equal partnership role from the alcoholic. Then the recovering spouse may share a litany of grievances from the past. These failures generally draw forth reminiscences from the respective families of origin, as well as childhood hurts and disappointments. Each historical period — family of origin, drinking past, present and future — is explored in the therapy as the source of interferences with the couple's ability to provide shared parental leadership for their children.

Resistances During Middle Phase of Therapy

Because the predominant affect associated with the control phase of family processes is *anger*, the parents in recovery retreat from dealing openly with emotions and issues. Confrontation, which is a way of facing anger, is also avoided. Negatively tinged feelings towards the spouse and children have historically been expressed destructively. The success of the control phase and the family's ability to move into the phase of intimate relating are dependent on family members' being able to integrate both negative and positive aspects of others.

Splitting. One of the major resistances occurring at this point is the splitting of the therapeutic modalities. As the parent has come to internalize the all-good, always available selfobject milieu of the twelve-step program and sponsor, the more "controlling" (less frequent meetings, less availability and accessibility, fee-for-service) nature of the therapy is experienced as negative, or all-bad.

Splitting is a psychological defense mechanism which is common in long-term alcoholism and addictions recovery work. The splitting results from an inability to integrate ambivalent images, attitudes or emotions. Impressions which are both negative and positive towards the same person (institution, agencies, etc.) are not experienced simultaneously. Rather, these images tend to be split into their black-white, good-bad components. The unconscious, defensive operation of splitting occurs in an effort to avoid intense, ambivalent interpersonal conflicts.

Because the success of the control phase therapy work is dependent on the parent's being able to experience and accept both negative and positive components of himself and others, it is imperative that the splitting be resolved. Otherwise, splitting results in a premature disruption of the therapeutic relationship.

One of the suggestions which I offer to the client is that the A.A. sponsor be invited in for one of the family meetings. The influence of this sponsor, who is so integral to family functioning, needs to be acknowledged in the therapy. An Al-Anon sponsor (or other key twelve-step person) also may become a part of this family conference. Regardless of whether the sponsor is being perceived as the idealized or disappointing object, if the sponsor's participation can be enlisted, the client's interpersonal experiences will become more integrated and therefore more reality-based.

Another suggestion offered to the recovering parent when the therapist is experienced as the disappointing selfobject is an individual session. At this time, the therapeutic failures which may have led to the client's disappointment are discussed and acknowledged and amends made. Even the most unintentional — and hence unacknowledged — breaches in therapeutic empathy can have a disruptive effect on the therapeutic alliance with a parent, particularly at this critical therapeutic juncture.

Parent/sib resistances. A parent/sib dynamic, when one or both parents have been functioning in a sibling-type relationship with their children, is one of the major difficulties in helping a parent to accept family leadership responsibilities. The parent/sib will make tentative bids towards leadership, but then report how difficult a particular leadership function was to execute. Helplessness and a continuing expression of the need to be parented by the therapist, or spouse, or a family sibling leader will be expressed through covert parent/sib dynamics. In addition, the parent/sib usually demonstrates a bickering, sibling-like quality to the interactions with the children, confusing issues, distracting, shifting to irrelevancies, being accusatory, etc. Finally, the parent/sib has begun therapy with an almost immediate elevation of the therapist to the all-good, all-powerful role of family messiah. Avoided completely are those negative feelings or disappointments when the therapist does not act in accordance with these expectations. Rather, the parent/sib will act out by not complying with what she believes are the therapist's expectations of her (to parent her children).

The resolution of parent/sib dynamics during the control phase occurs through work with the marital dyad, as well as through sibling group interventions which lead to reorganization and negotiation. Material from the original family addictive system is usually most effectively worked through during individual sessions with the parent/sib. The recognition and acceptance of the adult child-self of the parent/sib is important before moving this individual into marital dyad work.

Since the parent/sib's dynamics occur at an unconscious level, there is rarely a direct interpretation of the parent's role relationship to her children. This kind of interpretation is far too threatening even to be understood, let alone integrated by the parent/sib.

The following case illustrates a parent/sib resistance during the control phase of therapy.

Case Illustration — Violette

Violette was an eleven-year-old sibling caretaker for her two younger sisters, Mimette and Suzette, who were nine and five. The family had immigrated from Canada as a type of "geographic cure" for the father's alcoholism. However, the father was not any more successful after the move, being able to maintain sobriety only for brief periods of a month or two. At the time of the referral, he had just been ordered into treatment by the employee assistance program at his job.

When the spouse and children arrived for the first interview, Violette's mother gained my attention through her parent/sib dynamics in the waiting room. Looking very much like the oldest sister, the mother wore her hair in long black braids and was dressed in jeans — a carbon copy of her three daughters. Mother and daughters exchanged sheepish glances, as if to question who should speak first, and then they all began speaking at once. Finally, the group deferred to Violette, who explained that she would have to be the spokesperson because of her mother's very obvious French accent: "She's a little too shy."

During the child recovery work, Violette complained about the squabbles between her sisters. Mimette, especially, was having a lot of problems in school, and Suzette was always staying home from school, pretending to be ill. Violette appeared overwhelmed, as her mother sat nodding in agreement that, indeed, these problems existed in the family. When Violette complained about being burdened with too much responsibility, her mother's supplication to the therapist was for perfect understanding. What an impossible task it was to raise three daughters when one's husband was a drunkard! She had to rely on Violette to cook the meals and do the family laundry and help the younger sisters because there was no one else available. Violette and her mother argued in the session about which of them actually did the most. Her mother pointed to her all-consuming work schedule, including overtime hours, as an electronics assembler in a factory. Violette's mother also complained of many vague somatic complaints, which appeared not to have a physical basis but had been present since childhood — stomach cramps, headaches, dizziness, etc.

When it was suggested that Violette could be relieved of some of her chores, and these could be delegated to the other two daughters, the mother became very anxious and Violette stiffened. Violette appeared to be just as frightened of relinquishing control as she was of not being taken care of adequately and of seeing the entire family fall apart.

After this family had been in recovery for about eight months, Violette's father began to exert pressure for his wife to assume more leadership in the family. The mother continued to turn to the therapist to rescue her from these adult demands. Her excuses continued to be many and varied as to why she needed to rely on Violette. Although she blamed many of these failings on her husband's alcoholism, she admitted that his sustained sobriety changed the picture somewhat.

In a private session with me, Violette's mother admitted tearfully that she had many leftover resentments from her family of origin. Her father had died from alcoholism, and she had been overburdened by family responsibilities as the oldest child caretaker for her mother and siblings. She simply could not understand why Violette complained so much when she, the mother, had effectively assumed the care of *six* siblings! This mother also admitted that her husband reminded her of her own alcoholic father, and that—while she really did love her husband—she also was terrified of him. She admitted that her long hours on the job amounted to a type of workaholism which allowed her to escape from the family pressures.

When Violette's mother was able to express her fears and helplessness openly—not only in the session with me, but also to her husband—she began to be free from her bondage to her past. Gradually, with her husband's support, she was able to move into a position of shared parental leadership.

Resistances to Making Amends. Midway into the control phase the parent usually begins to examine his failures with his children and to use the forum of the therapy to acknowledge these failures. These are the important parent-child processes of the middle phase of therapy. However, before the parent makes the amends, there should be a resolution of ambivalent feelings toward the child. This means that, in some individual forum, the parent is going to need an outlet for angry, hostile, bitter feelings toward the child. When a parent retains a jealous relationship with a child, such as a mother may have towards her incest-victim daughter, any amends to the child will not be authentic. The child will continue to be blamed, and the amends will be an exercise in the parent's efforts to look good for some external authority. Amends based on empathic attunement involve the parent's humility.

CHILDREN'S THERAPY—MIDDLE PHASE

Stage II — Verbal Rehearsal

In the previous chapter we learned that the first stage of child therapy during the recovery process focuses on the child's *disavowal*. During the Stage I process, play therapy procedures concentrate on stabilizing the child's traumatized condition. Soothing interactions with the therapist promote ego strengthening and increase the child's ability to use the therapist as a source of calm and strength.

The Stage II process of verbal rehearsal now makes use of the child's increased resilience. Play therapy now comes to be a backdrop for increased verbal interactions between the child and the therapist. Whereas previously the therapist had maintained a low profile in the play therapy setting, allowing the child's natural responses to unfold, the therapist now encourages verbal participation. Projects, crafts, artwork, and even role-playing situations are all ways that a child can become more fluent verbally with an adult. These "verbal rehearsals" are expected to prepare the child for sibling group verbal interactions as well as eventual family sessions.

Games, particularly, can be introduced to help a child work through the middle phase of control phase family dynamics. Since rules now take on an increasing importance for the child as the parent begins to introduce the new rules for family functioning, a game playing activity with the therapist can assist the child to become verbally adept in discussing rules. For example, one little boy of nine used to stagger the imagination by introducing numerous arbitrary rules every time we became involved in the board game Parcheesi. My verbal interactions with the child would help clarify how very much he enjoyed establishing *rules* which gave him the clear advantage. When he responded that he didn't like the "regular rules" of the game because they were "boring," I would reply how his family life must have seemed almost exciting with so many arbitrary rules when his parents were drinking and using drugs. Now, in recovery, his parents with their "regular family rules" must be creating a family life which, compared to the pre-recovery chaos, seemed "boring." Thus, the child's resistance to family rules could be discussed in the less threatening play therapy milieu, rehearsing him for the family meeting which soon was to follow.

While a therapist and child are engaged in a board game in the play therapy room, I often encourage a sibling and parent to become involved in a board game in an adjoining room. These occasions are often the first time that children and their parents may have played together for many years, if ever. Here, the child — independent of the therapist — encounters the parent in a play situation which has to do with understanding and following rules.

During a particularly tense period of family sessions, a more traditional play therapy session (designed for the purposes of soothing and relieving tension) may be scheduled for the child. It is important for the child to continue to experience the therapist not only as an advocate, but also as a continuing source of calm and soothing. The changing shifts in family homeostasis which occur during the control phase are reflected by problems of inner self-regulation for the child. The use of play to coincide with the control phase has been explained by Anna Ornstein (1985):

> . . . during play the child is *in control* of his physical surround and can use his imagination, he can "rehearse" anticipated relationships and events that could otherwise prove to be overwhelming. (p. 350, italics mine)

Self-Esteem Regulation

Self-esteem is strengthened during this phase by increasing the child's capacity to withstand family tensions. Strengthening the body-self through exercises intended to provide an integrative function to the mind-body-self is not only tension reducing but also just plain fun. A small trampoline kept in one corner of the office catches the eye of even the most apathetic or listless child. Now, jumping on the trampoline, a child comes to feel more in *control*. Therapy with the trampoline can also facilitate more modulated emotional functioning in a hyperaroused child.

The trampoline procedure is variable, depending on the creative interaction between therapist and child. It is usually begun by having the child jump while the therapist provides a mirroring function, counting the number of times that the child is jumping to mirror his vigor, or reciting with him a little rhyme as he jumps to mirror his specialness and greatness:

> Me, me,
> one, two, three,
> you and me,

> together we see,
> See *me*!
> Four, five,
> I'm alive,
> jump so high,
> up to the sky.

A youngster may come into a session droopy and lifeless from a major self-esteem loss—such as when a drinking parent has not remembered a birthday—but leave the session after the trampoline work feeling strengthened and exuberant.

During the period of ego strengthening procedures, it is important to keep in mind that the end goal is to achieve more coordinated and balanced functioning in the child. Another body-mind-self activity involves anger release work with a foam rubber baseball bat. This is particularly helpful with the child sexual or physical abuse victim, who needs to feel empowered at a body level, as well as in psychological functioning. Often, role-playing of situations to empower the child is critical before the abusing parent begins to make amends. When a parent begins to address the child about issues of past abuse or traumatic scenes involving the child and parent, that child's ego needs to be able to withstand these interactions. Otherwise, post-traumatic scenes of the original trauma are revived, and the child is essentially retraumatized by the parent's intrusiveness. In such instances, the child's rapid regression results in a weakening of the stress barrier and ego disorganization. Emotions which belong to the parent are absorbed by the child and confused as originating from within herself. Or, the reliving of traumatic events produces in the child new waves of shock and fear. A more resilient ego, however, is able to use the parent-child interactions to even further empower the child-self or to enhance the child's perceptions of the parent as a compassionate selfobject.

Improving the child's self-esteem becomes the central concern of the therapy at this stage. If psychoeducational assistance is needed, for example, the child may be recommended for tutoring, speech therapy, or other special assistance in an effort to continue to strengthen educational functioning.

Sibling Interventions

Sibling rehearsal is accomplished by having the siblings meet together in pairs or as a group to discuss their conflicts. This goal is in keeping with the overall child therapy goal of this phase, "verbal

rehearsal." As the siblings discuss their conflicts or even their agree-
ments with each other, they are preparing for the family therapy
sessions which follow. Rallying the siblings to come to the defense of
a sibling in trouble or a sibling who has been diminished in some
extrafamilial pursuit (such as bullied by peers) strengthens the siblings' ability to relate in a positive manner.

Sibling reorganization is a way of actively intervening during sibling
group meetings, as well as in the family meetings, to alter the sibling
bond. When parents refer to the children as undifferentiated, such
as "the kids" or "the girls" or "the boys," the therapist may even
physically move the children in the session, so that they are viewed
more as individuals. Siblings who typically perform certain family
functions, such as family chef or dishwasher, may be instructed to
relinquish these duties to another sibling or parent. Sibling reorganization is a critical intervention during the control phase, which seeks
to interrupt the covert source of power in the sibling subsystem.

Sibling negotiations come to occupy a central place in the family
therapy sessions of the control phase. As the children become more
adept verbally, they learn that they can take responsibility for de-
claring the agenda in the family meetings. Sibling quarrels and
disagreements can be brought before the family group and negotiations used to solve problems, with weekly reports back to the
group.

Children's Rules and Requests

Two important notions, rules and requests, are stressed during
this early control phase. These are intended to gradually move the
parent into effective leadership functioning.

The first notion is that of "rules," or, *the parent has a right to parent*!
This notion, simple though it sounds, appears to baffle many recovering parents. Their old, unworkable model of parenting borrowed
from the family of origin usually drifted from chaotic to tyrannical.
The recovering parent eventually abrogated responsibilities for parenting to the nonalcoholic parent or one of the siblings. Now, the
introduction of the idea that there are legitimate parental rights is
both reassuring and anxiety-provoking. Families whose leadership
patterns have been distorted by incest and child physical abuse are
the ones who have the most difficulty with these control phase
issues.

The parental rights intervention, which is directed to the children
in a family group meeting, goes something like this:

Every family has a leader. In this family there are two leaders (in the case of two-parent families). In the school, there also is a leader. Who is the leader in the school?

The children will usually answer that "the principal" is the leader in the school, or "the teacher." The idea of a shared leadership model is then introduced.

Yes, the principal is the leader in the school. But there also is a leader in the classroom. Who would that be?

As this discussion is extended to other social groups, such as the church, clubs, or organizations to which the family may belong, the children are rehearsed, along with the parents, about the notion of effective organizational leadership. This work continues to develop the skills which the children have been practicing in verbal rehearsal meetings.

Having established the idea of the parents as leaders, the therapist begins to educate the family about the differences between "rules" and "requests."

Every group has rules as to what we may do and what we may not do. What are some of the rules in your school? Church? [And so on . . .] In the family, there are also rules. These rules mean that the family can be strong and happy when everyone is doing what he or she is supposed to do. In the school, the principal and teachers make the rules for the children. In the family, who makes the rules?

By this time, the children will usually answer that the parents are the ones who make the rules, although occasionally a sibling leader may be named. As inquiry is made about the rules for behavior, a great deal of confusion usually surfaces. Children stare blankly, and even parents look mystified. It soon becomes apparent that the rules for family functioning have never been clearly articulated. The therapist continues,

Some of the rules which parents make for children have to do with what time they must come home after school, what time they must go to bed, and so on. . . .

A rule is different from a request. A rule must not be changed or broken by the child. A request may be changed when the child and parent agree. For example, if your parents tell you that you must

come home from school by 5 o'clock, you cannot change that rule one
day when your friend asks you to stay out later.

A request is something that a child can make to the parent about
something he wants, or something he wants to do, or something he
wants the parent to do. Sometimes, a child may request to have a rule
changed. If you *request* that you be allowed to come home by 5:30
instead of 5:00, your parent may not agree to that request, but you
may ask. If your parent agrees, the rule is changed. If you change the
rule without asking, you are breaking the rule.

Simplistic though these rehearsals may seem, when we bear in
mind the deficits in verbal informational abilities shown by children
in alcoholic/addictive families (see Chapter 7), we will realize the
importance of rehearsing basic family life information. The recovering alcoholic/addictive parent, too, suffers a deficit, not only in
cognitive functioning but also in an internal repertoire of parenting
skills which was not provided in the family of origin.

We must continue to be empathic with a child's needs for self
articulation, but we also must be empathic with the parent's need to
understand how to parent when a child poses problems. The reality
of family life is that little children do pose problems for their parents
when they become recalcitrant, oppositional, destructive, or defiant.
Parents have realistic needs to set rules and limits as guidelines and
standards for behavior. Indeed, children are reassured by these
structures, which are usually construed as expressions of the parents'
concern for the child. It is not pedagogical to set limits.

> A further statement on the question of limit setting seems in order
> . . . the child *perceives* the difference between firmness which is moti-
> vated to calm and to comfort him from that which is retaliatory in
> intent and he will respond accordingly. It is at moments like that that
> parental empathy may be the most severely taxed! "Giving in" to a
> child's unacceptable behavior expresses contempt rather than empa-
> thy toward the child and has severe consequences for later develop-
> ment. Guilt and self-contempt is then added to the child's already
> negative self-image which most likely is the source of his aggressive,
> self-destructive behavior to begin with. (Ornstein, 1976, p. 25)

Research examining parental styles (Barnes and Windle, 1987),
particularly with respect to the prevention of alcohol and drug problems by adolescents, found that "a high number of rules for adolescent behavior" along with parental nurturance and low coercive pun-

ishment contributed to a reduction of substance abuse and other problem behaviors in the teenagers.

Just Say "No"

Parents in recovery also have the right, indeed are encouraged, to say "no" to their children. The most common problem I have found with parents in recovery is not of the pedagogical type, but just the opposite: Parents do not know that they have the right to *deny* a child's requests. The most recent evidence (Hayden, 1988) indicates that it is not only psychologically healthy, but indeed *mandatory*, that children begin to experience their parents as in control of setting required limits and boundaries. Hayden (1988) notes that the parenting of the 1960s and 1970s was characterized by permissiveness and a narcissistic "do-your-own-thing" approach to child-rearing. This laissez-faire approach is no longer tenable.

> The world of the eighties is a fragmented social milieu to MTV, AIDS, drugs, sex, and too many choices for children who are in no way developmentally ready to make these choices. Along with this cultural chaos, children have to deal with the physical chaos of their own changing bodies. The result is a desperate situation in which the child needs to impose some sort of structure on the environment. (p. 1)

When parents are able to tell a child "no" without experiencing guilt, this very act of limit-setting helps the child define his own boundaries.

I have known parents in recovery who looked bewildered in the face of an angry child's belligerent demands: "You said you were going to let me stay up until midnight and watch the late show, so why are you complaining?" A parent's tentative explanation, "Well, yes, dear — I did that *one* night, but I didn't mean every night . . . " is simply more fuel for the child's manipulation. The parent in recovery is supported in articulating a firm but caring "no." Parents are discouraged from issuing their "no" in anger or punitively, then retracting it in a moment of weakness. The boundary which is established by the *no* needs to be firm and reliable.

Lasch (1979), writing on the "culture of narcissism," discusses *permissive parenting* as it relates to the whole notion of control:

> The appearance of permissiveness conceals a stringent system of controls, all the more effective because it avoids direct confrontations between authorities and the people on whom they seek to impose their

will. Because confrontations provoke arguments about principle, the authorities whenever possible delegate discipline to someone else so that they themselves can pose as advisers, "resource persons," and friends. Thus parents rely on doctors, psychiatrists, and the child's own peers to impose rules on the child and to see that he conforms to them. (p. 310)

Confrontation is a prominent feature of the control phase. The parents of children in recovery need to learn how to confront one another and their children directly and effectively. This type of parenting, of course, means *involvement* with the child. The involvement should not cross generational boundaries, as in a laissez-faire or "buddy" relationship. Rather, effective control phase parenting *establishes* generational boundaries. The majority of parents in recovery have been only tangentially involved in the lives of their children in the establishment of healthy guidelines and boundaries.

During this control phase, parenting classes may be recommended. I also maintain a reading list for parents, including two books by Faber and Mazlish *How To Talk So Children Will Listen and Listen So Kids Will Talk*, and *Siblings Without Rivalry, Your Child's Self-Esteem* by Briggs, and *If You Love Me, Don't Feed Me Junk* by Gooch. Parents are even asked to consider this period as a type of family life education. They are neither criticized nor evaluated for their lack of understanding or their failures in implementing effective interactions. They are simply encouraged to continue to learn.

ONGOING RECOVERY

Gradually, the parents come to work together more cooperatively in fulfilling joint leadership functions. The children are no longer assuming positions of power and dominance over their siblings, nor do they look to siblings to perform major caretaking functions.

The family processes usher in the phase of "affection," where the primary concerns have to do with intimate relating. As individuals within the newly recovering family system come to experience *belonging*, they recognize that there is responsible *leadership* which sustains the family, and now it is becoming safe to both give and receive love and *affection*. The question is, how?

Parent Sessions — Affection Phase

Marital dissension between the spouses has lessened, now being accepted as an inevitable part of human interactions which must be faced, acknowledged, and resolved. Each partner recognizes his ability to be both a frustrating and a supportive, loving selfobject in the marital dyad as well as with the children.

During this phase, work with the marital dyad involves facilitating the recognition of the adult (child) present in each of the partners. Recognizing that one retains aspects of the self which have been preserved in the original childhood form may not be a revelation for either member of the couple. However, when one is led to the recognition that this also holds true for the mate, there is usually surprise. Heretofore, each of the partners had held in mind the fantasy of the spouse as an idealized parent image, capable of providing love and protection, but choosing to be punitive and depriving. Past failures in selfobject relating were generally followed by massive disappointments. These feelings were assuaged by many of the former addictive practices.

When the marital partners begin to realize that their relationship is not comprised of "just we two," but actually involves *four* entities ("we two adults"+one child-self of each), their interactions take on more realistic colorations. By acknowledging the damaged child-self of the other, partners recognize that they often will be desired to serve a parenting-type function for the other. They will, like Adam, be expected to fill in the missing or damaged part of their co-dependent-Eve when she becomes empty and depleted. Or, like Eve, they will be expected to enhance their Adam's wisdom and potency. No sexism is intended here, for there is a continual requirement for both of these strengthening and mirroring functions in each spouse. To have mirroring provided for one's specialness and greatness when self-esteem lags *or* to have another upon whom to rely for wisdom and power when one feels ineffectual is legitimate in any marital relationship. When such needs are not met optimally, there is disappointment, hurt, even narcissistic rage. The challenge is to learn to honor the child-self of the other (without yielding to its tyrannical demands) by forming an empathic bond which transcends yet respects personal boundaries. This is the beginning of intimacy; that is, the key to intimate relating is *empathy*.

The developmental arrest which gave rise to the adult-child dilemma is never completely repaired. I believe that recovery is an ongoing process of repairing this damaged child-self. It seems unrealistic to me to impress upon couples the notion that their more independent functioning will diminish the importance of the child-self demands during their marital interactions. Suggesting to either parent that the child-self is immature or otherwise abnormal creates defensiveness. The old, false-self walls suddenly reappear. Ashamed of the existence of this childish self, the spouses allow defensive functioning to interfere with further intimacy. *Accepting* the existence of the child-self leads to more spontaneously occurring mature levels of functioning as the self regains cohesion. Creative ways of expressing the child-self needs for affirmation, playfulness, and mirroring are encouraged.

When the marital partners begin to understand that the child-self of the other has been unintegrated into the personality because of the abusive, unempathic conditions of the past, new levels of compassion usually occur. Each partner becomes more tolerant of the childish insecurities and fears of the other. The establishment of an empathic milieu, a healing environment, for one another offsets the tendency to discount or lay blame.

I do not believe that these levels of intimate communication can be accomplished by a couple in recovery overnight—but I also do not believe that it takes a decade! There is a long, slow process of dealing with past and present oscillations until a convergence of issues results.

Most parents in recovery are also suffering from the adult-child dilemma; therefore, most are suffering from different levels of a posttraumatic stress condition which may become reactivated during the recovery work of their children. This type of intensive recovery work requires time for the new psychic shifts to adjust, gradually.

The road to family recovery involves building new levels of trust where intimate relating can occur with safety guaranteed. For example, a co-dependent spouse who was exceedingly controlling in managing the family finances was able to reveal to her recovering alcoholic husband that underlying her need for control was her deepest insecurity—that she would wind up "a bag lady." In her own family of origin, she had been a helpless child witness as her drug-abusing father squandered most of the family paycheck on his heroin habit. The family had lived in deprivation and squalor. When this woman's husband understood the basis for his wife's extreme control, he became reassuring and actually protective of his wife's frightened child-self. Able to feel empathy for this part of his wife's experience, he was also able to provide her with the reassurance necessary to help free her from the delusion of living in the past, allowing her to function more fully in the reality of the present moment.

Parent-Child Intimacy

When parents are ready to make amends to children for the wrongs they may have committed, a type of verbal rehearsal occurs with the parent before that parent ever meets with the child. Facilitating the parent's ability to see the *impact* of his *amends* on the inner self of the child is crucial. I do not agree with approaches which teach parents that making amends is really for themselves—to rid themselves of guilt—and that they are not responsible for the child's reactions. I have known of cases where a child's life had been devastated by a parent, such as in severe, ongoing incest. When that parent came forth to make amends to the youngster, it was no more than a mere, "Sorry, kid!" This constitutes the severest form of narcissistic injury to the child and is another example of retraumatization. Such a parent is myopically bewildered when the child becomes angry and enraged with the "Sorry, Kid!" amends.

Other parents go to quite the opposite extreme. When a parent has not been prepared for empathic relating to the inner self of the child, he may turn the amends session into a maudlin exhibition. Crying and sobbing, the parent overidentifies with the child, but travels so far back in time to his own childhood injuries that he loses sight of his own child in the present. Thus, the session becomes a type of catharsis for the parent, albeit self-indulgent and not at all in touch with the needs of the youngster.

Still a third type of amends is made by the parent who, unaware of the need for empathic attunement to the child, uses the amends session for self-justification, explaining to the child motives—why the parent did this or that, all the extenuating circumstances, justifying and rationalizing—and overburdens the child with his own agenda. When the facilitator may interject, "What are you trying to say to your daughter, Mr. Jones?" the parent looks annoyed, "Why, I'm making amends, of course!"

A final type of amends is one which is written out by the parent and simply left on the breakfast table in hopes the child will read it. While the statement may be eloquently worded and sensitively phrased, the parent is unavailable to the child, once again, as a source of calm and support.

To ensure that the parental amends facilitates the healing of the damaged parent-child relationship, parents are "rehearsed" in the amends process or prepared to make empathic contact with the child. The literature of Alcoholics Anonymous which pertains to step nine, making amends, is recommeded reading. Another resource, *Liberated Parents/Liberated Children* by Faber and Mazlish, is also recommended. It is essential that the parent be empathic with the child's inner state. The actual words which the parent says to the child need to be succinct, though specific to this inner state (rather than concentrating on the parents' position). For example:

I'm sorry that I burdened you many times, Johnny, when I left you alone at night with your baby sister. You were too young for those responsibilities, and you must have been very frightened and angry with me. I was wrong to leave you alone when I went out partying. I want you to know that I will not hurt you in this same way again.

The reassurance which is offered through the parental amends convinces the child that the parent does know and understand him.

Child Recovery Work — Affection Phase

This phase is marked by the children's increased verbal skills and the parents' increased ability for empathic relating. Children are now more able to use the family and sibling meetings as problem-solving forums. They are guided increasingly by the parents, who are functioning in a leadership role in the therapy. Within the family group meetings, as well as within the family home environment, the parents take on a facilitative role — settling disputes, exploring family processes, providing empathic attunement.

Now the therapist begins to take a less active role in the family and sibling group meetings. Individual child therapy sessions are scheduled only as needed from time to time to provide tension reduction for the child or to maintain rapport. The therapist's most active role occurs in the parent sessions scheduled before or after the family meetings. Acting as a type of clinical supervisor to the parents, the therapist processes with the parents their observations and their understanding of their children's problems. As they come to better understand the inner world of their child, the parents become empathically attuned, able to guide the child through recovery. The continuing reminder to the parents is that they can have a "therapeutic" effect with their own children.

TERMINATION

By the time the family is ready for termination from therapy, both parents and children have been sufficiently skilled in recovery as a *process* for each member of the family, which is now to be guided forward by the parents. There is an open door policy about returning for brief consultation, or when family life crises occur, or when child developmental issues confuse and perplex, or at any other time the family unit becomes sufficiently stressed. Post-traumatic stress symptoms and relapse dynamics (both individual and family) have been elaborated throughout the therapy. Now family members are asked to spend some time in problem-solving sessions discussing how they will cope with these difficulties in the future. Community resources, such as twelve-step programs, aftercare programs, children's services, and other helping agencies are all identified for the family.

SPECIAL SITUATIONS IN RECOVERY

Foster Home Placement of Children in Recovery

When children in recovery must be removed from the parental home, individual child recovery work must often proceed without the parents' involvement. At such times, children are treated according to individual child therapy procedures outlined in the early, middle and ongoing phases of recovery. Initial work to stabilize the child will consist largely of efforts to decrease tension and induce calm and soothing. The success of early recovery phase work with a child depends on ameliorating the symptoms of chronic trauma, or the practicing alcoholic/addictive parent (PAAP) symptoms. An important step is to work with the foster parent and pediatrician to assess the child's nutritional status. Even a child in foster care or other extrafamilial placement can benefit from dietary adjustments to improve home and school adjustment. Many foster parents benefit from education and counseling about the child's nutritional needs.

Special problems arise when a child is known to be in an abusive foster placement, or when the foster parent is also thought to be chemically dependent. At such times, the therapist must make a decision to advocate for the child, always running the risk that: (1) the child's version of what is occurring in foster care will be denied and the child will be seen as a troublemaker; (2) the therapist and foster parent will enter into an adversarial relationship; or (3) if the situation as described by the child is not interrupted, the therapist will end up witnessing the child's retraumatization.

Although a foster parent may become involved in the child's recovery process, usually the PACT (parents as co-therapists) model must be adapted to the foster care situation. Unless the foster placement is to be long-term and the foster parent is able to commit fully to the child in recovery, the involvement of that foster parent in the child's recovery is largely superficial. Supportive and educational methods may be used with a foster parent; however, the *family process* issues do not progress beyond the inclusion phase. Although each of the other two family process issues of control and affection may surface from time to time, the predominant theme will have to do with *belonging*. (Child: "How long am I going to be in this foster home?" Foster parent: "How long is this kid going to stay?" Natural parent: "When will my child be returned?")

A child who settles into a more permanent foster arrangement will experience a revival of inclusion issues anytime foster sibs come and go. Often, these inclusion themes may be mistaken for control issues. For example, a foster boy of nine years (who had been removed from the home of his drug-addicted parents) appeared to defy his foster parent by reverting to not coming home after school. While this behavior problem had not been present for several months, the addition of a new foster sister to the home had been the catalyst for the boy's seeming defiance. Rather than defiance, the boy's behavior was translated by the therapist to the foster parent as arising from feelings of loss and rivalry. Excluded from the foster mother's attention by the chatty, clingy foster sister, the boy's earlier exclusion by his natural parents was rekindled. Through the middle phase of child recovery work, this boy was assisted to use words to describe his negative feeling states to his foster mom. "It just bugs me when I come home after school and have to listen to Sally yap-yap-yap in your face. I'd rather just hang out after school than have to come home and listen to her blab. It makes me feel bad—like how I used to feel when my Dad was high on speed and always blabbing to my Mom. Or, she'd get drunk and blab to him. They never listened to me."

As the boy's self-esteem was strengthened by the foster mother's reassurance, he became more accepting of her limit-setting. He learned that acting-out his anger by staying after school was not an option in the foster home. He was expected to follow a rule. Sibling interventions with the two foster sibs assisted these children to develop a bond and to lessen their competition.

Any child in an extrafamilial setting can be assisted through the middle phase of child recovery work. Verbal rehearsal, self-esteem regulation, sibling interventions, children's rules and requests, and parental limit-setting are important features of the middle phase, regardless of whether the child is residing with the natural parents or living apart from them. While it is true that the *family process* issues will remain primarily those of inclusion, a child can be assisted to use words to talk about his problems in belonging.

Social, or external, sources of control also have the effect of keeping the family at the inclusion phase. Although there may be the illusion of control or affection phases processes, the family in recovery does not proceed naturally through these phases until the external control has been removed. Thus, inclusion phase issues will be salient until the family in recovery has the benefit of stable family group membership. An example is the incest family. When a father's only contact with the family is through child sexual abuse treatment, the family cannot move spontaneously to control and intimacy phases. Until that father has been granted legal sanction to rejoin the family or have regular, ongoing contact with the family outside the therapy setting, the family processes will remain centered on inclusion issues. Although superficial negotiations may be transacted between the parents around parenting issues, there is an "as if" quality to these transactions. Until leadership is tested through practical application, the issues of power and dominance are largely intellectual arguments. A father who has been removed legally from the family has little actual power and status until the legal restrictions are removed.

A somewhat opposite situation occurs with parents who are divorced. When external authorities stipulate a split physical custody arrangement, they tend to unwittingly provide a covert source of power to an extrafamilial individual (the divorced spouse). A written legal document stipulates that this divorced parent must remain an integral part of the child's (hence family's) life. This often occurs as a source of major life stress to the family.

One-Parent Families

Single-parent households are becoming as common as families where there is both a mother and father (Morrison, 1986). For children in recovery, the single-parent family poses special problems. While a recovering or co-dependent parent may form a PACT agreement for herself and her children to receive ongoing care, that agreement may be confounded by the children's visitation with a practicing alcoholic/addicted parent. Often, these visits continue to retraumatize the children. The therapist must advocate for the children; however, she is likely to encounter frustration and professional denial in the larger social system. Denial on the part of other professional helpers often supports a rigid "letter of the law" stance with respect to the children's "need" for visitation, despite the fact that the children are being victimized by the visitation.

Case Illustration — Willie

Willie, the eight-year-old son of a recovering alcoholic mother and a practicing alcoholic/marijuana-addicted father, was required, with his two younger siblings, to have weekend visitations with his father. The mother feared that her ex-husband was continuing to drink and smoke while driving with the children in the car. The mother, who was on welfare, sought through legal aid to obtain a more carefully monitored visitation for the children.

On one occasion, Willie came in to our session appearing to be in acute shock after a weekend visit with his father. He claimed that the father had been drunk, driving with the children on the freeway, playing "dodge 'em" in the traffic. The case worker who investigated my complaint of child abuse believed the father, who denied everything, claiming that his wife was simply trying to "stack the deck" so she could "win" during conciliation court. When this information was provided conciliation court counselors, they, too, believed the father that the mother was simply being punitive by "coaching" her son. Unrestricted weekend visitations were therefore ordered continued. Willie and his two sisters continued to show severe emotional and behavioral disturbances, particularly after weekend visits with their Dad.

Unfortunately, in cases such as the one just described, the report from the treating therapist who substantiates the child's traumatization may be considered "biased" information in favor of — not the child — but the *mother*. Thus, the relevancy and value of the therapist's information are completely dismissed. Another opinion is sought from an outside, "neutral" evaluator who doesn't even know the child and may have no expertise in treating either the childhood trauma *or* chemical dependency. The report then comes back to the Court:

> This is just a fight between the two parents where the kids are being used by the mother. Even though the boy, Willie, *says* he doesn't want to visit with his father, he appears to be saying this because of pressure from his mother.

Children continue not to be taken seriously as separate selves, as independent centers of initiative by professional helpers. (Recall that we *live* in an addictive society.) Children will continue to be victimized by parental chemical dependency as long as these problems are denied by professional helpers.

Sometimes the problems for single-parent recovering families appear insurmountable. The parent's employment requires a great deal of time away from the children. With the demands of physical recovery, the parent's coping resources may be exhausted. That parent may be suffering from one or a combination of adult child syndromes (adult child of alcoholism/addiction, adult incest survivor, physical abuse survivor, etc.) *together* with post-traumatic stress symptoms *and* their own addictive processes. The need for a supportive, twelve-step network must be stressed to assist the single parent with continuous, outside assistance.

Historically, professionals have criticized the use of Alcoholics Anonymous as "a substitute addiction." The alcoholic was seen as an individual with "tremendous dependency needs" who really should learn to grow up, stand on her own two feet, and strive for more independent functioning. This attitude seems almost medieval now in the light of our modern understanding of chemical dependency recovery, incest, child abuse, and post-traumatic stress reactions. Research tells us that we can interrupt the cycle of abuse in families when we provide a parent in recovery with a strong, available, supportive network. Professional debate about the superiority of some therapy modality over the Anonymous programs needs to be laid to rest *unless* the modality offers intensive, available, accessible community support for its members. Therapy and twelve-step programs are not equivalent, although therapeutic effects are generally derived from both. They are mutually compatible approaches.

Parent's Refusal for Treatment

At times even the best therapeutic gestures will fail to motivate an alcoholic or addicted parent to become involved in recovery. A codependent spouse may be the one who ushers the children into a recovery process, and the PACT model will have to proceed, despite the ongoing addictive practices in the home. In other instances, when a parent eschews treatment, there will be separation and divorce, but the children may still enter recovery. Family instability, including divorce, is cited in the literature (Nylander, 1960) as escalating the problems in children of alcoholics. These deleterious effects can be lessened when children enter recovery.

Our final case involves a high-risk, single-parent family and illustrates the *long-term* issues in a nonalcoholic parent and her children in recovery.

Case Illustration — Xavier, Yolanda and Zeke

These three youngsters were eleven, ten, and five when their mother sought "divorce counseling." She identified her husband as a chronic alcoholic, unwilling to seek treatment, who could be mean and brutal to her and the children. He was becoming increasingly cruel to Xavier, demeaning him, calling him names, undermining his self-worth, and slapping him around.

Early phase therapy. Zeke, the chubby five-year-old, was the natural child of the father, "Big Ezekiel," an ex-marine. The mother admitted that she had not wanted to marry this man but did so in order to provide a home for Xavier and Yolanda shortly after their father had been killed in Viet Nam. Xavier, a handsome boy with the dark Hispanic features of his mother, as well as her intense demeanor, readily agreed to therapy because he stated that he felt "battered" by his stepfather. Yolanda, who called her stepfather "Papa," was not happy about the divorce; she blamed the therapist and did not want to become a part of the sessions.

Early children's meetings were filled with bitter exchanges among the sibs. Yolanda could be quite sadistic, teasing her older brother, calling him "Fag." In a mocking tone she called her younger brother "Daddy's baby boy." Yolanda secretly longed for visitation with her stepfather, but he never invited her to go along when he came to pick up Zeke.

Xavier was filled with quiet, seething rage. He wished that his stepfather would die. He felt sorry for his mother, he said, and he was "glad" to help her whenever he could. Xavier, an honor student in parochial school, used his early sessions to ventilate his anger.

Play therapy sessions with Zeke during this period were filled with hostile, destructive play. He was restless, bored easily, and had developmental lags in several areas of intellectual functioning. He had had difficulty adjusting to first grade, being loud and bossy with his peers and aggressive on the playground.

The mother was depressed throughout the several months that the divorce process required. She began to experience grief related to the death of her first husband, and then a resurgence of traumatic feelings associated with her childhood, when she had been severely abused physically by her mother. She overidentified with "poor little fatherless Zeke," which justified allowing the boy to sleep with her. She felt ashamed of Yolanda, whose obesity had become a serious problem. She said that she felt like throwing up her hands and "running away from home." The ex-husband's support payments had become irregular, and the mother had to obtain public assistance. Concerned over finances, she decided to economize by giving up her addiction to cigarettes. Within a few weeks she was able to stop smoking for the first time in twelve years.

During the early recovery phase of therapy, the family unit consisted of four individuals who appeared to lack any kinship ties: the mother, Xavier, Yolanda, and Zeke. The mother would have preferred to surrender leadership functions to Xavier, particularly the fathering role of Zeke; however, Xavier became increasingly reclusive. Yolanda also spent more and more time alone in her room, and Zeke monopolized the television set.

Middle/control phase therapy. The ongoing support of the Al-Anon program and sponsor to the mother strengthened her ability to finalize the divorce. Better able to speak in her own behalf, she sought and obtained from the court visitation for Zeke which stipulated that his father would have to be alcohol-free during these visits.

Gradually, the mother became more firmly established in the children's eyes as their family leader. This led Yolanda to show her mother a new type of respect. Xavier had the most difficulty accepting his mother's leadership. He showed a passive-aggressive disregard for her rules. Family finances had prevented Xavier from continuing parochial school with his peers, and his junior high school adjustment to public school was rocky. He could not seem to fit in, and his grades began to slide. He blamed his mother for being home-bound and not getting a job so that he could return to parochial school. A crisis during this phase occurred when the mother caught Xavier smoking marijuana in the bathroom: "So what's the big deal about weed?" Xavier confronted his mother in a specially arranged therapy session. "*You* used to smoke those cancer sticks. And you let Zeke keep a shelf full of booze, and his dad even lets him drink it!"

This is when I first learned that Zeke had a hobby — collecting miniature liquor bottles given to him by his father — and that his father allowed him to sip the sugary, sweet liqueurs. The mother had not told me of her youngest son's budding interest in alcohol, and she blushed shamefacedly when the information was leaked by Xavier. She stammered and tried to make excuses. It was apparent that the mother hated to deny Zeke anything, even the identification with his father's alcoholism. Throughout this period, Zeke's problems in the first grade continued. His conduct was worse after weekends with his father. The father still practiced alcoholism, though he claimed not to drink during Zeke's visits.

Yolanda's substance abuse problem remained food. Her weight continued to wall her off from others throughout her pubertal years. She obstinately refused any individual therapy; however, with their strengthened verbal skills, Xavier, Yolanda, and Zeke began to participate in an alcohol/drug awareness series in their group meetings. These continued for several weeks, with the children exploring their personal values about substance use and how their lives had been affected already.

Family negotiation meetings during this phase led the mother to improve her ability to provide clear, firm messages to her children about family rules. Increasingly, the family began to rely on these meetings to bring forward sibling complaints, questions, and disputes. One such meeting led to the mother and two older siblings confronting Zeke about his liquor collection, which he then agreed to gather up and return to his father. Conflict resolution as a way of family life replaced the divisiveness which had occurred during the first year of therapy.

Affection phase therapy. The mother had entered a training program for medical office assistants, which she completed in six months. Improved self-confidence led her to seek and obtain a job as an office assistant to a physician. The mother's increased empathy for each of her children enabled her to express to Xavier her regret about what he had suffered as a result of his stepfather's psychological abuse. She also recognized his fear that she was not capable of providing for him, but she reassured him that *she* was *the parent* in the home. The mother apologized to each of the children for her part in not recognizing their emotional distress over the years, especially to Yolanda, whose low self-esteem continued to be expressed as obesity. It was at this time that the family as a group began to rally on Yolanda's behalf, supporting her in her effort to improve dietary practices. The mother enrolled the girl in a self-improvement program for teenagers which provided nutritional counseling.

An increased capacity to serve as a support group for one another had been developed by the end of two years. Xavier's entrance into high school was successful and he was once again an honor student. Yolanda's self-esteem improved with her improved appearance, and she began to show an interest in boys. Zeke was being provided with special tutoring at a learning center. The mother continued in Al-Anon with a large network of Al-Anon friends. Therapy with the family was terminated at this time.

Ongoing Recovery. Four years after this family had completed initial recovery work, the mother recontacted me about Yolanda, who was then just beginning her senior year in high school. Yolanda, still slim and quite pretty by now, had been caught shoplifting at a local bargain store. The mother was angry and baffled. She demanded to know the reason that Yolanda had stolen a cheaply made pair of women's panties, which she didn't even need.

Yolanda screeched at her mother, "How do *I* know why I took them? I just spaced out! Sometimes I do *that*, OK? I just spaced out, and then — I — I *take* things." Yolanda broke into sobs, asking her mother to leave the room so that she could speak to me privately.

In her first individual session since the family's initial contact seven years earlier, Yolanda disclosed that "Papa," her alcoholic stepfather, had sexually molested her when she had been six years old, about the time that her mother was pregnant with Zeke. The fondling and masturbation made her feel guilty and ashamed, but, she admitted, she had felt "kinda special, too," as though Papa preferred her over her mother and brother. She had played the "secret game" with Papa up until after Zeke was born. She had believed it was as much her fault as Papa's. That's what he had told her when he slipped into her bedroom at night, "All little girls like this game, but it has to be played secret. You can't ever tell your Mama. She'd whip you and send me away." All these years, Yolanda had believed that the divorce was *her fault*, that Mama must have found out about the game. She was terrified that I would find out too, by guessing her dark, guilty secret if she were ever alone with me in therapy. Now, at last, she wanted to try to understand, to see whether the shoplifting was not in some way related to her "secret."

The incest report temporarily restricted Zeke from contact with his father. The family (with the exception of Xavier, who was living on his own) reentered therapy. Zeke was angry and hostile, blaming Yolanda for being a troublemaker, for "telling big fat lies" about his Dad "coz you're just jealous." The mother also blamed Yolanda for keeping the secret so long. Once again, this was a loosely organized group of three individuals (Yolanda, Zeke, and the mother), who began family processes at the inclusion phase. This time, however, they were able to work through their difficulties in a relatively short period of time, by the end of one year.

Two years later, the mother again made contact. Now she claimed that 16-year-old Zeke had a "drinking problem," consuming heavy amounts of beer during weekend keg parties with his peers. The mother had resumed smoking for the first time in ten years "out of desperation." She had then realized that their problems must be "nipped in the bud." The mother claimed that she had been better able to *see* Zeke's problem with alcohol after her remarriage a few months earlier. Her recovering alcoholic husband, with ten years' sobriety, was heavily involved in Alcoholics Anonymous. He expressed genuine concern and a desire to help Zeke. However, the 16-year-old was isolated from others by a wall of hurt and resentment towards Big Ezekiel, who, after Yolanda's disclosure, had never resumed father-son contact. A new family of loosely knit individuals (the mother, stepfather, and Zeke) began again at the beginning, at the inclusion phase of their family's processes. . . .

(By this time, Xavier, a young Naval officer, had begun his career after graduating cum laude from the state university. He neither drank alcohol nor used drugs. Yolanda, newly wed, was expecting her first child.)

The preceding vignette was drawn from the case material of one family's life history over eleven years. Several important points were illustrated relevant to what has been discussed about children in recovery:

1. *This was a poly-addicted family:* the stepfather's alcoholism and incestuous abuse of Yolanda; the mother's cigarette smoking; Yolanda's eating disorder; Xavier's marijuana use; and Zeke's alcohol abuse.
2. *An alcoholic/addictive family situation creates an environment where children tend to be abused — physically, sexually, morally, psychologically, and emotionally:* the alcoholic stepfather's physical and psychological abuse of Xavier; sexual abuse of Yolanda; substance

abuse introduced to Zeke at an early age; and finally, parental abandonment. The children were not viewed as autonomous selves, deserving of respect, but were used and discarded.

3. *When the two-person, marital system fails, the risk factors are increased for the single parent from an addictive/abusive family of origin to become abusive.* This family had several predictors to make them at high risk for severe problems: single parent, low socioeconomic status, ethnic minority, blended family, previous physical abuse in a parent (mother), no recovery in alcoholic parent, and multiple family addictions.

4. *Risk factors were offset by the establishment of a firm, supportive network for parent (Al-Anon) and early recovery work.* These supports enabled the family to function at a relatively high level, addressing the various life crises in a responsible, problem-solving manner.

5. *Children who are not the biologic offspring of an alcoholic parent are also affected adversely by an alcoholic/addictive family environment.* They, too, become at high risk for substance abuse.

6. *Despite bitter sibling dissension and rivalry, secretiveness and divisiveness, the children can be assisted to function more supportively.*

7. *An alcoholic/addictive family remains vulnerable throughout its life history.* Recovery at one phase of family development, such as when the children are school age, does not mean that they will not need assistance at other points of family stress and crisis. However, the impact of early recovery strengthens (and shortens) the interventions at each of the successive points along the way.

8. *The initial recovery effort may help the family function more adaptively, but it does not mean that all of the children's problems could or should be solved.* Yolanda had to be ready to deal with her molestation issue; however, her earlier exposure to recovery work primed her for trust in the process when she was in crisis and in need of support.

9. *As family members come and go, the family will continue to rearrange itself around new issues.* The family at the beginning phase of initial recovery was not the same family which had first entered treatment eleven years earlier, although the same alcoholic/addictive family processes were still operative, and the impressions left upon the family by earlier members still influenced these processes.

10. *While each of the children fit the stereotype of his/her respective birth order position, the greater influence upon the family was the unique, individual*

selfhood which each of these children contributed. Seeing Xavier as the parentified child, or Yolanda as the middle child, or Zeke as the youngest, or as any other role, would merely obscure each child's separate pain and suffering.

11. *While the therapist remains ready to serve as educator, guide, coach, resource person, even leader initially, it is ultimately the parent(s) who must guide the family through successful recovery.*

12. *The fact that the two adult children had passed through adolescence and young adulthood with actually a minimum of problems raises the question, "Would this family have coped as well if there had been no initial recovery effort?"*

SUMMARY

If the description of a long-term therapy case which spanned eleven years is discouraging to those who support brief psychotherapy for the children of alcoholism and addiction, then I have succeeded in stating my case. Brief intervention will *not* be sufficient to assist the recovering child and parents.

Whatever treatment paradigm we wish to use, we will have to employ some way of conceptualizing the traumatic response of the child-self to events beyond the normal range of childhood experience. I do not believe that damage to a child can be corrected by brief interventions or a few sessions of family therapy.

To the extent that it is possible, parents need to be involved in a child's recovery. For those of us who are professional caregivers, it is important to begin to recognize the boundaries of our competence, as well as our limitations. Although our own ego needs may be gratified by the creative work which we are able to do with children, we need to understand that the *real* healing for the child comes from healing the troubled parent-child relationship. When we see that the child's healing is going to require slow, steady, ongoing recovery — and lots of love — we recognize that the parent is the best person to provide that care and healing. Although we may not always be able to engage a parent in long term child recovery work, when we can, the benefits are enormous. The children's PACT (parents as co-therapists) model is one way that this therapeutic work can be accomplished with the child and the parents.

Barnes, G. M., & Windle, M. (1987). Family factors in adolescent alcohol and drug abuse. *Pediatrician, 14*, 13–18.

Basch, M. F. (1983). The perception of reality and the disavowal of meaning. *The Annual of Psychoanalysts, XI*, 125–153.

Bell, B., & Cohen, R. (1981). The Bristol social and adjustment guide: Comparison between the offspring of alcoholic and nonalcoholic mothers. *British Journal of Clinical Psychology, 20*(2), 93–95.

Bennett, L. A., Wolin, S. J., & Reiss, D. (1988). Cognitive, behavioral and emotional problems among school-aged children of alcoholic parents. *American Journal of Psychiatry, 145*(2), 185–188.

Billings, A. G., Kessler, M., Gomberg, C., & Weiner, S. (1979). Marital conflict resolution of alcoholic and nonalcoholic couples during drinking and nondrinking sessions. *Journal of Studies on Alcohol, 40*, 183–195.

Black, C. (1979). Children of alcoholics. *Alcohol Health and Research World, 4*, 23–27.

Black, C. (1981). *It will never happen to me*. Denver: Medical Administration Co.

Black, C. (1985). Children of alcoholics. In *Growing in the shadows*, R. J. Ackerman (Ed.). Pompano Beach, FL: Health Communications.

Boszormenyi-Nagi, I., & Ulrich, D. (1981). Contextual family therapy. In *Handbook of family therapy*. A. Gurman and D. Kniskern. (Eds.). New York: Brunner/Mazel.

Byrne, M. (1980). Helping children to cope with alcoholic parents. Presentation at Helping children to cope with stress. Lesley College, Cambridge, Mass., January. In A. Brenner *Helping children cope with stress* (151–164). Lexington, MA: Lexington Books.

Brant, R., & Tisza, V. (1977). The sexually misused child. *American Journal of Orthopsychiatry, 4*(1), 80–90.

Briggs, D. C. (1975). *Your child's self esteem*. Garden City, NY: Doubleday.

Brown, S. (1985). *Treating the alcoholic: A developmental model of recovery*. New York: John Wiley.

Burk, E. (1972). Some contemporary issues in child development and the children of alcoholic parents. *Annals of New York Academy of Sciences, 197*, 189–197.

Cantwell, D. (1975). Familial-genetic research with hyperactive children. In *The hyperactive child: Diagnosis, management and current research*. D. Cantwell (Ed.). New York: Spectrum.

Cermak, T. L. (1988). *A time to heal*. New York: Jeremy P. Tarcher.

Cohler, B. J. (1980). Developmental perspectives on the psychology of the self in early childhood. In *Advances in self psychology*, A. Goldberg (Ed.). New York: International Universities Press.

Coleman, S. B. (1985). The surreptitious power of the sibling cohort. In *Failures in family therapy*. S. B. Coleman (Ed.). New York: Guilford.

Cork, R. M. (1969). *The forgotten children*. Toronto: Addiction Research Foundation.

Courtois, C. A. (1988). *Healing the incest wound*. New York: W. W. Norton.

El-Guebaly, N., & Offord, D. (1977). The offspring of alcoholics: A critical review. *The American Journal of Psychiatry, 134*(4), 357–365.

Erikson, E. (1950). *Childhood and society*. New York: W. W. Norton.

Ervin, C., Little, R., Streissguth, A., & Beck, D. (1984). Alcoholic fathering and its relation to child's intellectual development: A pilot investigation. *Alcoholism: Clinical and Experimental Research, 8*, 362–365.

Evans, R. E. (1988). Why teenagers smoke and what can be done about it. *The Brown University Child Behavior and Development Letter, 4*(5), 1–2.

References

American Medical Association. Committee on Alcoholism, Mental Health Council. Hospitalization of patients with alcoholism. (Reports of officers.) (1956). *Journal of the American Medical Association, 162,* 750.

American Psychiatric Association (1987). *Diagnostic and Statistical Manual of Mental Disorders* (3rd ed., rev.). Washington, DC: author.

Anderson, E. E., & Quast, W. (1983). Young children in alcoholic families: A mental health needs-assessment and an intervention/prevention strategy. *Journal of Primary Prevention, 3*(3), 174–187.

Anthony, E. J. (1976). Freud, Piaget, and human knowledge: Some comparisons and contrasts. *The Annual of Psychoanalysis, IV,* 253–257.

Aronson, M., & Gilbert, A. (1963). Preadolescent sons of male alcoholics: An experimental study of personality patterning. *Archives of General Psychiatry, 8,* 235–241.

Aronson, M., Kyllerman, M., Sabel, K. G., Sandin, B., & Olegard, R. (1985). Children of alcoholic mothers: Developmental, perceptual, and behavioral characteristics as compared to matched controls. *Acta Paediatrica Scandinavia, 74,* 27–35.

Bank, S. P., & Kahn, M. D. (1982). Psychotherapy with siblings. In *The sibling bond.* S. Bank & M. Kahn (Eds.). New York: Basic Books.

Faber, A., & Mazlish, E. (1975). *Liberated parents/liberated children*. New York: Avon Books.

Faber, A., & Mazlish, E. (1980). *How to talk so kids will listen and listen so kids will talk*. New York: Avon Books.

Faber, A., & Mazlish, E. (1987). *Siblings without rivalry*. New York: W. W. Norton.

Farber, E. A., & Egeland, B. (1987). Invulnerability among abused and neglected children. In *The invulnerable child*. E. J. Anthony and B. J. Cohler (Eds.). New York: Guilford.

Feldman, W. (1988). Culture versus biology: Children's attitudes toward thinness and fatness. *Pediatrics, 81*, 190–194.

Fine, E., Yudin, L., Holmes, J., & Heinemann, S. (1976). Behavioral disorders in children with parental alcoholism. *Annals of the New York Academy of Sciences, 273*, 507–517.

Finkelhor, D. (1979). *Sexually victimized children*. New York: Free Press.

Fox, R. (1962). Children in the alcoholic family. In *Problems in addiction*. W. C. Bier, Jr. (Ed.). New York: Fordham University Press.

Fox, R. (1968). Treating the alcoholic family. In *Alcoholism: The total treatment approach*. R. J. Catanzaro (Ed.). Springfield, IL: Charles C. Thomas.

Freud, A. (1927). Four lectures on child analysis. In *The Writings of Anna Freud, 1* (pp. 3–69). New York: International Universities Press.

Freud, A. (1966). *The ego and the mechanisms of defense* (Rev. ed.). New York: International Universities Press.

Freud, S. (1920). Inhibitions, symptoms and anxiety. In *The Standard Edition of the Complete Psychological Works of Sigmund Freud*, Volume 18, (pp. 75–175). J. Strachey (Trans. and Ed.). New York: W. W. Norton.

Freud, S. (1926). Inhibitions, symptoms and anxiety. In *The Standard Edition of the Complete Psychological Works of Sigmund Freud*, Volume 18, (pp. 3–64). J. Strachey (Trans. and Ed.). New York: W. W. Norton.

Gabrielli, W. F., & Mednick, S. A. (1983). Intellectual performance in children of alcoholics. *Journal of Nervous and Mental Disorders, 171*(7), 444–447.

Gallant, D. M. (1987). *Alcoholism: A guide to diagnosis, intervention, and treatment*. New York: W. W. Norton.

Garbarino, J. (1987). What is psychological maltreatment? In *When children need help*. L. P. Lipsitt (Ed.). Providence: Manisses Communications Group.

Gibbs, N. R. (1988). All fired up over smoking. *Time Magazine, 131*(6), 64.

Gooch, S. (1983). *If you love me, don't feed me junk*. Reston, VA: Reston Publishing.

Gorski, T., & Miller, M. (1982a). *Counseling for relapse prevention*. Independence, MO: Herald House-Independence Press.

Gorski, T., & Miller, M. (1982b). *Family recovery: Growing beyond addiction*. Independence, MO: Herald House-Independence Press.

Gorski, T., & Miller, M. (1982c). *Learning to live again: A guide for recovery from alcoholism*. Independence, MO: Herald House-Independence Press.

Gorski, T., & Miller, M. (1983). Relapse: The family's involvement. *Focus on Family*, Sept./Oct., 17–18.

Gorski, T., & Miller, M. (1986). *Staying sober: A guide for relapse prevention*. Independence, MO: Herald House-Independence Press.

Haberman, P. W. (1966). Childhood symptoms in children of alcoholics and comparison group parents. *Journal of Marriage and the Family, 28*, 152–154.

Harrity, A. S., & Christenson, A. B. (1987). *Kids, Drugs, & Alcohol*. White Hall, VA: Betterway Publications.

Hayden, B. C. (1988). "No" is not negative when rearing children and adolescents. *The Brown University Child Behavior and Development Letter, 4*(4), 1.

Hennecke, L. (1984). Stimulus augmenting and field dependence in children of alcoholic fathers. *Journal of Studies on Alcohol, 45*(6), 486–492.

Herjanic, B., Herjanic, M., Wetzel, R., & Tomelleri, C. (1978). Substance abuse: Its effect on offspring. *Research Communication in Psychology, Psychiatry, and Behavior, 3*, 65–75.

Herman, J. L. (1981). *Father-daughter incest.* Cambridge, MA: Harvard University Press.

Herman, J. L. (1987). Child abuse prevention and treatment: The great social experiment: Presentation. Sponsored by the North Country Child Abuse Coalition of the San Diego Community Child Abuse Coordinating Council, San Diego, CA, October.

Hughes, J. M. (1977). Adolescent children of alcoholic parents and the relationship of alateen to these children. *Journal of Consulting and Clinical Psychology, 45*, 946–947.

Jacob, T., Favorini, A., Meisel, S., & Anderson, C. (1978). The alcoholic's spouse, children and family interactions: Substantive findings and methodological issues. *Journal of Studies on Alcohol, 39*, 1231–1251.

JAMA. (1985). AMA Diagnostic and treatment guidelines concerning child abuse and neglect. *Journal of the American Medical Association, 254*(6), 6.

Jesse, R. C. (1975). *Children of alcoholic fathers: A concurrent investigation of personality, behavior, attitudes, and values with implications for family therapy.* Dissertation proposal, California School of Professional Psychology, San Diego, CA.

Jesse, R. C. (1977). *Children of alcoholics: A clinical investigation of familial role relationships.* Doctoral Dissertation. California School of Professional Psychology, San Diego.

Jesse, R. C., McFadd, A., Gray, G., & Bucky, S. (1978). Interpersonal effects of alcohol abuse. In *The impact of alcoholism*, S. F. Bucky (Ed.). Center City, MN: Hazelden.

Jesse, R. C. (1985). The narcissistic self structure of the eating disordered individual. Delivered paper. San Diego: Harborview Medical Center.

Jesse, R. C. (1987). The child in recovery. *Alcoholism and Addiction, 8*(2), 19.

Jesse, R. C. (1988). Children of alcoholics: Their sibling world. In *Siblings in therapy*, M. Kahn & K. G. Lewis (Eds.). New York: W. W. Norton.

Jesse, R. C. (In press). *The care and feeding of children of alcoholics.*

Johnson, V. E. (1973). *I'll quit tomorrow.* New York: Harper & Row.

Kagan, J. (1984). *The nature of the child.* New York: Basic Books.

Khan, M. (1963). The concept of cumulative trauma. *The Psychoanalytic Study of the Child, 18*, 54–88.

Kelly, G. A. (1955). *The psychology of personal constructs: A theory of personality.* New York: W. W. Norton.

Ketcham, K., & Mueller, L. (1983). *Eating right to live sober.* New York: Madrona Publishers.

Kluft, R. P. (1985). *Childhood antecedents of multiple personality.* Washington DC: American Psychiatric Press.

Kohut, H. (1971). *The analysis of the self.* New York: International Universities Press.

Kohut, H. (1977). *The restoration of the self.* New York: International Universities Press.

Kritsberg, W. (1985). *The adult children of alcoholics syndrome.* Pompano Beach, FL: Health Communications.

Krystal, H. (1978). *Self representation and the capacity for self care. The Annual of Psychoanalysis, VI*, 209–246.

Kyllerman, M., Aronson, M., Sabel, K. G., Karlberg, E., Sandin, B., & Olegard, R. (1985). Children of alcoholic mothers. Growth and motor performance compared to matched controls. *Acta Paediatrica Scandinavia, 74*(1), 20–26.

Lamar, J. V. (1987). Kids who sell crack. *Time Magazine, 131*(19), 24.

Lasch, C. (1979). *The culture of narcissism.* New York: W. W. Norton.

Lawson, G., Peterson, J., & Lawson, A. (1983). *Alcoholism and the family.* Rockville, MD: Aspen Publications.

Lipsitt, L. P. (1987). Sugar and hyperactive behavior. *The Brown University Child Behavior and Development Letter, 3*(9), 5.

Lipsitt, L. P. (1988a). New laws on child abuse and family violence. *The Brown University Child Behavior and Development Letter, 4*(5), 3.

Lipsitt, L. P. (1988b). Early hyperactivity and later difficulties. *The Brown University Child Behavior and Development Letter, 4*(4), 7.

Lipsitt, L. P. (1988c). Children and alcoholism. *The Brown University Child Behavior and Development Letter, 4*(8), 6.

Lipsitt, L. P. (1988d). Children and liquor advertising. *The Brown University Child Behavior and Development Letter, 4*(9), 7.

Lutey, C. (1972). *Individual intelligence testing.* Greeley, CO: Carol Lutey.

Marcus, A. (1983). A comparative study of maternal alcoholism and maternal child-rearing attitudes, child perception of maternal behavior, child's academic achievement and school attendance. *Dissertation Abstracts International, 44.*

Margolis, M. (1977). A preliminary report on a case of consummated mother-son incest. *The Annual of Psychoanalysis, V*, 267–294.

Masterson, J. (1985). *The real self.* New York: Brunner/Mazel.

Michalik, M. A. (1981). *The impact of an alcoholic father on the adjustment of adolescent sons.* Doctoral dissertation. California School of Professional Psychology, San Diego.

Miller, A. (1981). *Prisoners of childhood.* New York: Basic Books.

Miller, A. (1983). *For your own good.* New York: Farrar, Straus, & Giroux.

Miller, D., & Jang, M. (1977). Children of alcoholics: A 20 year longitudinal study. *Social Work Research and Abstracts, 13*, 23–29.

Moos, R. H., & Billings, A. G. (1982). Children of alcoholics during the recovery process: alcoholic and matched control families. *Addictive Behaviors, 7*, 155–163.

Moos, R. H., Finney, J. W., & Chan, D. A. (1981). The process of recovery from alcoholism. *Journal of Studies on Alcohol, 42*(5), 383–402.

Moos, R. H., & Moos, B. S. (1984). The process of recovery from alcoholism: III. Comparing functioning in families of alcoholic and matched control families. *Journal of Studies on Alcohol, 45*(2), 111–118.

Morrison, J. R., & Stewart, M. A. (1971). A family study of the hyperactive child syndrome. *Biological Psychiatry, 3*, 189–195.

Morrison, M. (1985). Physiology of addiction in women. Presentation at Fifth Annual Betty Ford Center Conference on Alcoholism and Chemical Dependency: Women. Palm Springs. Annenberg Center for Health Sciences, Eisenhower Medical Center.

Morrison, P. (1986). *Changing family structure: Who cares for America's dependents?* Santa Monica: Rand research report. Rand Corporation.

McCord, J. (1972). Etiological factors in alcoholism: family and personal characteristics. *Quarterly Journal of the Studies on Alcohol, 33*, 1020–1027.

McKay, J. R. (1960). Clinical observations on adolescent problem drinkers. *Quarterly Journal of the Studies on Alcohol, 22*, 124–134.

Nace, E. P. (1987). *The treatment of alcoholism*. New York: Brunner/Mazel.

Nichols, M. P. (1987). *The self in the system: expanding the limits of family therapy*. New York: Brunner/Mazel.

Norton, R., & Noble, J. (1987). Combined alcohol and other drug use and abuse: a status report. *Alcohol, Health and Research World, II*, 78–82.

Nylander, I. (1960). Children of alcoholic fathers. *Acta Paediatrica Scandinavia, 49*, (Suppl. 121), 1–134.

Nylander, I. (1982). A comparison between children of alcoholic fathers from excellent versus poor social conditions. *Acta Paediatrica Scandinavia, 71*(5), 809–813.

Obuchowska, I. (1974). Emotional contact with the mother as a social compensatory factor in children of alcoholics. *International Mental Health Research Newsletter, 16*(4), 2–4.

O'Gorman, P., & Oliver-Diaz, P. (1987). *Breaking the cycle of addiction: a parent's guide to raising healthy kids*. Pompano Beach, Florida: Health Communications.

Orford, J. (1975). Alcoholism and Marriage: the argument against specialism. *Journal of Studies on Alcohol, 36*, 1537–1563.

Ornstein, A. (1976). Making contact with the inner world of the child. *Comprehensive Psychiatry, 17*(1), 3–36.

Ornstein, A. (1985). The function of play in the process of child psychotherapy: a contemporary perspective. *The Annals of Psychoanalysis, 12–13*, 349–366.

Paolino, T. J., & McCrady, B. S. (1977). *The alcoholic marriage: alternative perspectives*. New York: Grune & Stratton.

Piaget, J. (1952). *The origins of intelligence in children*. New York: International Universities Press.

Piaget, J. (1964). *The child's conception of the world*. London: Routledge & Kegan Paul.

Ryan, W. G. (1984). Practically everything practical the clinician wants to know about substance abuse. *Voices: the art and science of psychotherapy, 20*(1), 29–47.

Sarnoff, C. (1976). *Latency*. New York: Jason Aronson.

Sarnoff, C. (1987). *Psychotherapeutic strategies in the latency years*. New Jersey: Jason Aronson.

Satir, V. (1967). *Conjoint family therapy*. Palo Alto: Science and Behavior Books.

Schaef, A. W. (1987). *When society becomes an addict*. San Francisco: Harper & Row.

Schrenk, L. (1985). *Psychotherapists' attitudes toward alcoholics and their treatment: Toward development of a treatment model*. Doctoral dissertation, California School of Professional Psychology, San Diego.

Schutz, W. S. (1958). *FIRO: a three dimensional theory of interpersonal behavior*. New York: Holt, Rhinehart & Winston.

Schultz, W. S. (1967). *Joy: Expanding human awareness*. New York: Grove Press.

Schuckit, M., & Chiles, J. (1978). Family history as a diagnostic aid in two samples of adolescents. *Journal of Nervous and Mental Disease, 166*, 165–167.

Shepard-Look. (1987). The sexual victimization of children. Presentation: California State University, Northridge.

Smith, S. M., & Kunjukrishnan, R. (1985). Child abuse: Perspectives on treatment and research. *Psychiatric Clinics of North America, 8*(4), 49.

Steinglass, P., Bennett, L., & Wolin, S. (1987). *The alcoholic family*. New York: Basic Books.

Steinhausen, J. C. (1982). Psychopathology and mental functions in the offspring of alcoholic and epileptic mothers. *Journal of the American Academy of Child Psychiatry, 21*(3), 268–273.

Steinhausen, H. C., Godel, D., & Nestler, V. (1984). Psychopathology in the offspring of alcoholic parents. *Journal of the American Academy of Child Psychiatry, 23*(4), 465–471.

Stolorow, R. D., & Lachman, F. M. (1980). *Psychoanalysis of developmental arrests.* Madison: International Universities Press.

Straus, M. A. (1980). A sociological perspective on the causes of family violence. In *Violence and the American family.* M. R. Greer (Ed.). Washington, DC: American Association for the Advancement of Science.

Terr, L. (1979). Children of Chowchilla: A study of psychic trauma. *The Psychoanalytic Study of the Child, 34,* 552–563.

Terr, L. (1981). Psychic trauma in children: Observations following the Chowchilla school-bus kidnapping. *The American Journal of Psychiatry, 138,* 14–19.

Terr, L. (1983a). Life attitudes, dreams and psychic trauma in a group of "normal" children. *Journal of the American Academy of Child Psychiatry, 22,* 221–230.

Terr, L. (1983b). Chowchilla revisited: The effects of psychic trauma four years after a school-bus kidnapping. *The American Journal of Psychiatry, 140*(12), 1543–1550.

Terr, L. (1984). Children traumatized in small groups. *In Post-traumatic stress disorder in children,* S. Eth and R. Pynoos (Eds.). Washington, DC: American Psychiatric Press.

Terr, L. (1988). What happens to early memories of trauma? A study of twenty children under age five at the time of documented traumatic events. *Journal of the American Academy of Child and Adolescent Psychiatry, 27,* 96–104.

Ticer, S., & King, R. (1987). No smoking sweeps America. *Business Week,* July 27, pp. 40–52.

Tiebout, H. M. (1954). The ego factors in surrender in alcoholism. *Quarterly Journal of Studies on Alcohol, 15,* 610–621.

Tyndale House Publishers. (1983). Genesis 2:03. *The Living Bible.* Wheaton, IL.

Tyndale House Publishers. (1983). Matthew 18:04. *The Living Bible.* Wheaton, IL.

Vandell, D., Minnett, A., & Santrock, J. (1987). Age difference in sibling relationships during middle childhood. *Journal of Applied Developmental Psychology, 8,* 247–257.

vonBertalanffy, L. (1968). *General systems theory.* New York: George Braziller.

Webster's Dictionary of the English Language. (1988). New York: Lexicon Publications Inc.

Werner, E. E. (1986). Resilient offspring of alcoholics: a longitudinal study from birth to age 18. *Journal of Studies on Alcohol, 47*(1), 34–40.

Whalen, T. (1953). Wives of alcoholics: Four types observed in a family service agency. *Quarterly Studies on Alcohol, 14,* 532–641.

Williams, C. N. (1981). Child care practices in alcoholic families. *Alcoholic, Health and Research World, 11,* 74–77.

Willingham, L. (1988). Requisite training for juvenile court ordered therapists for child abuse victims and families. Presentation at conference. University of San Diego, San Diego, CA: 30 January.

Winnicott, D. W. (1965). Ego distortions in terms of true and false self. In *The maturational processes and the facilitating environment.* New York: International Universities Press.

Winnicott, D. W. (1986). *Home is where we start from.* New York: W. W. Norton.

Woititz, J. G. (1983). Adult children of alcoholics. Pompano Beach, FL: Health Communications.

Ziegler-Driscoll, G. (1979). The similarities in families of drug dependents and alcoholics. In *Family therapy of drugs and alcohol abuse.* E. Kaufman & P. Kaufman (Eds.). New York: Gardner.

Index